Universal Praise for Bestselling Author Dr. Ruth K. Westheimer

"Dr. Ruth writes the way she talks — enthusiastically, nonjudgementally and informatively . . . ."

> — *Booklist,* 1994

"Her energy level is higher than that of a charged particle."

> — *People Magazine,* 1985

"Dr. Ruth Westheimer is the Stealth fighter of sex education."

> — *San Jose Mercury News,* 1995

"She can seemingly say things on the air that no one else can. This could be because she is short and sweet and takes her job seriously . . . ."

> — *New York Times,* 1985

"America's star sexologist . . . ."

> — *TV Guide*

"Her manner is down-to-earth and reassuring . . . she tries to make people feel better, value themselves, trust their instincts . . . ."

> — *Ladies' Home Journal,* 1986

"If height were measured in courage, determination and hard work, this little lady would be 10 feet tall."

> — *Newsday,* 1987

"Her image is synonymous with sex . . . ."

> — *Time,* 1987

"Her name and the distinctive thrill of her voice have become inextricably linked with the subject of sex."

> — *New York Times,* 1992

TM

References for the Rest of Us!™

BESTSELLING BOOK SERIES

Do you find that traditional reference books are overloaded with technical details and advice you'll never use? Do you postpone important life decisions because you just don't want to deal with them? Then our *…For Dummies*® business and general reference book series is for you.

…For Dummies business and general reference books are written for those frustrated and hard-working souls who know they aren't dumb, but find that the myriad of personal and business issues and the accompanying horror stories make them feel helpless. *…For Dummies* books use a lighthearted approach, a down-to-earth style, and even cartoons and humorous icons to dispel fears and build confidence. Lighthearted but not lightweight, these books are perfect survival guides to solve your everyday personal and business problems.

"More than a publishing phenomenon, 'Dummies' is a sign of the times."

— The New York Times

"…you won't go wrong buying them."

— Walter Mossberg, Wall Street Journal, on IDG Books' …For Dummies books

"A world of detailed and authoritative information is packed into them…"

— U.S. News and World Report

Already, millions of satisfied readers agree. They have made *…For Dummies* the #1 introductory level computer book series and a best-selling business book series. They have written asking for more. So, if you're looking for the best and easiest way to learn about business and other general reference topics, look to *…For Dummies* to give you a helping hand.

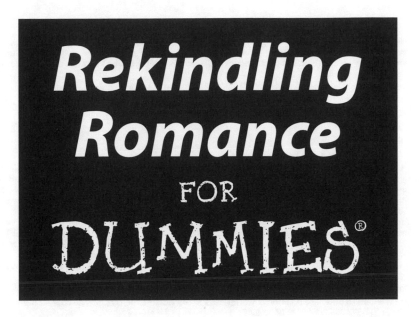

by Dr. Ruth K. Westheimer
with Pierre Lehu

IDG Books Worldwide, Inc.
An International Data Group Company

Foster City, CA ◆ Chicago, IL ◆ Indianapolis, IN ◆ New York, NY

Rekindling Romance For Dummies®

Published by
IDG Books Worldwide, Inc.
An International Data Group Company
919 E. Hillsdale Blvd.
Suite 300
Foster City, CA 94404
www.idgbooks.com (IDG Books Worldwide Web site)
www.dummies.com (Dummies Press Web site)

Library of Congress Control Number: 00-108208

ISBN: 0-7645-5303-8

Printed in the United States of America

10 9 8 7 6 5 4 3 2 1

1B/TQ/RR/QQ/IN

Distributed in the United States by IDG Books Worldwide, Inc.

Distributed by CDG Books Canada Inc. for Canada; by Transworld Publishers Limited in the United Kingdom; by IDG Norge Books for Norway; by IDG Sweden Books for Sweden; by IDG Books Australia Publishing Corporation Pty. Ltd. for Australia and New Zealand; by TransQuest Publishers Pte Ltd. for Singapore, Malaysia, Thailand, Indonesia, and Hong Kong; by Gotop Information Inc. for Taiwan; by ICG Muse, Inc. for Japan; by Intersoft for South Africa; by Eyrolles for France; by International Thomson Publishing for Germany, Austria and Switzerland; by Distribuidora Cuspide for Argentina; by LR International for Brazil; by Galileo Libros for Chile; by Ediciones ZETA S.C.R. Ltda. for Peru; by WS Computer Publishing Corporation, Inc., for the Philippines; by Contemporanea de Ediciones for Venezuela; by Express Computer Distributors for the Caribbean and West Indies; by Micronesia Media Distributor, Inc. for Micronesia; by Chips Computadoras S.A. de C.V. for Mexico; by Editorial Norma de Panama S.A. for Panama; by American Bookshops for Finland.

For general information on IDG Books Worldwide's books in the U.S., please call our Consumer Customer Service department at 800-762-2974. For reseller information, including discounts and premium sales, please call our Reseller Customer Service department at 800-434-3422.

For information on where to purchase IDG Books Worldwide's books outside the U.S., please contact our International Sales department at 317-572-3993 or fax 317-572-4002.

For consumer information on foreign language translations, please contact our Customer Service department at 1-800-434-3422, fax 317-572-4002, or e-mail rights@idgbooks.com.

For information on licensing foreign or domestic rights, please phone +1-650-653-7098.

For sales inquiries and special prices for bulk quantities, please contact our Order Services department at 800-434-4322 or write to the address above.

For information on using IDG Books Worldwide's books in the classroom or for ordering examination copies, please contact our Educational Sales department at 800-434-2086 or fax 317-572-4005.

For press review copies, author interviews, or other publicity information, please contact our Public Relations department at 650-653-7000 or fax 650-653-7500.

For authorization to photocopy items for corporate, personal, or educational use, please contact Copyright Clearance Center, 222 Rosewood Drive, Danvers, MA 01923, or fax 978-750-4470.

 is a registered trademark under exclusive license to IDG Books Worldwide, Inc., from International Data Group, Inc.

About the Authors

Dr. Ruth K. Westheimer: Dr. Ruth Westheimer is a psychosexual therapist who helped pioneer the field of media psychology with her radio program, Sexually Speaking, which first aired in New York in 1980. Within a few years, she had built a communications network to distribute her expertise that included television, books, newspapers, games, calendars, home videos, and computer software.

Dr. Westheimer received her Master's Degree in Sociology from the Graduate Faculty of the New School of Social Research and her Doctorate of Education (Ed.D) in the Interdisciplinary Study of the Family from Columbia University Teacher's College. Working at Planned Parenthood prompted her to further her education in human sexuality by studying under Dr. Helen Singer Kaplan at New York Hospital–Cornell University Medical Center. She later participated in the program for five years as an Adjunct Associate Professor. She has also taught at Lehman College, Brooklyn College, Adelphi University, Columbia University, and West Point. She is currently an Adjunct Professor at New York University.

Dr. Westheimer is a Fellow of New York Academy of Medicine and has her own private practice in New York. She frequently lectures around the world, including at universities, and has twice been named "College Lecturer of the Year."

Dr. Westheimer has written 18 books. Some of the others include *Dr. Ruth's Encyclopedia of Sex, Dr. Ruth's Pregnancy Guide For Couples, The Art of Arousal, Dr. Ruth Talks to Kids,* and *Rekindling Romance For Dummies.*

Pierre A. Lehu: Pierre Lehu has been Dr. Ruth Westheimer's "Minister of Communications" for 20 years. He is the co-author of *Dr. Ruth Talks About Grandparents: Advice for Kids Making the Most of a Special Relationship* and *Dr. Ruth's Guide to College Life: The Savvy Student's Handbook.* He lives in New York City with his wife and two children.

ABOUT IDG BOOKS WORLDWIDE

Welcome to the world of IDG Books Worldwide.

IDG Books Worldwide, Inc., is a subsidiary of International Data Group, the world's largest publisher of computer-related information and the leading global provider of information services on information technology. IDG was founded more than 30 years ago by Patrick J. McGovern and now employs more than 9,000 people worldwide. IDG publishes more than 290 computer publications in over 75 countries. More than 90 million people read one or more IDG publications each month.

Launched in 1990, IDG Books Worldwide is today the #1 publisher of best-selling computer books in the United States. We are proud to have received eight awards from the Computer Press Association in recognition of editorial excellence and three from Computer Currents' First Annual Readers' Choice Awards. Our best-selling ...For Dummies® series has more than 50 million copies in print with translations in 31 languages. IDG Books Worldwide, through a joint venture with IDG's Hi-Tech Beijing, became the first U.S. publisher to publish a computer book in the People's Republic of China. In record time, IDG Books Worldwide has become the first choice for millions of readers around the world who want to learn how to better manage their businesses.

Our mission is simple: Every one of our books is designed to bring extra value and skill-building instructions to the reader. Our books are written by experts who understand and care about our readers. The knowledge base of our editorial staff comes from years of experience in publishing, education, and journalism — experience we use to produce books to carry us into the new millennium. In short, we care about books, so we attract the best people. We devote special attention to details such as audience, interior design, use of icons, and illustrations. And because we use an efficient process of authoring, editing, and desktop publishing our books electronically, we can spend more time ensuring superior content and less time on the technicalities of making books.

You can count on our commitment to deliver high-quality books at competitive prices on topics you want to read about. At IDG Books Worldwide, we continue in the IDG tradition of delivering quality for more than 30 years. You'll find no better book on a subject than one from IDG Books Worldwide.

John Kilcullen
Chairman and CEO
IDG Books Worldwide, Inc.

IDG is the world's leading IT media, research and exposition company. Founded in 1964, IDG had 1997 revenues of $2.05 billion and has more than 9,000 employees worldwide. IDG offers the widest range of media options that reach IT buyers in 75 countries representing 95% of worldwide IT spending. IDG's diverse product and services portfolio spans six key areas including print publishing, online publishing, expositions and conferences, market research, education and training, and global marketing services. More than 90 million people read one or more of IDG's 290 magazines and newspapers, including IDG's leading global brands — Computerworld, PC World, Network World, Macworld and the Channel World family of publications. IDG Books Worldwide is one of the fastest-growing computer book publishers in the world, with more than 700 titles in 36 languages. The "...For Dummies®" series alone has more than 50 million copies in print. IDG offers online users the largest network of technology-specific Web sites around the world through IDG.net (http://www.idg.net), which comprises more than 225 targeted Web sites in 55 countries worldwide. International Data Corporation (IDC) is the world's largest provider of information technology data, analysis and consulting, with research centers in over 41 countries and more than 400 research analysts worldwide. IDG World Expo is a leading producer of more than 168 globally branded conferences and expositions in 35 countries including E3 (Electronic Entertainment Expo), Macworld Expo, ComNet, Windows World Expo, ICE (Internet Commerce Expo), Agenda, DEMO, and Spotlight. IDG's training subsidiary, ExecuTrain, is the world's largest computer training company, with more than 230 locations worldwide and 785 training courses. IDG Marketing Services helps industry-leading IT companies build international brand recognition by developing global integrated marketing programs via IDG's print, online and exposition products worldwide. Further information about the company can be found at www.idg.com. 1/26/00

Dedication

My beloved has gone down to his garden to the beds of spices, to browse in the gardens and to pick lilies.

Song of Songs

To the memory of my entire family who perished during the Holocaust — I am thankful that they had the opportunity to instill in me the much cherished values of the Jewish Tradition before they were lost to me. And to the memory of my beloved late husband, Manfred Westheimer.

To my wonderful family of now: my daughter, Miriam Westheimer, Ed.D; my son-in-law, Joel Einleger; my grandson, Ari Einleger; my granddaughter, Leora Einleger; my son, Joel Westheimer, Ph.D.; my daughter-in-law, Barbara Leckie, Ph.D.; and my granddaughter, Michal Leckie!

Authors' Acknowledgments

From Dr. Ruth Westheimer: Pierre Lehu and I are now entering our twentieth year of working together! A special toast to Pierre and to many more years of cooperation.

I have so many people to thank it would require an additional chapter, so let me just mention a few: Martin Englisher; Richard Freese; Cynthia Fuchs Epstein, Ph.D. and Howard Epstein; Gabe Erem; Josh Gafni; Ellen Goldberg; David Goslin, Ph.D.; Amos Grunebaum, M.D.; Alfred Kaplan; Steve Kaplan, Ph.D.; Ronnie and Michael Kassan; Bonnie Kaye; John Kilcullen; Larry Kirshbaum; Marga and Bill Kunreuther; Rabbi and Mrs. William Lebeau; Lou Lieberman, Ph.D. and Mary Cuadrado, Ph.D.; John and Ginger Lollos; Sanford Lopater, Ph.D.; Jonathan Mark; Dale Ordes; Henry and Sydelle Ostberg; Bob Pinto; Fred and Ann Rosenberg; Cliff Rubin; Jonathan Sacks; Tim Satterfield; Rose and Simeon Schreiber; Daniel Schwartz; Amir Shaviv; Richard Stein; Hannah Strauss; Romie and Blanche Shapiro; John and Marianne Slade; Greg Willenborg; and Ben Yagoda.

To the IDG Books staff: What a terrific, hard working, competent, and expert group you are to work with! Thanks especially to Stacy Collins, Tracy Boggier, Joan Friedman, Ellen Considine, Rowena Rappaport, and Janet Withers.

From Pierre Lehu: Thanks to my wife Joanne, who rekindles our romance every single day. Thanks to my children, Peter and Gabrielle, my mother, Annette, and my in-laws, Joe and Anita Seminara, for their support. I join with Ruth in thanking everyone at IDG Books, though I must add my special thanks to Joan Friedman, who was my all-in-one lifeline, phone-a-friend, and ask the audience. And, of course, to Dr. Ruth Westheimer, for all she's done to rekindle romance in the entire universe.

Publisher's Acknowledgments

We're proud of this book; please register your comments through our IDG Books Worldwide Online Registration Form located at `http://my2cents.dummies.com`.

Some of the people who helped bring this book to market include the following:

Acquisitions, Editorial, and Media Development

Senior Project Editor: Joan Friedman

Acquisitions Editor: Stacy S. Collins

Copy Editors: Ellen Considine, Janet M. Withers

Managing Editor: Tracy L. Boggier

General Reviewer: Diane L. Brashear, Ph.D.

Permissions Editor: Laura Moss

Editorial Manager: Christine Meloy Beck

Editorial Assistant: Jennifer Young

Production

Project Coordinator: Maridee Ennis

Layout and Graphics: Amy Adrian, LeAndra Johnson, Erin Zeltner

Proofreaders: Susan Moritz, Nancy Price, Charles Spencer, York Production Services, Inc.

Indexer: York Production Services, Inc.

Special Help
Robert Annis, Gwenette Gaddis, Rowena Rappaport

General and Administrative

IDG Books Worldwide, Inc.: John Kilcullen, CEO; Bill Barry, President and COO

IDG Books Consumer Reference Group

Business: Kathleen A. Welton, Vice President and Publisher; Kevin Thornton, Acquisitions Manager

Cooking/Gardening: Jennifer Feldman, Associate Vice President and Publisher

Education/Reference: Diane Graves Steele, Vice President and Publisher; Greg Tubach, Publishing Director

Lifestyles: Kathleen Nebenhaus, Vice President and Publisher; Tracy Boggier, Managing Editor

Pets: Dominique De Vito, Associate Vice President and Publisher; Tracy Boggier, Managing Editor

Travel: Michael Spring, Vice President and Publisher; Suzanne Jannetta, Editorial Director; Brice Gosnell, Managing Editor

IDG Books Consumer Editorial Services: Kathleen Nebenhaus, Vice President and Publisher; Kristin A. Cocks, Editorial Director; Cindy Kitchel, Editorial Director

IDG Books Consumer Production: Debbie Stailey, Production Director

IDG Books Packaging: Marc J. Mikulich, Vice President, Brand Strategy and Research

◆

The publisher would like to give special thanks to Patrick J. McGovern, without whom this book would not have been possible.

◆

Contents at a Glance

Cartoons at a Glance

By Rich Tennant

"My wife and I were drifting apart. We decided to go back to doing what we used to do when we were first married. So we called her parents and asked to borrow money."

page 7

"THEY'RE A VERY PROGRESSIVE COMPANY—IT COMES WITH MATCHING COLORED CONDOMS."

page 295

"MOM AND DAD GET LIKE THIS EVERY TIME THEY WATCH BACK-TO-BACK EPISODES OF 'THE LOVE BOAT'."

page 63

"I couldn't find any rose petals, but I figured corn flakes make more sense in a milk bath anyway."

page 167

"JUST TO SPICE THINGS UP, I THOUGHT I'D WEAR THE FRENCH TICKLER INSIDE OUT THIS TIME TO ADD TO MY EXCITEMENT."

page 119

"I don't know, Mona—sometimes I get the feeling you're afraid to get close."

page 251

Fax: 978-546-7747
E-mail: richtennant@the5thwave.com
World Wide Web: www.the5thwave.com

Table of Contents

Introduction

• •

*A*llow me to play fortuneteller for a moment. I'm going to gaze into my crystal ball and analyze the state of your relationship with your significant other. Here I go. At the moment the picture is a bit murky — hold on while I concentrate. Ah, there we are. Hmmm, from what I can see, it looks like your relationship could use a bit of tweaking.

How did I know this? First, if everything were perfect, you probably wouldn't have picked up this book. But my crystal ball has another source of inside information. All I have to do is look out the window of my office and see all of the people hustling and bustling down the street. That vision tells me that stress and lack of time are negative influences wreaking havoc with everybody's relationships — be it with their spouses, their lovers, their children, or even their pets.

Seeking Solutions versus Throwing in the Towel

Most people who come to see me in my office have sexual problems, though I also see couples who have other marital problems. What I always tell them is that by calling to make an appointment, they've taken the most important step toward fixing the problem, whatever it is. Sadly, most people don't reach out for help when their relationships turn sour; they either live with the problem or allow their relationships to deteriorate completely. They end up leading miserable lives because of it, or they eventually separate from people they once loved. But after you admit that you have a problem and begin the process of getting help, then you've already made an enormous stride in arriving at a solution.

If your romance is showing some signs of weakness, chances are good that you don't have a serious relationship issue to overcome. More likely, your brain, which is the seat of all emotions, is overwhelmed by other aspects of your life. If you're constantly putting out one fire after another, it's easy to understand why you might have trouble keeping your romantic flame from blowing out. It's easy to shove romance into a dark corner, rationalizing that you'll get to it next week. But all too often a week turns into a month and then a year, and at some point it might just be too late: Your romance will have grown so cold that it will be beyond help.

Some people just give up on their relationships. They feel that they can barely cope with everything else on their plates, so they cut the cord and watch the dinghy that holds the remnants of their romance float off toward the horizon. They figure at least it's one less thing to worry about, especially because the situation feels hopeless.

Using the Ingredients You Have

I'm here to tell you that your relationship struggles are not hopeless. Why am I so confident? Because of the title of this book. If you and your partner had a romance once upon a time, you don't have to start from scratch. All the ingredients are still there. With some directed effort, I feel very strongly that you can rekindle that romance of yours. And congratulations are in order because you've already taken that very important first step: You picked up this book.

Let me be clear: I'm not promising an easy fix; rekindling definitely takes some work. You're going to have to push romance higher up on your priority ladder. But I'm also not going to suggest that you push it all the way to the top. You have to be a realist; if you and your partner have been together for some time, it's natural for you not to feel the overwhelming rush of romantic emotion that you experienced when you first met. On the other hand, all relationships need some romance to survive, so it's vital that you find a happy medium.

In order to rekindle your romance, you and your partner must undergo a two-step process. First, you have to realize that you've let your romance slide, and then you have to go about purposefully putting it back into its rightful place. As you read through this book, focus in on the subjects that apply most directly to your life. Maybe you want to underline or highlight suggestions you find particularly helpful or problems I define that seem to resonate with your relationship; that way, you can share your concerns or ideas with your partner by encouraging him or her to read those passages.

How This Book Is Organized

Rekindling Romance For Dummies can help you identify possible sources of stress in your relationship and offer you suggestions for ways to tackle those problems. Like all *For Dummies* books, this one is designed to let you pick and choose what you need to read; you don't need to read it cover-to-cover in order to glean lots of great advice. Use the table of contents, the index, or the headings in the chapters to hone in on the particular situations I describe that apply most directly to your circumstances.

Rekindling Romance For Dummies is divided into six parts. The chapters within each part cover specific topics in detail.

Part I: How to Win Your Mate All Over Again

In this part, I ask you to do some serious soul-searching in order to identify sources of trouble between you and your mate. I show you the importance of using open communication to overcome those potential sore spots, and I discuss the roles that conflict and mutual respect play in a successful relationship.

Part II: Inspiring a Romantic Revival

Chapter 5 offers a definition of romance to ensure that we're clear on our terms. After I define what I mean by romance, I discuss ways to strengthen your relationship by giving it the proper attention. Part of that strengthening may involve a renewal ceremony if you've been married for many years, and I discuss the reasons to take that step in Chapter 7. Chapter 8 offers suggestions for ways to plan a romantic escape from the stresses of everyday life.

Part III: Heating Up Your Sex Life

Many couples struggling to keep the heat in their romance also struggle to keep the heat turned up in the bedroom. The biggest stumbling blocks to a hot sex life? Boredom and insecurity. In this part, I show you how to strut your stuff — after you've identified exactly what your best stuff is — and how to spice things up between the sheets well into your golden years.

Part IV: Romancing Real Life

The stresses of life threaten romance at every turn. In this part, I show you the impact of having children, from the changes that take place during and after pregnancy to the lack of privacy that comes from having kids to the silence that can overwhelm a home after the kids have left. I also walk through other sources of romantic strain, from work stress to financial conflict, and offer solutions for working through them together.

Part V: Troubleshooting Your Love Life

Do you lose your partner to the TV or the computer every time he or she walks in the door? Is golf or shopping a bigger part of his of her weekend than time spent with you? If so, turn to Chapter 19 for some practical advice for overcoming these types of distractions. Chapter 20 offers guidance for determining when to seek professional help for your relationship and where to look. And Chapter 21 outlines some common medical problems that can impact the state of your relationship, so you know when a doctor's care is in order.

Part VI: The Part of Tens

Every *For Dummies* book has The Part of Tens. In this one, you get great advice about romantic getaways, unusual dates to plan with your mate, ways to add some zing to your sex life, and Web sites to visit for even more romantic ideas.

Icons Used in This Book

To highlight information that may be of particular importance to you, I've inserted icons in the margins throughout the book. Here's what the various icons signify:

This icon alerts you to a useful tidbit of information.

This icon sits next to paragraphs that contain ideas that help you create an especially sensual aura.

This icon points out stories involving couples that can help you cope with similar situations. The names used are not those of real couples, and the situations described are composites derived from various therapy sessions.

This icon points to practical advice and my personal thoughts about the state of romance today.

This icon signals behaviors that could cause trouble, either for you or your relationship.

Open Your Matchbooks

At the Indy 500, they say, "Start your engines" — I'm going to revise that to "get those matchbooks ready." Keep in mind that if the first match doesn't light the fire under your romance, keep trying. Your romance is too important to give up without putting up one heck of a fight.

Part I

How to Win Your Mate All Over Again

The 5th Wave   By Rich Tennant

"My wife and I were drifting apart. We decided to go back to doing what we used to do when we were first married. So we called her parents and asked to borrow money."

In this part . . .

Before you can start repairing some of the cracks in your romance, you have to understand the tools required for the job. One of the most essential tools is honesty, which allows you to evaluate your relationship fairly. Another is communication, both through the things you say and the things you do. A third is, believe it or not, conflict — a necessary part of every relationship, but one that often is allowed to overwhelm romance. And a fourth is respect, without which a couple can never experience the thrill of romance.

This part helps you understand the necessity of each of these tools and the ways they can be applied to the task of rebuilding your romance. Chapter 1 asks you to take an honest look at the state of your relationship, including improvements you can make in relating to your partner. Chapter 2 tackles the all-important subject of communication, from finding topics to talk about to setting aside the time to discuss them. In Chapter 3, you discover why you cannot — and should not — eliminate all conflict from your relationship, as well as how to prevent conflicts from turning too ugly too often. And Chapter 4 offers suggestions for improving the respect you show for yourself as well as for your partner, so you both can feel bolstered by your relationship.

Chapter 1

How Does Your Relationship Rate? A Self-Assessment

*A*sking yourself the question "How does my relationship rate?" is important, but be advised that assessing your relationship is a little like opening Pandora's box. Perhaps you've previously taken one of those tests that women's magazines are fond of touting on their covers. Maybe you thought nothing of the results — it's all innocent fun, right? Wrong. These types of personal tests ask you to question the status quo, and any time you do that, you can feel like you're on shaky ground.

I'm not saying that you shouldn't take a closer look at your relationship. The fact that you're reading this book tells me that you've probably already asked yourself whether some sprucing up is in order. But once you start asking questions, there's no telling where the answers will lead. You may even decide that the state of your relationship is so bad that you need to put it out to pasture. Ideally, things have not gone that sour, so you still have the opportunity to make significant improvements. To do that, you need to find answers to your questions. Luckily for you, you're not just filling out a magazine questionnaire that leaves you hanging; you get the support of an entire book that deals with such issues.

Is Assessment Worth the Risk?

With all the dangers inherent in relationship tests, you may wonder why I'm asking you to rate your relationship. The need to assess what is going on in your life is critical. When people come to my office for counseling, the first thing I do is have them take a sexual status exam. I ask them all sorts of very personal questions about their sex lives, because if I don't know what the problem is, I can't help them solve it.

The same principle applies to your relationship. If you just have a vague sense that your relationship needs some repair work, how can you decide what you need to do? But just because an assessment is a step you should take doesn't mean that you should do so lightly. There are pitfalls, but now that you know what they are, I trust that we can proceed — with caution.

Steering Clear of Comparisons

Part of the danger posed by magazine pop quizzes arises when you assess your answers. The editors give you some sort of scoring system to rate your answers, and after you calculate your score, you naturally start comparing the state of your relationship to the standards set by the editors. Remember that old saying "the grass is always greener on the other side of the fence"? That deep green hue you admire when peeking through a knothole is (more often than not) an illusion.

Coveting your neighbor's relationship

When it comes to relationships, people know that they are being watched, so they put on a show. If you think about it, you've probably done the same thing. For example, say you were arguing with your spouse in the car. When you got home, you would stop until you were in the house and the door was closed, right? Your neighbors may think that they know what the two of you are like, but you hide certain details from public view.

But what if the couple next door always keeps the windows wide open so that their life is an open book (perhaps *The Joy of Sex*)? The shade of their grass isn't important; it doesn't get rid of the weeds in your own lawn. Let me give you a concrete example. Suppose that you've never heard the couple next door fight. You may think that this means their relationship is in great shape. But perhaps instead of yelling and screaming at each other when they're angry, these two people give each other the silent treatment. Comparing how many fight nights you have to the seemingly harmonious aura of their home could lead you astray.

Even if it's true that your neighbors never fight and you occasionally do, how does that change your situation? It doesn't. Nor should it make you feel better if the couple on the other side of your house has nightly brawls. The relationship between the two of you matters; nobody else's scorecard counts.

Real life versus the media

When it comes to making comparisons, another pitfall is to compare yourself to the families that inhabit your TV set and cinema multiplexes. Placing your life next to a fictional creation can only cause problems. When you see an action hero dive through a plate glass window, does it make you want to embark on a similar shattering experience? In that case, you know "it only happens in the movies." So why is it that when you see two people making love on screen, you begin to wonder why the activity in your bedroom doesn't duplicate what you're watching? After all, those love scenes are just as fictional as the action scenes in *Die Hard* or the aliens in *Star Wars*.

Of course, having sex is a bit more commonplace than hurling yourself through a window. In fact, there are probably a million or so people engaging in this pleasurable pursuit somewhere in the world as you read this page. But that doesn't mean that what you see on screen reflects reality. Directors have to hold your interest, and to do so they resort to all sorts of tricks. For example, that famous actress starring in the movie may not be the person between the sheets in the love scene; a body double may be taking her place. Directors also have to condense time so a plot that spans days or weeks can fit within a couple of screen hours. That's why within seconds of falling down on the bed, the screen couple is moaning and groaning without any thought of foreplay. In real life, when you and your partner lie down together, you may not have finished your discussion of who left the hall closet light on for a whole week, and you won't get down to business for a few more minutes.

One category of films that can be especially dangerous is erotic videos. I'm not against watching them, but I do wish that they would cast people who resemble the general population a bit more. Young men see these films and worry about the size of their organs. And women worry about the size of their breasts and their thighs. Both sexes wonder why their bedroom activities don't resemble the steamy scenes depicted in between those short spurts of terrible dialogue. But remember, these actors aren't making love; they're working. They're under hot lights with a team of people looking on, and they have to perform whether they like it or not. Don't compare yourself to the people in these films; they're just following a script, whereas you are living a real life.

Comparing Past and Present

If you're not going to compare your relationship to anyone else's, either real or fictional, then what comparison are you going to make? The obvious answer is to compare your current relationship to the relationship you used to have. I have to assume that if you are part of a couple, married or not, at some point in time you voluntarily made a commitment to each other. Each of you found a sufficient number of attractive characteristics in the other to justify the decision to become a couple.

Some relationships start off being very romantic: You bring each other flowers regularly, candlelight dinners are a regular part of your agenda, and holidays are celebrated with gifts and passion. If this describes the start of your relationship and now you barely say two words to each other, then clearly you have a problem. But what if at the beginning of your relationship you both were working 12 hours a day, seven days a week, and decided to move in together just so that you could see each other slightly more often? Now two years have gone by, and you still are like two ships passing in the night. Can you say your relationship needs rekindling if the romance quotient was never very high to begin with?

To start this evaluation process, you need a good dose of realism. If you've been looking back at the beginning of your relationship through a pair of those legendary rose-colored glasses, then any dissatisfaction you now feel may be based on a faulty premise. Or if you have been busy under the covers and now have six small children running around, it should be obvious why you don't visit Victoria's Secret very often.

Waiting for your partner to change

Cathy and Jim

When Cathy first met Jim, she thought of him as a diamond in the rough. He was sweet and hard working, but he dressed badly and his manners needed work. After six months, she moved into his apartment and did her best to straighten it out. She wasn't worried that it seemed a fruitless exercise because she figured they'd eventually get married and have a place of their own that she'd keep neat.

Jim did agree to get somewhat spruced up for the wedding, but because they wanted to save up for a house, they stayed in the same apartment after they married. Cathy began to try harder to put her mark on the apartment, but Jim resisted many of her efforts. He didn't see his piles of old magazines as dust-gatherers but as valuable reference tools, and because they'd always been there, he saw no reason for them to be thrown out. The more Cathy realized how difficult it was going to be to make the place "homey," the more frustrated she became. The two of them began to fight constantly, not just over the mess, but about almost everything.

The belief that marriage (or any sort of commitment) will change one partner's personality is a dangerous trap. If someone is messy before he says "I do," he's going to stay messy afterwards. If she has always pinched pennies, she's not going to loosen the purse strings after tying the knot. And if your partner has never acted romantically, that behavior is not likely to start just because you now have a ring on your finger.

What should you do if your partner doesn't have a romantic bone in his or her body and you crave it? Are you destined to never have a romantic moment in your life? The answer is no, but you do have to have realistic expectations. For example, say you love having flowers in the house, but your partner would sooner have a tooth extracted than step into a flower shop. What should you do? Buy them for yourself. You can pretend that he gave them to you or just bask in the glow of their beauty. Don't sit there feeling miserable and refusing to buy flowers because you insist that they be a gift.

When you assess your relationship, keep it within the parameters of what you started with. Don't expect to discover a prince after you've wedded your toad.

Dealing with dwindling romance

A more common situation that couples face is that whatever level of romance existed early in the relationship has since dwindled. The extent of this decline can depend on many factors, including the following:

- **The length of the relationship.** Twenty or thirty years can do more than wrinkle your skin.

- **Whether or not the partners have married.** Some couples don't survive those steps down the aisle.

- **If one result of the union has been children.** This can be especially difficult if the children outnumber the parents.

- **What paths their careers have taken.** Dot.com employers are notoriously bad for a couple's love life.

The word *dwindling* may not be a scientific term, but a decrease in romance is not something that you have to calibrate to any particular degree. The only thing that counts is how you feel about it. If you're relatively satisfied with your life together, even if it is a bit less romantic than it once was, then there's no need to fret. The more dissatisfied you are, the more effort you need to put into the rekindling process.

Also be aware of the overall trend of the romance in your relationship. Perhaps you've been together for ten years, and there has been some lessening in the romance sector but it has leveled off over the years. That's a different situation than if you've been together two years and there has been a steady decrease that shows no signs of slowing down. The latter may require drastic action, possibly including a trip to a partnership counselor, whereas the former may just need a little tweaking.

Pencil and Paper Time

If you're looking for an actual questionnaire to fill out, I'm afraid you're going to be disappointed. Because each individual has such different circumstances, I really don't see the point of filling out a form, which can't possibly apply to each specific situation. All you need to make this self-assessment is some paper, a pencil, and some quiet time when you can think. If you insist on making your own questionnaire with dotted lines and lots of A, B, C, and Ds, be my guest. Just don't send it to me for official scoring.

Going it alone

DR. RUTH SAYS

I don't recommend that you begin this process with your partner. This is a case where one head is better than two. You're going to make some critical judgments, and criticism of any kind often makes people defensive, which can lead to arguments. We're trying to make improvements to your love life, not get you into a fight.

Keep in mind that certain aspects of your relationship may not need to be included in a discussion of potential improvements. For example, imagine that your wife's great passion is gardening, so that as soon as the first crocus pops out of the ground, she spends every Saturday morning tending to her blooms. To you, spring means allergy season, so you're forced to stay inside. Should you ask her to give up something she loves so much because of your allergies? The fact that you never spend Saturday mornings together unless it's pouring rain may be something you would plan to write down on your list of gripes. But if you love her, do you really want to make her stay indoors? I don't think so. This situation does not need to be brought up unless Saturday mornings are the only possible time when the two of you can spend some quality time together. In that case, reaching a compromise would be important to your relationship.

Another set of gripes that are difficult to deal with are those that are work-related. Some people are workaholics when they don't need to be. Some actually spend all those hours at the office in order to avoid their partners. Those relationships need special counseling if they're to survive. But other people have no choice about working long hours, and that certainly interferes with romance. Special problems arise when two partners work different shifts. But although these situations are complex, there are ways of alleviating the damage they can do to your relationship. We discuss this further in Chapter 16.

Step 1: Judge thyself

The first step in creating a fair assessment of your relationship is to examine your own behavior and create a list of things you can do to improve the quality of your relationship. Though you may have a very easy time composing a long list of complaints about your partner (we'll get to that in Step 3), it's a mistake to limit your analysis to your "better half." Nobody's perfect, so you can certainly make improvements that will enhance the romance level of your relationship. You're not showing this list to your partner until you have edited it, so go ahead and be as harsh on yourself as you can.

If you can't think of a single thing that you're doing wrong, then you're not trying hard enough. You may be afraid that by admitting a fault you'll be forced to correct it, but that's not necessarily true. You can't be perfect, so your partner has to learn to accept and love some of your imperfections. But if your list is as long as your arm, then maybe you do need to make some changes.

Step 2: Examining past attempts to rekindle

It's quite possible that somewhere along the way, you've already made some attempts to heat things up between the two of you. Because you're reading this book, I have to assume they weren't successful. Write down what you did, and perhaps what your partner did, and why the attempt didn't work. I'm not suggesting that you do this as preparation to throw the problem in your partner's face. I know it may be tempting, but that is also self-defeating.

Such a list is useful because it may show you certain patterns. For example, say everything you tried before was aimed at getting your partner away from watching football. His love of sports may be a sore point with you, but just because you don't like it doesn't mean that the situation is going to change. What this pattern should tell you is that you need to look for other areas to improve, assuming that you're not so annoyed by this particular habit that you want to end the relationship.

Step 3: Listing your relationship gripes

This task is pretty easy for most people. Following are some fairly common types of complaints, though I'm a little hesitant to make such a list because I don't want it to turn into a self-fulfilling prophecy. In other words, perhaps you were totally satisfied with one of these areas before, but then when you start to think about it, you find some little things to complain about. Steer clear of that temptation. Don't nit-pick; only add things to your list that are existing problem areas.

- ✔ Decreasing communication
- ✔ Not enough time spent together
- ✔ Lack of physical contact (not including sex)
- ✔ Too few signs of affection (including saying "I love you")
- ✔ Fear of commitment (for those not married)
- ✔ Declining sexual intimacy
- ✔ Too much argument

When you conclude your gripe list, categorize it. You need a column for those things that can't be changed, such as your partner's allergies that prevent you from sharing your favorite outdoor activity. You need a column for items that you can easily change, like taping your favorite TV show so you can free up a Saturday evening for romantic dinners. And then you need a column for those items that are up for discussion. Exactly how to make that discussion take place productively is covered in Chapter 2.

Kick-Starting Your Romantic Momentum

Naturally, you don't want to take your entire list of gripes and throw it in your partner's face. Even if you are a lot more gentle than that, if you present a long laundry list of gripes, you're much more likely to get a negative reaction than a positive one. The reaction you should aim for is *not* instant change. Instead, your goal is for the two of you to calmly sit down and discuss situations that need improvement.

To achieve the goal of communicating about certain problems, your first step needs to be to pare down your list of complaints. If you narrow your list down to one or two items that your partner can easily manage to change, then the result of your relationship analysis will lead the two of you in the right direction. One or two small changes may not seem like much progress, but in fact it's a giant stride.

Certain laws of physics apply just as much to relationships as they do to concrete objects. One of these is the law of inertia. Basically, this law says that it takes a lot more energy to get an object that is standing still to start moving than it does to increase the speed of an object that is already moving. If you both have been ignoring your relationship problems, then taking the first step is tantamount to overcoming the inertial forces. If you can get your relationship heading in the right direction, then momentum will be in your favor, and the next steps won't be nearly as hard to undertake.

Of course, you can also get off on the wrong foot, and then you're dealing with negative momentum. That's why it's very important that you don't take a negative attitude and start blaming your partner for everything. A little tact can go a long way towards a positive conclusion.

You also need reasonable expectations. If you make a request for a small change in your relationship and get a quick compliance, then you can use that momentum to make bigger improvements in your relationship. So think small, and you may win big.

Give Yourself a Gold Star

When you embark on a journey to improve your relationship, there's no way to foretell how it's going to come out. But you deserve a gold star for trying instead of stoically remaining in a relationship that leaves you unsatisfied. Relationships are complicated and require some hard work to maintain in tip-top condition; too many couples choose to ignore the tears in the fabric of their relationship until they get so big that they can't be repaired.

Chapter 2

Say It and Show It: Improving Communication

The new millennium offers so many new ways to communicate that you would think two lovers could never be out of touch, and yet communication issues remain problematic. Wires get crossed easily, especially for couples who are not on the best of terms, but even those who want to share every thought sometimes have trouble. One reason for this is that the same creative geniuses/nerds who brought us all these new ways to stay connected, like e-mail, beepers, and cell phones, also created an even longer list of distractions, like video games, 250-channel satellite dishes, and the Internet.

Many people think the expression "use it or lose it" applies to a person's sexual prowess, but it has equal relevance to a couple's vigor in more cerebral pursuits. If, as time goes by, the two of you exchange fewer and fewer words, then it becomes harder and harder to communicate. Without good communication, romance doesn't have a chance.

Are You from Different Planets?

I never jump on bandwagons. I know that some books assign various alien life forms to men and women, and I fully admit that the two sexes do have other differences besides their external appendages and cavities. The problem with bandwagons, however, is that they can become self-fulfilling prophecies. If you assume that you and your partner are in different planetary orbits, then don't be surprised if it turns out that your intercoms aren't in synch.

Need proof that assumptions can be limiting? In 1980, if you had asked a passerby whether I was on the verge of becoming a famous celebrity, he would have laughed out loud at the idea that this 4'7" college professor with a Germanic accent was heading for stardom. Yet a few years later, there I was on the cover of *People Magazine.* If I had assumed that celebrity was beyond me, then I wouldn't have the opportunity to write this book.

While gender differences may seem apparent, especially to anyone who lives with a member of the opposite sex, nobody knows for sure whether their origin is more culturally based or hard-wired into our genes. I advise you to assume that the cause is the former and not the latter. If we give in to stereotypes, then there is no hope of ever effecting any change. Less than a generation ago, many men would have said that males just don't know how to change a diaper; these days, millions of men are experts in the diaper-changing field. So while I think you can't help but be aware of the differences, don't look at them as impenetrable barriers.

On the other hand, the impact these differences have on male-female relationships is not all negative. For example, if a woman likes being in the protective arms of her he-man, and the man feels good about his ability to make his woman feel secure, then their romance is going to be enhanced by these differences, not damaged.

Rather than assuming that gender differences are insurmountable, I prefer to emphasize that as inhabitants of planet Earth, we're all capable of communicating our thoughts and feelings to a partner. Sure, some people are such chatterboxes that they could spend all day talking to a lamppost, while others could lean on one all day without saying a peep. That doesn't mean these two types of people have nothing to say to each other.

If your partner has trouble expressing his or her thoughts verbally at this point in time, then he or she probably wasn't hosting a talk show when you met; yet, you fell in love and became a couple. Communications may have deteriorated a bit since the relationship began, but you can work to repair them — that's the goal for which you should be aiming.

Coping with Communication Breakdowns

If you find that the communications between you and your partner have lost much battery power, especially if you feel the verbal void is harming your relationship, then get out your tool kit. In many instances, the lack of communication results from not having enough free time to even string a couple of sentences together. To improve this situation, you need to make a concerted effort. You have to say to your partner, "We need more time to talk — where do we fit it in?"

When communications are already full of static, getting specific answers to a question like this can be tricky. "Later" won't do, because it's applicable 24 hours a day, 7 days a week. "Not now" is acceptable, as long as it is followed by a specific hour within your lifetime. If your partner begs off from being specific at that moment in time because you posed the question while peering around the shower curtain as he or she was lathering up, then make an appointment to talk about when to talk. Don't do this in an angry way, but do be firm.

Your partner may say that there's no need to talk any more than you already do. Your partner may even feel that the flow of words is turned up too high as it is. If that is the case, then your relationship may need more than rekindling and require actual repairs. Under these circumstances, I advise that you see a marital therapist. Making such an appointment sends at least one very important message to your partner: This issue is vital to the survival of your relationship. If your partner doesn't respond positively, then perhaps it's time to consider severing the connection. But hopefully that's not going to happen, and with the help of the therapist you can make some progress.

Making time for face-to-face time

One reason you want to ask your partner to choose the time and place for this conversation about communication is that it directly involves him or her in the process. Setting a time to talk is not a huge commitment to your relationship, but it's a start, and getting started is vital to making progress.

Perhaps this isn't the first time you've tried to have this powwow. Maybe you've asked for some face time many times before and have been rebuffed. Don't be too quick to take that rejection personally. Sometimes other factors are at play that aren't always apparent. For example, say that you always wake up in the morning full of energy and ready to tackle the big problems in the world. To you, having a discussion about your relationship over morning coffee is as natural as dunking a doughnut in it. But if your partner needs that time to get psychologically prepared for the rest of the day, then that might be the worst possible time to have this sort of talk. So you may be thinking that your partner is ducking you, when in fact the time of day is the main stumbling block. Timing is everything, so having a discussion about when to have a discussion solves at least one area of potential conflict right off the bat.

Of course, your partner may suggest a time that's not right for you. Maybe he or she is a night owl, and you can't keep your eyes open past 9:30 p.m., so 11 p.m. would be difficult for you. I recommend that you accept that offer for at least the first discussion. Take a nap that day if you need to, or go for a walk at 10 p.m. to get your blood flowing. Take a cold shower if you're still falling asleep. You're initiating this discussion, so you need to bend over a bit backwards to get things started.

"But Dr. Ruth," you say, "my partner picked that time knowing how difficult it would be for me." First, I say, calm down. You can't be sure that what you are surmising is true. If your partner is a night owl, that may really be the perfect time for him or her. You asked for a good meeting time, and your partner may just be giving you an honest answer. That's why you have to give it a shot. If your partner acts out of bad faith, then it will become obvious, and you have a bigger problem than perhaps you realized. But if not, maybe you've found just the way to start rekindling your romance — staying awake after the sun sets.

Managing miscommunications

The list for potential miscommunication is endless, so never "assume" anything, especially if you're communicating poorly. You can start imagining an insult or a cold shoulder that doesn't exist in your partner's mind at all. The longer such a thought lingers, the worse it becomes. It's similar to what can happen when a loved one doesn't show up at the expected time and doesn't call. As the hours pass, you start worrying and imagining the worst. By the time the person walks through the door, you're in an absolute panic, usually over nothing.

You may experience the same effect when the two of you aren't getting the right meaning of each other's words. If you don't talk it out, you can build up a miscommunication in your imagination to a point where you're ready to break up over absolutely nothing. And if you overreact when you finally do talk about it, your partner may have no idea what's going on. Matters may quickly escalate from there.

 If you get the urge to obsess over an issue that you're not sure really exists, use all of your willpower to push it aside. Assumptions can be very limiting. When you start to think about the issue, force yourself to think of something else. Sing a song in your head. Work on a crossword puzzle. Do some sit-ups. Bake a cake. Then when you do sit down to talk to your partner, your goal should be to clear it up so that you never have to worry about it again.

Separating Sex and Romance

One of the most widespread forms of miscommunication between men and women stems from the fact that too many people, especially men, equate sex with romance. They believe that if their sex life is adequate, then there's no need for anything beyond this one arena. Tied to this is the notion that romantic activity outside the bedroom is automatically a lead-in to sexual activity.

And by the way, this is a double-edged sword. Many people think of kissing and hugging as preludes to sex. As a result, when they aren't in the mood, they don't want to snuggle because they assume that it will lead to sex. This can be true of both partners in a relationship where a pattern has been established that kissing and hugging lead to sex. So the first batch of people may avoid physical contact if it's not attached to sex, and the second group may avoid physical contact because they fear that it will lead to sex at the wrong time. Either way, the partner who is looking for some physical contact that is not sex-related gets left hugging her knees.

Communication is vital in this arena. The partner who wants romantic touching has to explain that she would like some more physical contact that is not linked to sex. She has to explain to her partner that just the way a car needs oil to keep the engine running smoothly, she needs some hugs, kisses, and hand-holding in order to keep her spirits going.

Sports analogies sometimes work well when explaining things, so here's one: Just because you play catch doesn't mean that it's going to lead to an entire nine-inning game of baseball. Sometimes players do play catch to warm up before a game, but playing catch doesn't automatically lead to a complete game of baseball.

I don't want to put all the onus on men here. Some women crave romance but purposefully shut down their libidos once they get their fix because they're a bit busy or preoccupied. They are satisfied by the hugs and kisses, but they don't consider what will satisfy their partners. Although romantic interludes don't have to lead to sex, if they're heading in that direction, veering off the path every time is not a fair way to treat a man. If women allow themselves to become more aroused, they usually do enjoy having sex and have orgasms. But sometimes they stuff themselves on the appetizer and then don't feel they have room for the main meal. Their partners, who require more sustenance, are left feeling frustrated. If this scenario occurs too often, then clearly the relationship can suffer.

Decoding confusing signals

Another cause of confusion occurs when couples try to communicate with each other about which signs of physical affection will lead to sex and which won't. Two key facts need to be remembered: Men get aroused easily, and women can change their minds.

Even though a man may get aroused by some hugging and kissing and even have an erection, this doesn't mean that he'll start writhing on the ground or baying at the moon if he doesn't have sex. Men, particularly young men, get erections all day long and all night long as well (usually every 90 minutes during REM sleep). After a few moments, these erections grab a cab and head downtown of their own accord, providing that the man isn't getting further stimulation. If he is being constantly stimulated, then his arousal will reach a point where it is difficult for him to just say no. But the stimulation from a one-minute hug, providing that he and his partner are not in the nude and she keeps her hands above the belt, doesn't mean that the next step has to be a sexual encounter.

And a woman who was just looking for a hug may suddenly find that she is interested in sex, even though that was not on her mind beforehand. Women always claim the right to change their minds, and sometimes they're just too busy to realize that they were somewhat aroused. When they take a breather in the arms of their man, they relax a bit and suddenly realize that there was more to their desire for a hug than just romance.

You may think that two people who are part of a long-standing couple should know enough about each other to be able to judge when they are going to have sex and when they're not, yet they often act like a couple on their first date — he's on first base wondering if he'll get to second.

What's the answer? Improved communication. You have to be able to share your sensitivities with your partner without hurting his or her feelings. If a woman notices that her partner has an erection, she has to be able to tell him that she's not in the mood without him getting upset. And if she decides that she is in the mood and they do have sex, the next time they hug, he can't assume that it's going to happen again.

It's very easy for there to be crossed wires in this back-and-forth exchange, particularly if both people change their minds faster than an operator can plug in the connection. Avoid setting fixed patterns. Each party needs to show flexibility. That means if sometimes she asks for a hug without thinking about sex, she will let herself be brought over to the bed and try to enjoy it. At other times, even if a particular kiss drags on a bit longer than usual, she can go off to finish the paper without feeling guilty and without him donning his hangdog face. It also means that she should initiate sex from time to time, and he should initiate hugs. Good communication means a back-and-forth interaction. It means surprise. It means that your minds are engaged and that you're not acting out the same script over and over, like in the movie *Groundhog Day*.

Improving conversational content

This seems like the appropriate place to delve into the content of your communications. If all you do is talk about such superficial matters as the weather, the children's science fair project, and what to defrost for dinner, then your relationship is going to be rather superficial as well. That's not to say that you shouldn't talk about mundane subjects. A life is a bit like a business, and you need to deal with managerial matters. But conversations you have with your coworkers aren't likely to lead to sex, or at least I hope not. You can spend hours at the water cooler bantering about sports, politics, and office gossip without ever probing any depths. If your conversations with your significant other are equally superficial, then what does that say about the state of your relationship?

Admittedly, some people who have partners still pour their hearts out to their coworkers. Sometimes they've found someone who is simpatico and doesn't mind being a good listener. Or they've found a busybody who likes peering into other people's private lives. And sometimes the other person is bored to tears. But if the talker is baring his or her soul at the office and clams up at home, that's not a good omen.

Meaningful communications don't have to only be about personal crises. I would hope that your life is not in such turmoil that your only topics of conversation are problem-related. Endless talk of problems will turn off a partner, no matter how sympathetic he or she is. Rather, what is "meaningful" is what stimulates the intellect. For example, say you watch the news and the Supreme Court has ruled for or against some case. Talking about the pros and cons of that decision should be equally interesting to both parties. You shouldn't be so polarized that such a conversation creates an automatic fight. If that's the case, then I'd say to put those topics off limits. But there should be areas of discussion that allow you to learn more about your partner as you exchange ideas.

Experiencing Empty Nest Syndrome

Some couples spend the first 20 years of marriage relating to each other, for the most part, around topics connected with their children. That's not to say that Jane and Johnny's grades and hobbies aren't important to discuss. However, this type of couple runs into trouble when Jane and Johnny grow up and leave home and the parents are left staring at each other with nothing to talk about. Suddenly, it's as if they are two strangers who just happened to share the same roof for two decades. Both may become frustrated and end up sitting in silence, or in front of the TV, or fighting. After all this time spent together, they have nothing in common. This is called *empty nest syndrome*. I cover the topic in-depth in Chapter 15, but I want to introduce it here because communication is so crucial to preventing the problem.

Celeste and Vincent

When Vincent was 58, his company moved to another state. Between the severance package and his retirement income, he decided to skip making the move and take an early retirement. Vincent and Celeste's children were both out of college, and he figured that if he didn't need to work, why should he?

Celeste worked in the town library, but only three days a week, which meant the couple had four entire days to be with each other. It had seemed like a good idea when they talked about it, but the reality turned out far differently. After only a few weeks, they found themselves arguing more than they ever had, and arguing about stupid things. They would try to avoid making contact, but eventually they'd find themselves in the same room, and after a brief silence they would start to pick at each other until a fight had begun. It seemed that fighting had turned into their only means of communication.

It's very difficult, if not impossible, to fix a situation like this after it has occurred. A couple may stay together and muddle through to the ends of their lives, but it's not a very satisfying relationship. And their retirement years, instead of being more enjoyable because they can spend their days and nights together, turn into a battlefield.

Creating connections early in life

The secret to avoiding empty nest syndrome is to develop a relationship early on that is based on more than the children. Little tykes can take up all of your time, and they are very cute and cuddly. But as they grow up and start pulling away, the two of you have to create a life as a couple. That means you need some adult pursuits that are not linked to the children.

Let's say you like to go shopping for antiques. You both enjoy going for a drive and stopping at several shops, and you also buy books on your favorite types of antiques and study up so that you can spot the real thing from the fake. This is the type of hobby that can drive children up a wall. They're not going to have a good time going to shops full of fragile objects, and if they act up and break something, their presence could be very costly. Does that mean you have to give up this hobby? If you do, realize that you may be damaging your relationship down the road.

One alternative is to invoke your full powers as disciplinarians: Take the children with you and force them to behave. By bringing along some books and including a treat or two for them along the way, like a stop at a miniature golf course, you may be able to satiate your appetite for this pastime without regretting it. Alternatively, find some babysitters — grandparents, paid sitters, or neighbors who also want some time off now and then and will exchange with you — and go by yourselves. Or combine both approaches.

Improving your topical tan

What if you don't have any such shared interests? What if he occupies his free time watching every sports show known to man and she spends her spare time at the mall? Are you doomed to mope around that nest staring at those empty shells? Of course not. There's still time to develop a common interest. In fact, the search process can be quite entertaining all on its own.

There are no rules about whether the two of you should have one shared interest or twenty. For example, you both might enjoy traveling, but if you have responsibilities, you can't be gadding about all the time. The same is true for going to the theater or skiing, especially in summer. But you can read up on these subjects and discuss what you learn. You can go online and discover stimulating facts to share. And, if you do these activities regularly when you have the chance, then you have past experiences about which you can reminisce (and perhaps a photo album or two to spur your memories).

The two key words here are *share* and *stimulating*. If you can both talk about it, and you both become stimulated while doing so, then it doesn't matter what "it" is, as long as it gets you communicating.

This concept doesn't mean that you have to share every one of your pastimes. She doesn't have to learn to appreciate football, and he doesn't have to turn into a baker. What it boils down to is a question of moderation so that you have some pastimes that you share and some that you don't. If you can't decide whether one party or the other is too involved in his or her own preoccupations, then write down the hours you each spend at solitary pursuits; it will quickly become obvious if one person is not holding up her or his share of the relationship.

Tips for the Terminally Shy

Although stereotypically the male has problems communicating, either sex can be tongue-tied, especially when it comes to matters involving such personal areas as sex, love, and romance. Many women have issues of self-esteem that keep them from asking their partners for what they need, even if it's only a hug.

To start with, separate the issue of not being able to say something from not having anything to say. Most people who can't communicate to others have a steady stream of thoughts going through their heads. Their lack of loquaciousness doesn't mean that they're not bright or interesting, just that they have difficulties getting the words out. There may be many reasons for this, and it doesn't matter what they are as long as you find a way to loosen those knots in the tongue.

For some people, writing is the key to unlocking their thoughts. Writing gives one time to think, and erasers and delete keys prevent making major goofs. A letter or a note to your partner can trigger a conversation, and for many people the start of the conversation is the chief stumbling block. By establishing the subject matter in the written missive, you can cover some of the hardest ground before you have to engage in conversation. So if you are having difficulties raising a subject with your partner, by all means send him or her a note to get the ball rolling.

Even if you never actually give the person the note, writing down your thoughts gives you a mental road map that you can use during an actual conversation. If you want to cover certain points, you can tick them off in your head instead of fumbling around for the next thing to say. It even gives you the chance to prepare an opening, so that you're not stumbling over words to get things started.

You may not believe it, but many actors and actresses are actually quite shy. There they are on a stage in front of thousands of people speaking a mile a minute, and yet they may feel unable to handle a one-on-one conversation. The fact that they are repeating someone else's words, via a script, is what gets them through the play. Although I don't recommend trying to script out an entire conversation — that tactic won't work if the other party isn't reading the same script — it may help to pretend that you are someone else. Try it out in front of a mirror first. Pretend that you are one of your favorite performers having a conversation with your partner. Perhaps by enveloping yourself with this special cloak, you will find it easier to say the right words. If it does seem to work in rehearsal, so to speak, then give it a try during a real conversation.

Other people have trouble holding a conversation because they are easily distracted. Their antennae are always up, and so instead of paying attention, their minds start to roam and then they have nothing to say. For these people, I recommend having any important conversation in a place with few distractions. Go for a walk in the woods or a drive on a country road. Or call your honey into the living room and shut off most of the lights. If he or she asks you what's going on, say that his or her face is so gorgeous that it distracts you from what you have to say, so you needed to turn the lights down low.

If one of your concerns is having to ask for something, why not start out by admitting one of your own mistakes? If this was a business negotiation, the last thing you would want is to let the first words out of your mouth be "I'm sorry." But here you want to convince your partner to let his or her guard down a bit, so lowering your shield at the very beginning will give the signal that this conversation isn't about winning, but compromise.

Using Your Whole Body: Nonverbal Communication

If you believe that your mouth and ears conduct all your communications, I want to disabuse you of that notion. You actually send hundreds of signals to your partner (and to everyone else you encounter) all day long without once opening your mouth. The way you dress, your posture, your facial expressions, how you look at people (including not looking at them), your hand gestures, and the way you touch (or don't touch) are all ways you communicate to the people around you.

Decoding the messages you send

You may not be fully aware of what messages you convey with these nonverbal signals, but if communications are an issue in your relationship, then definitely try to assess exactly what messages you broadcast in this manner.

For example, have you ever thought about what you wear when you go to bed? If you cover yourself in several layers of wool and flannel, that outfit gives your partner a definite message, and it's not "Take me, I'm yours." So what if it's winter and you're trying to cut back on your heating bills? If you want a more active sex life, buy yourself an electric blanket and pare down your sleep wardrobe to a bare minimum.

Likewise, people like to wear sloppy clothes when they're hanging around the house, but if what you're wearing is in tatters, that also sends a message. Sure, you want to feel comfortable in your own home, but how is your partner supposed to find you sexy if you're always looking ragged?

When you're in close proximity of your partner, even just walking by, do you reach out and touch him or her? This type of communication doesn't cost a cent, but it can go a long way in conveying your feelings to this person you love.

And when you're actually talking, do you bother to look at your partner? If not, you're not giving the person your full attention, and your partner probably realizes that only half of your brain is engaged, if that.

In other words, just because you see your partner every weekend or have lived with him or her for 20-some years, don't treat your beloved like your old slippers. People you're close to are sensitive, and their feelings can easily be bruised, probably even more easily from you because their defenses are down.

Recognizing when words aren't enough

Harry and Betty

Harry was beginning to hate his neighbor, Bill. Bill was one of those guys who was always helping his wife. He was always volunteering to drive her places, or set the table, or fill the dishwasher. He and Bill would be watching a football game when suddenly Bill would leave to help her carry something and miss a big play. Harry didn't get it.

But the worst part was that Harry's wife, Betty, was always throwing Bill up into his face. He'd be reading the paper after a long day in the office, and she'd carry on about how Bill would never just sit like that while his wife was cooking. Harry would end up getting up to help but with a sour look on his face, thinking that the only reason he wasn't sitting there reading was because of his neighbor.

Some methods of communication require specific actions. A couple of traditional ones include sending a box of candy or a bouquet of flowers. But there are many other ways of letting a loved one know how you feel that don't cost a penny. Following are just a few examples:

- Help out with your partner's chores, like cooking dinner or helping the kids with homework.

- Accompany your partner to an event, even when you'd really prefer to stay home.

- Be extra attentive to your partner's relatives, even if you don't particularly like them.

I suppose the key word that applies to all of these gestures is *sacrifice* — be it of your time, your energy, or both. Such gestures are truly appreciated, and if you don't feel so comfortable saying how you feel, they can go a long way towards communicating your inner thoughts.

If you're on the receiving end of such kindness, let your partner know how much you do appreciate him or her. Don't go overboard in your praise because that can make the do-gooder feel uncomfortable. It may even make some people feel they were too generous. But definitely let the generous person know that you noticed what he or she did for you.

Tackling Thorny Topics

No matter how close the two of you are, one or both of you will always have a thin skin about some topics. Finances, for example, can send some people over the edge. Religion is another sticky issue. And, of course, there's sex, but that's for another chapter.

Sometimes a thorny topic can be avoided, but other times there's no getting around it. If you notice that whenever you raise one subject you get into a fight, then you probably want to change your line of approach. For example, the very word *taxes* can light a fuse under some people. Yet you may have to talk to a spouse about planning for estimated payments. Instead of avoiding the subject or exploding in return at your partner's outburst, why not just let the storm cloud blow over? Sometimes after people have a chance to vent about their favorite government agency, they calm down sufficiently to discuss which child to sell in order to pay those pesky taxes.

Don't allow repeated patterns to act as road blocks to conversation. Find a way around them so that you can proceed to accomplish whatever you need to get done.

Perfecting your communications etiquette

As important as communicating is for a couple, remember that there is a time and a place for it. The amount of privacy and time needed depend on the subject matter and the intensity of the emotions likely to be stirred. If you're discussing where to go on your next vacation, then doing so while enjoying a meal at your favorite restaurant is perfectly acceptable. But if the subject is whether to engage in oral sex, then a restaurant may not be the proper environment, despite what you may have seen in *When Harry Met Sally.*

When one or both partners spend a lot of time on the job, you have no choice but to have certain discussions over the phone during office hours. So be aware that the location from which messages are delivered naturally influences their content and tone. It's certainly appropriate to convey pure information, like when to meet for dinner, but if you need to make an important decision that may involve some differences of opinion, the setting may very well influence the outcome.

If you have something important to discuss with your partner that can't be tabled until you're both under the same roof, call to make an appointment to speak when he or she can get away from the desk to use a cell phone or a nearby phone booth. Just remember that cell phone calls can be picked up by others, even accidentally, so don't say anything that requires absolute privacy.

Avoiding firestorms

Some people can't seem to have a simple discussion. They insist on always being right, and rather than listening calmly to what you have to say, they escalate any disagreement into World War III. They may think that yelling the loudest makes them victors, when in fact they may be big losers.

We live in the information era; everyone realizes how valuable information is. Closing off discussions by throwing a temper tantrum prevents you from hearing the information you need in order to have a good relationship. To be a good conversationalist and to pick up the vital information you need, you have to be a good listener. Listening to what someone else has to say doesn't mean that you're admitting that the other person is right, only that you are open to hearing what he or she has to say.

If you think about it, argumentative people don't act out of inner strength; they act out of fear. They are terrified of ever being wrong. If your partner is like this, there are no easy solutions. People don't change their personalities overnight, if ever. You can suggest that he or she go for some therapy, though it's admittedly difficult to convince those who say they are always right that they need some repairs upstairs.

Perhaps the best thing you can do to handle a person like this is to seek some therapy yourself. The underlying issues that may have caused your partner to take on such personality traits are usually not easy to figure out. Even if your partner never joins you in the therapist's office, a therapist can guide you through some of the mine fields that lie ahead and help maintain your own sanity as you navigate through them.

Chapter 3

Conquering Conflict

· ·

In This Chapter

▶ Venting anger without losing control

▶ Learning to let go of grudges

▶ Maintaining your privacy during a conflict

▶ Recognizing and conquering repeat offenses

▶ Becoming an active peacekeeper

· ·

Although communicating better helps many couples, sometimes communication alone can't get to the heart of a problem. The two of you aren't Siamese twins (just try to imagine the complications if you were), and from time to time you are going to disagree. You can't (and shouldn't) eliminate all conflict from your relationship. You can, however, improve the ways that you and your partner deal with problems when they arise.

In this chapter, I help you recognize the role that conflict plays in your relationship, find ways to vent your frustrations without causing permanent relationship damage, and take steps toward avoiding unnecessary or excessive explosions.

Understanding the Necessity of Conflict

A little conflict can be a good thing. The stereotypical henpecked husband and doormat wife who never speak up for themselves are hardly romantic roles. Some men may have an idealized vision of a wife as a geisha, whose role is to serve hand and foot and to obey her husband's every command. But if a relationship does not allow give and take, it becomes boring. By standing up for yourself, you can make your relationship stronger. Respect is a vital ingredient in a successful relationship; if one party always gives in at the least hint of conflict, then respect disappears and the relationship suffers for it. Also, constantly bottling up feelings can result in a major explosion, which may be less easily overcome than a series of small spats.

Some people avoid conflict because they don't have confidence in their relationship. They fear that they may lose their partner just because they have a few fights. What sometimes happens in these situations is that such deep-seated insecurity becomes a turn off to that person's partner, who ends up dissolving the relationship precisely *because* the insecure person refuses to deal with any disagreements.

Don't misunderstand; I'm not saying that your relationship is about to explode because you and your partner don't engage in a daily brawl. It's certainly better to live in harmony, but almost all couples show some frayed nerves now and then. Look at it this way: You probably get angry with yourself once in a while, so why wouldn't you get angry at somebody with whom you share so much time and who's not your mirror image?

The flip side of avoiding conflict altogether is giving in to your anger too often. Although engaging in some conflict can be good, too many battles can leave your relationship scarred and war-weary. If combat continues for an excessively long time, your relationship will need a United Nations peace-keeping force instead of just some rekindling.

Blowing Off Steam

Volume alone doesn't necessarily indicate anger. Some people need to scream out loud to release inner tension. It may seem like they're itching for a fight, but by the time they're done with their ranting and raving, they're back to being their normal pussycat selves.

Learn to recognize when your partner is venting dissatisfaction with people or things that don't relate to you; even though you're the person hearing that frustration, you're not the real target of the anger. If you react to your partner's tantrum, then he or she might turn that anger on you. But if you simply listen (and maybe respond in a supportive way), you can probably avoid turning one person's blowout into a head-on collision.

Controlling your words

Whether you're blowing off steam or feeling truly angry at your partner, never let your brain lose control of your mouth. It's easy to say something that you don't really mean in a fit of anger, but the consequences of such a lapse can last, literally, a lifetime. The offended party may never believe that you didn't mean the nasty things you said. So the best course of action is never to say them at all. If you begin to feel so angry that you want to hurt the other person with your words, the best thing to do is to walk away. Those few steps may save you a lifetime of trying to make up for misspoken words.

In addition to being careful of what you say, be equally aware of how you say it. When tempers are high, many people resort to using expletives. But there's a difference between using an expletive for emphasis and directing it at somebody. If you want to repeat the F word five times in a row, that's one thing, but if you hurl it at your partner and follow it with a "you," that's another story.

Curse words generally get overused. If you hardly ever curse, then when you do it has an impact. But if you use curse words constantly, then no one will pay any attention if you say them a few more times. Try to use the extreme words as rarely as possible so that when they do pop out, they'll have the desired effect of conveying the degree of your emotions.

Overcoming the blame game

Tracing the source of a marital spat can be tough detective work. Some couples can wage a small war and then both sides forget all about it, while others find that even the tiniest skirmish has lasting effects. A major sticking point can be who started the brouhaha.

The tendency to assign blame may be a holdover from childhood, when Mom always wanted to know the source of a scuffle before doling out punishment. Without meaning to, Mom encouraged the "not me!" syndrome.

It's really not important who starts a fight unless one party is always launching attacks and the other feels constantly under siege. If that's the case, then you may need to call in a mediator. But if you have a run-of-the-mill blowup, then the question of who fired first is just not that important.

Finding the source of conflict *is* important. Fights can escalate quickly if both of you pitch every little fault that the other might ever have exhibited, starting with who hogged all the pillows on your wedding night. Although some of those other faults or past incidents may have some validity, you can never resolve all of them during one particular scrap. So if you can hone in on the real reason you're at each other's throats *at this moment,* you are more likely to come to a resolution.

If you can look at a fight as a way of problem solving, rather than as a way of hurting the other person involved, conflict can actually be useful. For example, perhaps you never realized how upset your partner feels when you are constantly late for dinner; what may be irrelevant to one person can be a real source of annoyance to the other. But if you discover this sore point during your partner's outburst, you can show your love by making a permanent repair.

If you have a gripe that you'd like to communicate with your partner, and you'd prefer to address it calmly rather than during an argument, perhaps a verbal request isn't the best way of handling it. Try writing a note or an e-mail, so that you both have time to digest the problem. You still may want or need to discuss it in person, but by giving your partner some warning, perhaps you can prevent your voices from rising too high in pitch during the discussion.

Chipping Away at That Chip on Your Shoulder

You can't heal the wounds from one of these battles unless both sides are willing to take part in the process. Holding grudges really hurts the person who can't let go of resentment, but he or she rarely realizes that. After a while, a grudge becomes like an old friend, and some people don't let go even if they can't remember exactly why it's there to begin with.

In situations where resentment has grown this much, one of you may have to decide whether the relationship is worth saving. If you reach the decision that it is, then you probably have to take several steps back from the front lines. You may have to admit that you're wrong, even if you're absolutely sure that you're not, just for the sake of making peace. If the person holding the grudge still won't let go, then a marital therapist may be in order.

Harboring Fury with a Vengeance

Holding a grudge can be a passive practice, but some people take a more aggressive approach and try to exact revenge for whatever perceived injury they feel has been inflicted upon them.

Linda and Ben

Ben had always been a car fanatic; he spent hours cleaning and waxing the car and vacuuming the inside. Ben rode the bus to work, and Linda used the car. Because she was always on the run, she often gobbled some fast food in between meetings with clients and didn't always take the time to clean up. When Ben used the car in the evenings, the garbage he found on the seats really annoyed him. He'd spoken to Linda about it several times, but it didn't seem to help.

Ben decided that the only way to get Linda to change was to teach her a lesson. Ben didn't particularly like watching TV, but Linda used it to relax, and she was an inveterate channel-changer. Ben purposefully hid the remote so that she couldn't change channels without getting up. After a few days, Ben realized that Linda didn't connect the missing remote with his gripe, so he told her what he did. Linda was furious, and the next day when he got home from work, not only was there more garbage than ever on the seat, but she'd driven the car through every mud puddle she could find.

Obviously, revenge is never an option within a loving relationship. Although you may take a while to forgive your lover, upping the ante by getting even won't strengthen your relationship.

Using sex as a weapon

One common area where lovers exact revenge is in the bedroom. Withholding sex is certainly a means of getting your revenge on the other party. If you're furious with your partner, it's understandable that you may not be terribly eager to make love, and that's okay. But if the next day, when tempers have cooled, you still refuse "out of principle" (namely to exact a penalty on the other person for his or her offense), then you are entering dangerous ground.

The danger posed by revenge is that rather than allow the wound to heal, the vengeful acts exacerbate the situation. Tit for tat gets out of hand, and the next thing you know, each of you is at the other's throat.

If you're upset at your partner, talk it out. If that doesn't work, then go for professional help. Getting even never fixes the situation.

Scripting an arousing conflict

Some people get so aroused by a fight that they wind up having great sex afterwards. I certainly don't recommend knock-down, drag-out combat, though if you want to try out how it makes you feel, you could do a professional wrestling imitation. Script out a simulated battle. You can even use props, but make sure they're soft! (Remember: Your chairs aren't the breakaway models the wrestlers use.) Your match can be X-rated, so wear some clothing that you don't care about; that way, if it gets ripped, you won't regret it. And if you do try this, be very careful. Remember this is play acting, not the real thing.

Keeping Feuds in the Family

It may be very tempting to talk about your latest family feud with other members of your family, friends, or office mates. However, hanging up your dirty laundry for others to paw and sniff at can add pressures that you don't need. Where you may be willing to forgive and forget, your confidante starts telling you that you're a fool to back down, and so you don't. Of course, you're the one who has to live with the results, so this sort of advice often causes even more problems.

Sometimes family members or friends grow to resent your partner for an argument that has long vanished from your own memory banks. Maybe they have something against your partner to begin with and are looking for excuses to think badly of him or her. Or maybe you exaggerated when reporting what happened, so their view is distorted. Whatever the cause, if they keep bringing an old argument up, it's likely to get back to your partner and cause further trouble. That's another reason to keep your fights private.

If you tell your partner what other people have said about your spat, he or she may feel ganged up on. So even if you do spill your heart out to someone else, don't bring that person's opinions back to the battle. If you agree with what some third party said, then incorporate it in your own arguments. If you're not sure that a friend's opinion is relevant, don't try to justify a particular line of reasoning by saying that it came from somebody else. If you believe strongly in your argument, that should be good enough. If you have doubts about it, then that subject doesn't belong in your discussion.

Keeping the Water Buckets Handy

Fights can be like real fires, which flare up at the least little spark but take a whole fire company to extinguish. Here are some tips that may help you facilitate the peace process:

- **Lower your voice.** People use an assortment of tactics when fighting with their mates, but probably the most common is to turn up the volume so that family feuds turn into shouting matches. Both sides may work under the assumption that whoever makes the most noise wins. By lowering the volume, you turn down the heat as well.

- **Take a deep breath.** Do this both physically and psychologically. When you take a physical deep breath, you may find that you've actually been holding your breath slightly, increasing the tension that you felt. A deep breath can help you to relax a bit, and with any luck, the change will show in your demeanor. If you appear calmer, so may your partner. A psychological breather means that you take a step back and listen to what you are saying. Are you accusing your partner of all sorts of horrendous behavior that in your heart you know is not true? Each one of these exaggerations can come back at you. By changing your perspective, you may be able to change your partner's as well.

✔ **Control your body language.** If your face is locked in a grimace and your arms are flailing all over the place, you can easily imagine that your body language is threatening. Make an effort to tone it down. That change can have an effect on your partner, who may have been matching your body language with a threatening one of his or her own.

✔ **Walk away if the temperature gets too hot.** Taking a breather doesn't mean that you're giving up; if you both cool off a bit, a resolution is more likely. So if it looks like the argument is heating up to the point where there's going to be a nuclear explosion, take your half of the radioactive material away before there's a meltdown. The discussion doesn't have to end when you take this break; it can simply serve as a postponement. However, when you've both cooled down, you may realize that this particular subject is not nearly as important as you had previously thought.

✔ **Pick a goal.** When two people argue, they often bring up old wounds, and pretty soon the fight is about one or more grievances that weren't there to begin with. That's when one person has to say, "Wait a minute, we've gone off the topic here. We need to decide *blah blah blah.*" Sometimes by selecting one reasonable goal, you can diffuse an argument that otherwise could drag on for quite some time.

✔ **Think positive thoughts about the other person.** Try to remember that you love this human being, a concept that may have taken a back seat to other opinions in the heat of the argument. A better attitude on your part may soften the attitude of your partner/opponent, and that can lead to a quicker solution.

✔ **Remember it's okay to disagree.** The final result of a fight doesn't have to be that you are on the same page. It's quite possible that you'll never agree on this particular subject, but you shouldn't let that affect your overall relationship. You're not supposed to be two peas in a pod; in fact, your relationship will be stronger if you have your own opinions. What is important is that you put this particular disagreement in its proper perspective as it relates to your relationship. If you allow the cause of this fight to overshadow how you feel about each other, then it can damage the relationship. But if you can chalk it up to "it's okay to disagree," then that should diffuse any danger the argument may pose to the two of you.

Recurring Nightmares

Some fights are like bad dreams that haunt you time and time again. The same subjects keep coming up and causing friction. If you, or both of you, feel that there is too much bickering going on in your relationship, then try to isolate these particular issues and do something about them.

What happens when the tag in a shirt bothers you — do you let it chafe your neck each time you wear that shirt, or do you tear it off? If you don't do something about that tag, after a while you never put that shirt back on. If you are always fighting with your partner, instead of wanting to be with that person, you'll want to run the other way. So although you could shrug these little arguments off as meaningless, if you don't solve them, they can turn into a type of water torture: One little drip drives a person crazy after a while. So don't think of them as unimportant; give them the attention they deserve.

This section describes some examples of this type of irritation, which can cause serious damage over time.

Celebrating special days

To some people, holidays, birthdays, and anniversaries are full of meaning. They look forward to those days and fantasize about how wonderful they'll be, while other people remain oblivious to their passage. Though neither extreme is good — the former usually experience some disappointment and the latter often miss out on much joy — if two such opposites are paired, then you can be sure there will always be fireworks whenever the calendar lands on one of these days.

Fran and Fred

Fran considered herself a romantic. As a little girl, she had always dreamed of finding her Prince Charming, who would give her boxes of her favorite chocolates every time he'd see her. Fred hadn't exactly stuffed her with chocolates while they were dating, but she also knew that as a college student he couldn't afford to do very much shopping at Godiva. He had always remembered her on holidays and her birthday, however, and she'd been satisfied enough with his attentions to get married.

Fred went on to become a trial lawyer, and when he was working on a case, he simply sealed himself off from the outside world. The only calendar he paid attention to was the court calendar; holiday after holiday passed without Fran receiving any acknowledgment that it was a special day. To Fran, each one of these missed opportunities became another nail in the coffin of their marriage, whereas Jack was totally shocked to get a letter in the mail from one of his fellow lawyers announcing the end of the union.

Most people are not as extreme as Fran and Fred, but special days do cause problems for couples if their expectations are very different. To some degree our expectations are inherited, if not genetically, then culturally. If you come from a family that makes a big deal about birthdays, and your partner's family barely notes their passing, then you can understand why you may experience some conflicting emotions when you share one of these days together.

Once again, communication is the key to solving this disparity. Listen to each other and try to understand why you have the attitudes you possess about each of these days. If you really love each other, then you can each make the appropriate compromises, but that can only happen if you understand the underlying reasoning behind the other person's reactions.

Grappling with bad habits

Bad habits may not seem that bad to the person who has them; your bad habit may even give you a lot of pleasure. But bad habits can certainly be a source of annoyance to your partner (and vice versa). Remember that the term *bad habit* is subjective: What you consider terrible may not bother many other people. Both of you may need to make compromises, but you also need to remember that one person can't really change another. If, like Oscar and Felix in *The Odd Couple,* one of you is an absolute slob and the other tidy as a pin, "Felix" shouldn't expect "Oscar" to become a neatnik: not overnight or ever. On the other hand, if one of you is always leaving shoes where they can be tripped over, you may be able to change that one particular habit.

Some people believe that their partners continue to exhibit particular bad habits solely as a means of torture. For example, if your partner burps at the dinner table, even at a fancy restaurant, it may seem as if each burp is an arrow aimed to hurt you. However, in most cases, the bad habit is just that: an act that over time became a habit that is not easily broken. So although bad habits can be annoying, don't take them personally. Your partner with the bad habit may be oblivious instead of malicious.

Of course, some bad habits may escalate into dangerous situations, including alcoholism, drug addiction, and spousal abuse. If your partner has a serious problem like this, remember that you don't need to face it on your own — and you probably can't. Don't continue to suffer needlessly, but go for help as soon as possible. Such situations usually only get worse if neglected, so the sooner you seek a solution, the more likely that you'll be able to help your partner and possibly the relationship. This is especially true when these problems are combined, such as alcoholism and abuse. You should not spend even one day worrying about your safety. If you do nothing, the situation will only grow worse and your own health may be on the line. By contacting the proper authorities, you'll not only be protecting yourself (and your children if you have them), you'll be sending a very strong message. It may be the only kind of message that will cause your spouse to realize how far things have gone and that it is time to get help.

Facing finances together

Many couples argue about money. Often one person likes to save his or her greenbacks while the other prefers seeing them disappear into merchants' cash registers. Credit cards can cause even more serious problems, especially if both partners abuse them.

If people are reticent to talk about sex, they're even more likely to clam up when it comes to discussing finances. Too many people get married without having a good idea of how their mate feels about money. He may have forced himself to spend a few bucks on flowers and dinners while they were dating, but after they move in together, he clamps down on all spending. Or she may have been parsimonious with her own funds, but after somebody else starts replenishing the bank account, she goes on frequent spending sprees.

I go into more details on this topic in Chapter 17. If finances are a major source of conflict in your relationship, be sure to take a close look at that chapter.

Unknotting family ties

When you become a couple, you may think that you're only associating yourself with the person you love. But unless you happen to fall for an orphan, he or she always comes with baggage — an entire extended family. And don't forget that you've got your own family standing in your shadow — or are you perhaps standing in theirs?

Families are inevitably a source of conflict, because any time you put more than one person in the mix, you create the potential for mischief. Human beings happen to be headstrong, and people get set in their ways. Just as your body may reject a new organ, a family (or at least some members) sometimes tries to reject an intruder.

I could probably write a whole book entitled *Dealing with Your Significant Other's Family For Dummies* and still not cover every possible problem. The key to surviving difficult in-laws, whether or not you are married, is to stay on neutral ground. Whether insults are said behind your back or to your face, it's up to your partner to deal with the situation. If you come on strong, you may manage to alienate the entire family, and then your partner may be pulled and twisted in so many directions that your relationship risks turning sour. So just keep smiling, and hopefully when they get to know you better, they'll come around.

If one particular family member refuses to make peace — for example, the stereotypical mother-in-law — then you may just have to grit your teeth and put up with it. Hopefully, you don't share your living space with this person, so that only the occasional visit has to remain tolerable. Admittedly, each time you see this person may be very trying, but there's no point in trying to force yourself between your partner and one of his or her relatives. The friction you cause may bring your relationship down in flames. So if your partner is worth having, then you have to accept the family that comes along hand-in-hand.

The pull of power struggles

If you work in a big corporation, you've probably noticed one manager or executive who has managed to climb up the corporate ladder by constantly trying to pull as much power into his domain as possible. Such a person never gives an inch, and often this individual manages to tire out the competition and may even make it to the top.

People who possess this type of personality often don't leave the power-grabbing habit at the office. Any time there is an issue of control, no matter how picayune, they have to come out on top. Doing everything to come out on top becomes second nature, and they won't let anyone stand in their way.

If the spouse of such a person has either a very strong ego or a very weak one, he or she may be able to live with this trait. In the first instance, the spouse probably pays little attention to the power-hungry partner's rantings and ravings. In the second instance, the spouse may constantly bow under the pressure. But for people whose egos are neither very strong nor very weak, power struggles can be an endless source of conflict, beginning with who gets to read the morning paper and ending with who sets the time for the alarm to go off. Such habits are likely to worsen with age, so you can't simply wait it out. Arguing probably won't get you anywhere either. This is another one of those situations where I suggest a professional mediator of some sort. Trying to solve such a situation on your own is just not likely to get you anywhere.

Diffusing distractions

Distractions include a wide array of activities that prevent a couple from spending enough quality time together. They include the following and many more:

- ✔ Watching too much television
- ✔ Surfing the Internet for hours on end every night
- ✔ Hanging out with the guys or gals too much
- ✔ Allowing the kids to take up so much time that the parents can never be alone together

If both partners have their own distractions, then the relationship may suffer a bit, but they probably won't fight about this issue. The partners may even be glad that the other person is occupied, because that way each can continue to pursue his or her own pastime. This may seem like a good arrangement, but be aware that this can erode a relationship. At one point, one or the other of you may come up for air, realize what you are missing, and seek companionship elsewhere.

I deal with this issue in greater depth in Chapter 19, because this is a common enough problem that it deserves individual attention.

Viewing the issue of pornography

I suppose that I could list this topic as a "distraction," but the angry feelings it can raise stem from more than just the time that may be taken away from the relationship. Many women feel hurt if their partners indulge in viewing erotica, even if it is only for a short amount of time, because they feel that it offers competition to their own sexual attractiveness.

The Internet has made this issue thornier than ever. Suddenly there is this vast library of erotic material available to anyone who is connected to cyberspace, and some men can spend an inordinate amount of time searching for the hottest babes online. And women are not immune to this problem, though women tend to be more attracted to chat rooms than porn sites. In chat rooms, they can form relationships with one or two men rather than stare at thousands on a porn site.

The fights that arise over this particular issue can become very bitter because the emotions, or maybe I should say passions (which include guilt), that are engendered add to the volatility of the fight. Because of this, I advise anyone dealing with this problem to tread carefully. It may appear like a simple issue, but fights about this can escalate quickly, and the relationship may well be very vulnerable.

If you can separate yourself from how you feel (even for a moment) and judge the severity of what is happening, try to see whether your partner's habit is hurting your sex life, has a neutral effect, or may even be making it better. This perspective may help you come to terms with this subject.

If one partner is truly hooked, the other shouldn't expect an immediate and complete turnaround. Take baby steps towards a compromise so that you can protect the relationship from crashing down around you. First, ask the person to voluntarily cut back his or her viewing time by half. But don't just leave your partner with nothing to do during those times. Rent other types of movies. Or go out to dinner. Or make love, but not just the usual way;

instead, try a different position or maybe a different location in the house. After a few weeks have gone by, see if your partner can cut back some more, and then, maybe, stop altogether.

Wrestling with religious differences

It's sad that so many of mankind's wars have been about religion, especially when so many of the combatants have claimed to worship the same God, whose first commandment is "thou shalt not kill." But with so much historical precedent, it's not surprising that religion can be a source of conflict between two lovers. Sometimes this conflict arises when one party changes his or her religious beliefs in mid-stream. Most of the time both parties knew exactly what their partner's religious beliefs were before they became a couple and felt that any differences would not present much of an obstacle, only to find out later that this assumption was off base.

The wedding ceremony can be the first source of conflict, which can set the opposing families at war even if the couple tries to stay on the sidelines. Another common source of trouble arises when it comes to the religious upbringing of children. One partner may have casually agreed to allow the children to be raised in the other's religion, but when a child's religious training begins, his or her feelings change. When a child takes on the customs of one partner's religion, the other partner may feel jealous. This can occur not only because of the actual religious connotations of this learning process, but because the partner feels as if the children are drifting more towards the "side" of the other parent.

DR. RUTH SAYS

Teaching two religions to children can defeat the belief system of both. For example, what is a child to think who is taught by a Christian parent that Jesus is the Messiah while a Jewish parent teaches him or her that the Messiah has yet to arrive? It may be better to choose one religion for young children, and then when they grow older and are better able to choose for themselves, they can make up their own minds. If that path is chosen, the parent whose religion is not taking the forefront may want to take on another activity with the children, like coaching their Little League team, for example. Just be careful not to pit the two, religion and sports in this case, against each other. Such competition puts unfair pressure on the children. In this case, both adults should try to act like . . . adults.

Fighting over food

Food can become an issue between partners in a couple of ways. One has to do with tastes or preferences, such as meat eaters versus vegetarians, and the other has to do with weight.

When it comes to tastes, each partner should try to agree to disagree and leave it at that. Neither one should make fun of the other, though if one person insists on eating nothing but junk food, then some prodding away from the soda and potato chip aisle may be in order.

The question of weight is a very complex one. To some people, eating has psychological implications that far outweigh the need to replenish lost nutrients. Self-esteem often plays a part, and if your partner is picking on you for your eating habits, that can cause even more self-esteem issues and aggravate the situation.

How can you approach this problem sensitively? Take positive actions rather than making negative comments. For example, if one person needs to lose weight, the other can encourage going for walks together, playing a game of tennis, or visiting the gym so that the beneficial activity becomes a shared and positive one. The person without the weight problem may also take on the food shopping duties, making sure that only healthy foods are brought into the home. And if the person with the weight problem isn't home for lunch on weekdays, the other can offer to make a balanced lunch to bring in every day to help his or her partner eat sensibly. Such activities show your partner that you care, and they give that psychological boost to aim for a healthy weight.

Struggling with stress

The homes of some couples are constant battlegrounds despite the fact that they love each other. A pattern develops, and the automatic response to any conflict is a spat, which often develops into a full-blown fight. Their love for each other gets overshadowed by their anger, which is mostly a result of tensions caused outside the relationship. Each wants what is best for the other, but after a while they can't express their love, only their anger.

Ann and John

Ann's grandchildren were staying over, and she had prepared a special meal. Her husband, John, walked in half an hour late. Ann had been worried that something terrible had happened, knowing that he would want to be there with his grandchildren, so when he walked through the door, she released the tension that had been building by screaming at him. He was late because his train had been delayed, and even though it wasn't his fault, he felt guilty about being late. That guilt made him defensive, so rather than simply apologizing for being late, he screamed back at his wife. With their grandchildren staring at them wide-eyed, this particular fight ended quickly. But it was part of a pattern that seemed to never end.

Every couple faces some moments of stress. Those moments may result in a sharp sentence or two, but usually the incident blows over quickly. If a couple that fights constantly can learn to recognize the cause of all this combative behavior, take a deep breath, and relax before launching a first strike, then they can overcome it. But if they each remain on a hair-trigger, then any little disagreement may spiral into a full-blown fight.

The best way to overcome this habit is for one partner to stop any nascent argument and ask the other what's wrong. In general, you usually discover that it has nothing to do with you; something may have happened at work, or some worry caused his or her blood pressure to skyrocket. If you can focus on the cause of the stress and talk calmly about it, then you can avoid attacking each other.

Blending personalities: Stay-at-homes versus party animals

When you first begin dating, you may need outside stimuli in order to prevent long stretches of silence from ruining the evening. That's why dates usually include some sort of activity, like dinner, the movies, a sporting event, or a show. But after you get to know each other better, and especially if you live together (whether married or not), such activities are no longer "necessary."

I put the word "necessary" in quotes because to some people, these activities absolutely are necessary. In fact, I'm one of those people. I don't like to sit home and just watch TV or the four walls. I like being around activity and other people and stimulating events. But not everybody is like that. Some people much prefer to veg out.

Of course, most people are a mix, combining a dash of daring-do with a pinch of mush. But because no two people have exactly the same mix, a couple may have problems blending the two personalities. Maybe you have to entertain clients every weeknight and want to simply fall asleep in your easy chair on Friday night, whereas your partner has spent those weeknights home alone and is dying for some adventure by the week's end.

If spontaneous dates with your partner are not happening, and one of you is becoming an unwilling stay-at-home, the best way to eliminate this set of conflicts is to sit down regularly and go over your schedules. Set aside time when you can go out together. Plan ahead and order tickets to a show. Make a dinner reservation and add it to date books and Palm Pilots. Although you may not agree on the number of outside activities desired, as long as you have some on the schedule, you can limit the severity of these arguments.

In addition, if you're the person who needs more outside stimulation, don't feel constrained to sit at home every evening just because your partner is a couch potato. Join clubs, take part in civic activities, go out with friends, volunteer at a hospital, join a bowling league, take a course, join a gym, and so on.

Remember to differentiate your own outside activities from those you do as a couple. A true sloth may say, "But you went out the past three nights, why do we have to go to the neighbor's pot luck dinner tonight?" The key word is "we." If one half the couple gets all his or her stimulation outside of the relationship, then that is going to spell trouble for the twosome.

Remember: Sex doesn't take place between the knees and the armpits, but between the ears. If you aren't tickling each other's intellects, then your libidos aren't likely to be stirred either, so both of you need to make an effort to spend some "quality" time together.

Adjusting schedules: Morning doves versus night owls

It's not easy adjusting your circadian rhythms, but it's also not impossible. I, for example, am not a morning person. Many times people ask me for a breakfast meeting, and most of the time I say "no thank you." But sometimes there's a breakfast meeting that features a speaker I want to see. Then it doesn't matter if I was out until 2 a.m. the night before — I'll go to that meeting. And if the speaker lives up to his or her reputation, then you won't hear me complain about how early I had to get up.

The point I'm making here is that although you and your partner may have some conflicts because of different internal clocks, you can't allow yourselves to become so rigid that such problems affect your relationship. You have to be ready and able to make exceptions, and that includes deciding when to have sex. If the two of you are on different schedules, make love at nights *and* in the mornings so that you're both satisfied. And while you're at it, I suggest that you also have some "afternoon delight" when you're both wide awake!

Planning a Peacekeeping Mission

Unless a couple is ready to divorce, all fights come to an end at some point. To prevent the next one, or at least to lengthen the time until it's *High Noon* again, each side needs to engage in some peacekeeping. Here are some suggestions for doing so:

✔ If you have a fight, agree to place the particular subject that started it off-limits for the rest of the day. Even if you think of a great retort, keep it to yourself.

✔ Exchange gifts of some sort — flowers or a favorite meal — to help heal the wounds an argument creates. Just make sure such gifts don't pop up *only* after a fight, or they may only reinforce the urge to do battle.

✔ Spend some quiet time together, which often means turning off the TV set, even if your favorite show is scheduled. (That's why you bought a VCR, remember?) If you don't want to talk, put a favorite, calming CD on and just listen together.

✔ Touch each other. This is very important. Reestablishing direct physical contact can go a long way towards triggering those fond memories of why you got together in the first place, and it can help to restore the relationship to something closer to its original form. If that touching leads to a session under the covers, great, but don't try to force it. It may take some more time until both parties are ready for that much intimacy.

Chapter 4

Renewing Respect

- -

In This Chapter

▶ Recognizing if your relationship lacks respect

▶ Showing pride for your partner

▶ Tooting your own horn

▶ Helping each other over self-respect hurdles

- -

As I mention in Chapter 3, if one half of a couple is doing a great imitation of a dish rag, then the other half won't exactly be worshipping the ground he or she walks on. For people to have real love for one another, they must have a mutual respect. While they don't have to put each other on a pedestal, they do have to find some personal characteristics to admire in each other that go beyond the physical. That's why having some conflict in a relationship can be a good thing. If you stand up for yourself, then that proves you have some backbone. That can help to increase your partner's respect for you.

What happens if one partner doesn't respect the other? Consider the following question: Can you imagine yourself having romantic feelings for someone for whom you have little or no respect? Distaste, maybe, but feelings of love or attraction? Of course not. If your partner doesn't respect you, then he or she doesn't harbor romantic feelings for you either. So establishing a relationship where both partners respect each other is vital to increasing the amount of romance in that relationship. If the two of you currently have very little respect for each other, the only way to rekindle the romance is to renew that respect. This chapter shows you how to get started down that path.

Lacking Respect from Day One

Not every couple has respect for each other in the first place. For example, if you have very low self-esteem, then you may allow yourself to fall into a relationship where you are taken for granted. In that situation, your partner may not feel love for you; he or she may be using you to satisfy his or her needs. These needs may include sex, financial support, ego building, or respectability in the public's eye.

When a partnership is founded on love, then both people involved are equals. But some people don't want equality in a relationship; they want to have the upper hand. By pairing off with someone of low self-esteem, this type of person can fulfill the need to take command. This pattern can begin during the dating period, continue into marriage, and maybe even last for a lifetime.

From a woman's perspective: The object of his frustrations

Certainly in the days before women had any rights, plenty of wives were locked into marriages that made them miserable. But because they and their children couldn't survive without their husbands, these women had no alternative but to stay where they were. Our society has made great strides, but it is often still more difficult for a woman to leave a relationship than a man, especially if there are children to take care of. Even if a couple has no children, or if the kids are all grown up, a woman who has counted on a man for her support and never pursued the training to get a decent job may feel stuck in her relationship. If a woman has low self-esteem because she never got praise and support from her parents while she was growing up, she's going to find it difficult to gather the inner strength needed to leave a man to whom she turned for support after leaving her parents' home.

If a man has never had any respect for his wife, then there's not much chance that he's going to change. Often, men who have little respect for themselves feel the need to belittle their wives. Maybe they were put down by their family members as children and are repeating the same pattern later in life, or perhaps they've been picked on at school or at work and require a punching bag of their own to make up for the psychological beatings they've received. Whatever the exact reasons, they take their frustrations out on their partners.

While some men like this are able to undergo a change of heart, it's a very difficult situation. In such cases, respect needs a lot more than mere rekindling. If a couple that fits this pattern is going to learn to respect and then love one another, they're going to have to start from scratch. Probably the only way they can do this is with professional help, such as a marriage counselor. That's why any woman trapped in such a situation should at least go for a consultation, if not with a therapist, then with a social worker or religious leader who'll be able to get her on the right path.

From a man's perspective: The hen-pecked husband

I believe that more women than men feel disrespected by their partners, if for no other reason than they usually have more responsibility for raising the children, which can limit their ability to earn a living. However, plenty of men also experience a lack of respect in their relationships; you've probably heard the terms "hen-pecked" and "p***y-whipped" used to describe them. Men may be the physically stronger of the two sexes, but that doesn't mean that women can't have a psychological edge with which they can successfully dominate their mates.

Because many women feel disrespected by their husbands, they can often find solace in each other. But men facing such disrespect may have a much more difficult time, because there is almost no place for them to get sympathy. Their friends may look down on them for not being strong. And if a male friend feels that the example being set by this weakling endangers his dominant status within his own family, then he may have very negative attitudes toward the man who is being treated poorly. So while it's easy to make fun of hen-pecked men (and sitcoms often do), they are under tremendous psychological strain. And there certainly isn't very much romance in a relationship with a husband who feels this way.

R-E-S-P-E-C-T: Find Out How It's Supposed to Be

I hope that you're not in a situation like the ones I describe above. Ideally, even if some repairs need to be made to increase the level of respect you get from or give to a partner, the situation remains within the bounds of the possible. You may just need to give a tweak to each other's egos so that you think in terms of having respect for each other.

Saying and showing it

Most couples rarely even think of the word "respect." You probably say "I love you" to your partner, but how often do you say "I respect you"? While you and your partner may feel that respect is a given, sometimes actions speak louder than words; how much respect you actually *show* towards each other may paint an entirely different picture of your relationship than your words do. And whether you realize it or not, that picture is a reflection of how romantic you feel towards each other. Here are some examples of common situations that show a lack of respect:

- ✔ She makes dinner every night and never receives a compliment, though she hears nasty barbs if the meal is not up to par.
- ✔ He comes home from a long day at work, and the first word out of her mouth is a complaint (or a whole string of them).
- ✔ She is trying to lose some weight, and instead of offering support, he constantly puts her down.
- ✔ He has put a lot of time into restoring an antique car (or any hobby), and when the project is done, she reacts by calling it a waste of time.
- ✔ His friends are never good enough.
- ✔ Her opinions are worthless.
- ✔ His taste in clothes is lousy.
- ✔ She's a lousy driver.

I think you get the picture. What's bad about most of these little digs is that they become part of a regular pattern and can go on all day long. Even if you do say "I love you" once a day, how effective is that at communicating your feelings of romance for one another if they're little islands of sweetness floating in a sea of criticism?

Creating a comfort zone

When you're at the office, your boss may jump down your throat any time you do something wrong and rarely give you a compliment. But your relationship is not a place of business. This is supposed to be a comfort zone, whether you live together or not. Everybody needs to hear compliments. If you can't get any ego stroking at your place of business, and especially if you're constantly being picked at for this little thing or that, then you need to get it from the one you love.

That doesn't mean that you can't issue the occasional complaint. Constructive criticism can help make your partner a better person. But if you love somebody, you also have to be able to forgive his or her little foibles. If nobody's perfect, that means you aren't perfect either. You need your partner's forgiveness just as much as he or she needs yours. Try to remember that the next time you start to pick at some little fault.

Pumping up your partner's self-esteem

If your partner doesn't believe that he or she is worthy of respect, then it's going to be harder for you to give the respect that's deserved. (And, of course, that works the other way around, too.) People with low self-esteem put themselves down continually, and they need a lot of support to change this habit.

Claire and Beau

It was love at first sight for Beau when he met Claire. Claire was a little overweight, but that did not bother Beau; in fact, he preferred her that way. But Claire had always been bothered by her weight, and despite all of Beau's attention, she couldn't quite believe that he really meant the compliments he kept giving her. Her reticence didn't bother Beau at first, but after a while he got tired of having his words thrown back at him. They fought about it a few times, and one day the filter of love seemed to drop from in front of Beau's eyes. Instead of liking what he saw, he began to feel repulsed by Claire. Her constant carping about her faults had pierced his armor, and he decided that he agreed with her. They broke up.

Let me be direct: Partners with low self-esteem need a stream of compliments, because they naturally tend to discount kind words. Only by causing your partner's compliment message center to overflow will he or she start to believe that you really think that way. (The fact that you've already chosen this person as your partner is not enough.)

On the other hand, people with low self-esteem tend to give those around them a lot of compliments, because they feel that everyone else is so much better than they are. This habit may tend to turn you off to the exchange of compliments in general, making you hesitant to return the favor lest you drown in praise. But if your loved one does have feelings of inferiority, then you can't turn off that tap. Eventually people with low self-esteem can learn to respect themselves so that they don't always need that pat on the back, but until that happens, you have to bend over backwards to help.

Actively admiring your partner

I'm certainly not advising you to utter a string of platitudes that you feel are false. Any compliment you give is credible only if you believe what you are saying. Therefore, the first step toward showing respect to your partner is to actually have respect for him or her. And to do that, you have to assess how you really feel. What are the things about your partner that you admire? Don't look at me for the answer. If you can't just rattle them off, then sit down with a piece of paper and make a list.

When you've done that, then make an effort to let your partner know how you feel at the appropriate moments. If you enjoy the way a meal has been prepared, say it out loud. If you appreciate that your partner spent the morning with your kids at the soccer fields, thank him. If she wrote a good letter to the local paper about some issue, tell her it was well written.

This will have a double effect. Obviously, your partner will enjoy this praise. But it will also make you more aware of his or her good qualities. It's easy to take people for granted when you see them all the time. Those special qualities that you found so attractive when you first met are bound to lose some luster along the way. But if you polish those qualities up to a high sheen with your praise, then you'll appreciate them more also. And that will go a long way towards raising your level of respect for your partner, and your romantic feelings as well.

Claiming your bragging rights

Polishing your partner's image needn't be something that stays within the walls of your home. Too many people think it's funny to put down their partners when they're in social situations. Talk about not showing respect! And what is especially counterproductive about this habit is that when you put down your partner, in a sense you're putting down yourself — after all, you chose to have a relationship with this person.

One unintended result of public putdowns is that your negative comments may start to spread. One person you complained to will speak to another friend and pass the word along that your partner is a lousy person, maybe even exaggerating what you said. Eventually, whatever flaws you make fun of grow to enormous proportions, doing grave harm to your partner's reputation, and not adding a lot to yours.

But now turn this scenario around. What if, instead of putting your partner down, you build him or her up? Try telling your friends and associates how great a mate you picked. Again this news will spread, but the magnifying effect will now paint an even more glowing portrait of your partner, and people will start to think of you as a really lucky person for having made such a great catch.

Resisting the tattletale temptation

I realize that if you've had a problem with your partner, there's an urge to want to unburden yourself by complaining to your friends and associates. You're looking for some reinforcement that you're right and your partner is wrong. Telling tales about your partner may bring you some short-term satisfaction, but the long-term effects can be serious.

Peter

When Peter came to work one morning, a coworker asked why he hadn't been able to stay at yesterday's meeting. Peter explained that his wife had forgotten her keys, and he had to rush home so that she could get the car to pick up their son at preschool. Peter went on to complain how his wife was always forgetting things and how it drove him crazy. In part, he did this to shift the blame for missing the meeting from himself to his wife. But he was also letting off steam because he was tired of his wife being so disorganized.

One problem with tattling is that the people you complain to will probably take your side. After all, they've only heard your version of the story. (For example, Peter didn't tell his coworker that he leaves the house early every morning, so his wife has to get their son clothed and fed before a neighbor drives him to school; that's why she is often frazzled.) But while you may draw some comfort from feeling "right," the long-term effect is not going to be a positive one. Any putdowns of your partner inevitably become exaggerated. And if tattling becomes a regular habit, there are other consequences.

If you do a really good job of convincing friends and coworkers that your spouse is a true dingbat, they're going to start putting pressure on you to make a change. With purely good intentions, they'll think that they should encourage you to get out of this relationship. All they've been hearing are bad things about your partner, so what other conclusion could they draw?

If things really are that bad between the two of you, then maybe these advice-givers are right. But what if you only open up to your friends or coworkers on bad days? What if you never say anything nice about your partner all those other days that are perfectly fine? Maybe those days aren't spectacular, so you don't come charging into the office with great news about your partner, but they are certainly more than adequate. All in all, you might be quite satisfied with your partner, but what are you going to say to the people who insist that you sever your relationship? If you stick up for your partner, they'll think you're being defensive or weak. Or they'll wonder why you complain so much if things are okay.

Keeping a relationship going is hard enough without a crowd in the bleachers egging on any conflict. Saying positive things about your partner can't cause you any harm. But when you put your partner down, even if the insult is deserved on that particular day, you're asking for trouble.

Shucking the "Aw, shucks" attitude

Some people don't necessarily have low self-esteem but still have difficulties accepting compliments. They have an "aw, shucks, it was nothin'" attitude. The problem with these people is that they enjoy receiving compliments but don't like to admit it. Maybe they don't like being the center of attention. Perhaps they have very high standards and feel that their work, no matter how well received, could have been better. Or maybe they grew up in families that never gave positive reinforcement, so compliments make them feel uncomfortable.

If you constantly tell people who give you compliments that they shouldn't, eventually that message is going to get through and people will stop patting you on the back. This can happen easily with a couple that has been together a long time. The person giving the compliments is going to tire of having them constantly thrown back, and he or she will give up. That doesn't mean that either partner has lost respect for the other. But if one partner really did want and need those compliments, then a problem might arise that needn't have.

People who have an aversion to receiving compliments may also feel uncomfortable giving compliments. Because it puts them on edge to be on the receiving end, they assume that others feel the same way. As a result, even if they would like to give their partners pats on the back, they hold back. If they feel less reticent in giving criticism (which again may stem from growing up in a family that would only criticize and never praise), then their partners could definitely get the impression that their efforts aren't being appreciated.

I don't know if such a person is ever going to change. If it's truly imbedded in someone's personality that giving compliments is not a good thing, then he or she won't overcome such feelings easily. But what if that person's partner feels badly about never being complimented? What if it makes him or her feel unappreciated? That type of conflict can escalate so that it severely impacts the entire relationship.

Patting yourself on the back

In Chapter 1, I advise that if you want flowers and your partner won't give them to you, you should buy them for yourself. In this situation, I say it's perfectly okay to go fishing for compliments. Ask your partner straight out: "Was dinner good?" "Did I do a good job?" "Do I look good in this outfit?" The person who is averse to compliments is only being asked to answer a question now. In all probability, your partner can do that honestly, and so you will get the appreciation you seek.

Is this as good as receiving a compliment that wasn't asked for? No, I can't lie and tell you that it is. But is it better than suffering in silence? Absolutely. So don't sit back and complain that you can never get a compliment; go ahead and ask for one. If you don't, then you'll start to resent your partner, and that will have a negative impact on your relationship. But if you can get the satisfaction you seek, even if slightly tarnished by the fact that you had to ask for it, then you'll have an easier time remembering that you love this person.

Embracing your partner's choices

What if you're not getting any respect from your partner because he or she doesn't believe you deserve it? While everybody deserves respect for simply being who they are, some individuals are not so quick to give respect without seeing some outward sign that it is deserved, like a degree of higher learning, a prestigious job, or a string of other status symbols. People who have opted out of the rat race can easily find themselves looked down upon by those who've chosen to compete.

Lila and Jeff

Lila and Jeff met in college. They got married a few weeks after graduation, and the next September Jeff started graduate business school while Lila worked as a receptionist in a doctor's office. After Jeff got his MBA, he got a job in a large corporation earning a good salary. Lila liked working for this doctor, and because Jeff was making lots of money, she didn't feel the need to change jobs or go for her own advanced degree.

Jeff quickly rose through the company ranks and then switched companies to get an even better job. He had long felt uncomfortable telling the people he met that his wife was a receptionist, and so after making the move, he made up a different job title for her. He was asked out to business dinners a few times and his wife was also invited, but he made excuses as to why she couldn't attend. Later, when an event came along that he couldn't attend alone, he had to tell her the lie that he had been using. Lila was devastated because she enjoyed working at this job for over five years, and suddenly her husband had made both it and her seem worthless.

Respecting your own potential

Certainly we should all be free to live our lives in whatever way we see fit. After all, no matter how much money you accumulate, you're still limited in the amount of time you have to live your life.

Not living up to one's potential is a different issue. If you choose not to drive yourself crazy to earn the most possible money, that may be admirable. But that decision taken to the extreme (so that your occupation is beach bum or something equivalent) does not deserve a tremendous amount of respect. On the other hand, the so-called "starving artist," who is working hard but just not getting any financial reward, is admirable because he or she still seeks to live up to full potential. Likewise, people who stay home to take care of their children are doing an important job despite the lack of pay.

Showing an interest in yourself

In my opinion, nobody should try to pressure anyone else to live up to a certain standard. If one person wants to work himself to the bone, that's his decision. He shouldn't force his partner to do the same. Yet the person who chooses the easier path may have to take some action in order to get at least the minimal amount of respect required to keep the relationship going. Here are some suggestions of what to do under such circumstances:

- **Keep your partner informed of what you are doing.** Don't allow him or her to assume that your work doesn't have much value. Paint a picture in your partner's mind that highlights your strong points.

- **Examine your life from the perspective of a stranger.** Could you improve the way you look? Does your life appear to be in a rut? Would you struggle to recall something you've done lately that would make for interesting conversation? If you answered yes to these questions, then it's time to make some changes.

- **Never let yourself become stagnant.** Maintaining the status quo is not good for you; you must always try to grow in some way. Even if you are satisfied with your job, take some courses so that you can enlarge your mind. Learn how to paint. Take up photography. Read books that will challenge you and teach you something. Remember, to keep your partner interested in you, you have to be interesting.

- **Share some interesting activities with your partner.** Go to museums. Attend lectures. Read a newspaper article and have a discussion. Go for a hike. Pack lunch and go for an all-day bike trip. Plan a trip together by learning all you can about the place you want to visit.

- **Think about your image.** Don't assume that because you are part of a couple, you don't have to worry about your image. While you certainly need to be able to relax around your lover, you can't let yourself slide entirely. Try to figure out why this person chose you to begin with — what was particularly attractive to him or her. Then do whatever it takes to make certain that you maintain, if not improve on, those qualities.

Combating a loss of respect

What if you find yourself losing respect for your partner? Should you just ignore those feelings? Definitely not, but you also can't just blurt out, "You're starting to bore me!" You have to use tact to convey your message.

Start by asking questions. If you believe that your partner's job is not suited to his talents, ask him whether he is content. And if he's not, see whether you can help him find new employment that will give him more satisfaction.

If you believe that your soulmate is stagnating, don't just let her continue to wallow in her mud hole. Drag her out, screaming and kicking if need be. Buy tickets to the theater for the two of you. Make a date to have dinner with some friends or neighbors. Call to get catalogues from local colleges that offer adult education classes, and spend some time going over them. Take her to a movie that everybody is talking about. Grab the remote and turn the TV to a program on the Discovery Channel or your local PBS station.

While your lover may balk at the beginning of this campaign, eventually I bet he or she will be very thankful. When people fall into ruts, they have difficulty getting themselves out. But once they've climbed out into the sunshine and can look around to see what the world has to offer, they should be very grateful to you for any assistance you provided. Then the two of you should be able to use that gratitude to light a very nice flame under that romance of yours.

Part II
Inspiring a
Romantic Revival

The 5th Wave — By Rich Tennant

"MOM AND DAD GET LIKE THIS EVERY TIME THEY WATCH BACK-TO-BACK EPISODES OF 'THE LOVE BOAT'".

In this part . . .

*W*ondering what romance really is? This part begins by defining our terms, so that you know what exactly you're trying to rekindle. Romance requires commitment from both partners, and this part shows how to overcome common doubts and other hurdles to make and carry out that commitment — from accepting the quirks of your partner's personality to finding ways to keep each other on your toes.

Marriage is often the natural outcome of romantic commitment, but sometimes after a number of years pass, married couples need to remind themselves of the spirit of that commitment. Chapter 7 details reasons why a renewal ceremony may be beneficial and offers advice for how to plan it. Chapter 8 offers suggestions for ways to plan a romantic getaway — whether you have a couple of hours or a couple of weeks to devote to rekindling.

Chapter 5

The Art of Romance: Keeping Love Fresh

It probably won't surprise you to hear that I get letters from teens wanting to remain virgins who ask for tips on how to please each other without going all the way. But those eyebrows of yours will probably raise when you find out that I also get letters (or more likely e-mails these days) from teens who are sexually active and worried that their love life is getting stale.

I don't receive hundreds of those types of letters, but they come in over the transom often enough to show that the situation is not a rarity. If teens, who are just discovering what it means to be in love and are at the peak of their sexuality, have difficulties keeping their romances fresh, then what can couples who have been together for decades do? Is their quest for romance hopeless? Should they throw in the towel and just accept whatever level of romance they have? I'm sure you realize these are rhetorical questions; if they weren't, I wouldn't have a book to write.

Isn't It Romantic?

So what is romance anyway? This is my definition: Romance is the context in which the emotion of love exists. We know that love can't exist in a vacuum because, to begin with, two people are required. Those two people need to communicate their love for each other. The sounds, smells, sights, and touches that define love must somehow be passed back and forth between the lovers. These transferals need a medium, and that medium is romance.

Fragile as ether

Before mankind visited space, people thought that space was filled with "ether." Whatever this ether was, it was assumed to be quite delicate, which is where we get the word *ethereal* from. Romance is very much like ether. It fills the spaces between two lovers, and it, too, is very delicate.

You mustn't ignore the romantic quotient of your love life, or it will evaporate. If romance is neglected, the two of you won't be able to communicate the love you have for each other. You must tend to romance, repair any rips to its surface, and make sure there is enough of this substance between the two of you to support as much love as you can possibly exchange.

Tough as armor

But like many mystical substances, romance has a dual nature. Despite romance's ethereal quality, it can also exhibit a certain toughness. We've all heard examples of how love can survive in horrible places, even amid pain and suffering. If you've ever read a romantic novel, you know the plots thrive on tragic circumstances. And in everyday life, when two lovers first meet, they're likely to endure sweaty palms and pounding hearts. So while the romance that exists between the lovers may be delicate, the romantic aura that surrounds them can be tough as armor.

Your personal romance needs some of both — the tenderness and the spark. As time goes by, most of us exchange much of the early drama of love for the peace and quiet of the hearth. But don't allow yourselves to become totally complacent, because love does need to be serenaded by the occasional blast of thunder and lightning.

Keep in mind that while romance may be universal, it is not uniform. Some couples are like two peas in a pod, and that makes them love each other. For other couples, dissimilarity is the glue that holds them together. There's no one magic formula, which explains why you may not always understand how two people remain coupled. Romance has a way of casting its own unique spells.

Posing the Question

As I emphasize elsewhere in this book — and in other books, columns, lectures (it's an important subject) — communication is the first and most crucial step toward solving the issue of too little romance. (Communication is crucial to most other problems that couples face, as well.) If the two of you want more romance in your relationship but sit there like statues never voicing your complaints, then you have no chance whatsoever of making any improvements. Only by talking about the issues can the level of romance start soaring like a hot air balloon rather than sinking like a stone.

You may think that two people who regularly take off their clothes and engage in intimate acts should have no difficulty communicating about the state of their romance, but that's not the case. People give several common reasons for not simply asking their partners, "What can we do to improve our love life?" Those reasons are spelled out in the following sections.

Assuming defeat

Many people have already reached the conclusion that there's no chance for any improvement in the level of romance in their relationship. They figure "why bother?" Such a defeatist attitude leads to — what else? — defeat. While you can't expect a sudden complete turnaround in a relationship, incremental changes are always possible. You must have hope in order for any change to be possible.

Dwelling on the past

Some people have tried to improve their relationships in the past and have gotten nowhere. They, too, take the "why bother?" attitude. But past failures don't necessarily mean that no future change is possible. Maybe that person tried the wrong approach the last time. Or maybe that person's partner didn't take suggestions seriously. Such obstacles can be overcome if you put your mind to it, especially with the aid of my suggestions or, if necessary, the help of a therapist.

Shying away

Some people are too shy to bring up such subjects. Maybe they're afraid of being rejected, even by their own partners. Or they feel silly asking for more romance in the relationship. If this describes you, keep in mind that better communications encourage all sorts of positive changes in your relationship. Maybe while you want more romance, your partner wants more sex (or more free time to go bowling). By talking about such issues, both you and your partner can get what you need without feeling guilty.

Looking for a mind reader

Some people feel that if they have to spell out their desires to their partners, that kills the romance. They expect their partners to be able to read minds, and if that doesn't happen, then they hold their resentment inside and refuse to speak about the issue. Such a view of how two people interact is idealistic; holding such expectations more likely leads to disappointment than anything else.

Sara and Lloyd

Sara and Lloyd lived together for three years before getting married. Both worked at jobs that demanded long hours, and the one thing that Sara looked forward to the most about their upcoming wedding was the honeymoon, which to her meant 10 days of being together, especially in the morning. Sara really enjoyed making love in a sunlit room, and for the six months that she was waiting for her wedding day to dawn, she fantasized daily about what those mornings would be like.

When the honeymoon finally arrived, Sara faced a situation that she hadn't expected. She knew how much Lloyd liked to play golf, and she realized that the resort they were going to had a golf course, but it never occurred to her that Lloyd would actually get up every morning at 6 in order to get in a round of golf. He was always back by 10, but by then Sara was already up and about, and so the languid moments she had anticipated evaporated.

After the newlyweds went home, Sara exploded into tears and told Lloyd how disappointed she was. Lloyd was flabbergasted. He had thought that by getting up so early, he could get in his round of golf and still have the whole day for them to be together. He had no idea that Sara had been looking forward to those mornings so much.

Sometimes the object of your desires falls into your lap, but usually you have to put in the requisite amount of effort to obtain life's pleasures. If you want a romantic weekend at a bed and breakfast, don't punish yourself by stubbornly saying that your partner should think of it on his or her own. Instead, open that trap of yours, talk about it, even make all the plans if necessary, and enjoy a wonderful weekend instead of sitting at home moping.

Keeping Disappointment at Bay

Just because you fantasize about some ideal romantic situation doesn't mean that you'll soon be swinging from a chandelier with your partner. (Not that such a feat proved very romantic for Michael Douglas and Kathleen Turner.) For example, you may fantasize about doing something special with your partner such as taking a cruise. You may build this cruise up in your mind until it's a romantic heaven, only to discover that your partner refuses to venture onto the high seas.

While it's okay to indulge yourself in a fantasy about your favorite movie star (because you know the fantasy will never come true), letting your imagination run too wild regarding your partner can lead to disappointment. If you request something simple from your partner, such as taking a bath together, you may be pleasantly surprised to find yourself the beneficiary of even more than you asked for. Keep your desires realistic, and you'll stand a better chance of making your dreams come true.

Differentiating Sex and Romance

Before I go any further, I need to make sure that we are on the same page of the dictionary. There's romance, and then there's sex. Obviously, they have certain connections, but they are not synonymous.

People who barely know each other can have sex during a one-night stand, but you can't say that they are romantically involved. If you think back, you can probably remember being madly in love with someone before you had sex, proving that romance can exist even when sex isn't part of the picture. So while sex may eventually become an integral aspect of a romantic relationship, you should think of them as two separate ingredients, like lox and cream cheese, that complement each other when placed on a bagel but which can also stand alone.

Desi Loves Lucy: Lessons in Eccentricity

We all love watching eccentric husbands and wives on television and in the movies; Desi and Lucy are a prime example. But those relationships are fiction, right? Could anyone really love someone like that in real life, or would their strange behavior eventually send their lover packing? In a *Vanity Fair* magazine interview, Alec Baldwin said about his wife, Kim Basinger, "The reason I fell in love with Kim is that she's so odd. My wife is one of those people — an absolutely maddeningly peculiar, exotic, lovely person." As one example, Baldwin cites being awakened in the middle of the night to find Basinger sobbing because she wished she had finished college.

You could say that any man would be willing to overlook some peculiarities in order to be with the delicious Kim Basinger. But the fact is that someone who is peculiar is also not boring, and boredom is one of the main unravelers of romance. So while it's great to dream of curling up by the fireplace every night, there are drawbacks to complacency. Romance can sustain being quirky, but it cannot survive a static existence.

Imagine romance as that flight of arrows pulled from Cupid's quiver that go back and forth between the lovers, plucking at one or the other's heart strings every time a bull's eye is hit. Every arrow won't hit its mark, and some arrows will be more potent than others. But both the man and the woman have to be pulling back on their bow string and letting loose some arrows on a regular basis, or their love will soon become more mythological than real.

Giving Romance the Hot Towel Treatment

What are Cupid's arrows made of, and how can you use them to freshen up your romance? As you might expect, the answer to this question is going to be different for everyone. While one person may feel that taking ballroom dancing lessons would be the perfect way to swing a relationship towards the moon, someone else may just want a weekend without their mother-in-law in the bedroom next door.

But just as every passenger feels fresher after using that hot towel provided by the airline attendant, some universal elements of romance apply to almost every couple. The following are some guidelines to freshening up your romance.

Finding time to be together

The old saying may state that familiarity breeds contempt, but these days too many couples just don't spend sufficient time with each other for romance to grow and flourish. No matter how full the appointment calendar is on your Palm Pilot, you must set aside some time to be together. Make this a priority. It may not be more important than feeding the kids, for example, but sometimes you can order a pizza instead of cooking. The kids will love the treat, and you and your spouse will have an extra half hour to connect.

Don't be afraid to actually make appointments to be together. Spontaneity is great, but waiting for those spontaneous moments may be futile. It's better to make plans that come to fruition than to hope that you'll find a moment or two to be together by chance. And, remember, if you schedule some time to be together, you'll actually be creating a framework for you to share spontaneous moments.

And don't confuse chores with romance. If you use your time together only to plan next week's dinner appointments, how romantic is that? You have to use personal time to be just that: personal. Ask each other how you feel. Stare into each other's eyes. Rub noses.

Seeking out privacy

Sitting together while the kids/your in-laws/the neighbors/the pizza delivery man are in the room will not be particularly conducive to romance. You need to be able to say what needs to be said, and maybe touch what needs to be touched, without interruption or observation.

It may be helpful to get out of the house altogether; a change in scenery may stimulate romance. At home, just catching sight of a pile of unpaid bills out of the corner of your eye can be enough to deaden any romantic impulses that may have been stirring.

But if you can't get out, then at the very least make sure you put the phone off the hook and, if you have kids, use that lock on the bedroom door. Romantic moments are very fragile. You must protect them, especially if they're hard to come by.

Concentrating on each other

It's all well and good to have that perfect moment when you're together, alone, and there's nothing on the schedule for the next 20 minutes. But if one or both of you lets that moment carelessly slip away, you can become even more frustrated. No matter how tired you are or what crisis is on the horizon, force yourself to concentrate on the here and now and that person sitting next to you. If you find your thoughts drifting off, bring them back to the moment.

This is a matter of prioritizing. Yes, the memo at the office is important, and so is Johnny's runny nose and your mother's trip to Florida. But you have to tell yourself that for this moment in time, your partner is of the utmost priority. Stay focused.

Increasing the energy level

Falling asleep in each other's arms may be considered romantic in some instances, but if you're trying to rekindle your romance, you need to put more energy into the process than that. Both partners have to take an active role. The more enthusiasm and spirit you put into any attempt to increase romance, the more likely your efforts will catch flame.

In addition to increasing your private time together, getting out of the house can increase your energy level. Just going for a walk together helps to clear the cobwebs from your mind and gives you more energy. And after you're out of the house, you'll be interacting with a dynamic world. That added stimulation keeps your energy up. Something as simple as a sunset can trigger the right emotions, as can some beautiful flowers or even a driving snow storm (if you're in a romantic mood and not worrying about having to shovel the driveway).

The process of raising your romantic energy has to be a two-party affair. One half of the couple can easily dampen the other's enthusiasm by sitting there like the proverbial bump on a log. Anyone may resist romance once in a while, but if you're never in the mood, then even the most ardent lover is going to eventually give up. So unless you're having a really bad day, try to find that second wind and join your partner in a romantic interlude.

Finding your special romantic focus points

To some people, reading poetry is very romantic. If your partner fits into that category, then go out of your way to read some poems out loud to him or her. Drinking a glass of champagne while watching the sunset may set someone else's heart on fire, so if that's the case, add such a toast to your daily (or at least weekly) agenda.

Don't assume that you know what your partner finds romantic. Actively try to discover what sets the right mood for him or her, and then do your best to meet those needs. One of the most basic aspects of romance is unselfishly doing something for the other person; the exact "something" you do isn't nearly as important as the effort you make. And if your partner responds to these special attentions the way you hope, then it won't take long before you find that activity romantic also, even if you never did before.

How do you find out what your partner finds romantic? Asking is one way. You don't have to be blunt about it, but if you think a certain circumstance is romantic, just say, "Isn't this romantic?" If your partner replies in the affirmative, then bingo: You've got at least one new arrow in your quiver.

You don't necessarily have to pose this question yourself. Let's say that you want to surprise your partner. That would be tough to do if you just had a lengthy conversation about how sexy he or she finds silk sheets. But if you asked your partner's best friend to do some prying on your behalf, then you could put together a surprise that would really take his or her breath away.

Of course your partner may also be leaving you a steady stream of clues, so that all you have to do is open your eyes and ears a little bit more to discover what he or she finds romantic. If your lover is reading the travel section and says something positive about a particular cruise, then store that information away. If you see him or her leafing through a catalogue, try to spot which items get the most attention.

Hey, big spender

I don't want to make it seem that being romantic necessarily involves spending big bucks. Carol Channing did sing "Diamonds Are A Girl's Best Friend," and some women love getting jewelry, but there are plenty of ways to be romantic that don't require much (or any) money at all. Here are a few:

- **Give a massage.** Massages are very romantic because they involve a lot of touching. It doesn't matter what type of massage you give — an all-over massage, a back rub, a foot massage, or just a few simple squeezes of the back of the neck. Any of these show you care and thus feed the romantic ether.
- **Pitch in around the house.** Do some of your partner's household chores without being asked.
- **Cook your partner's favorite meal.**
- **Watch your partner's favorite TV show with him or her.**
- **Support your partner's interests.** For example, go to the library to borrow a book on a favorite topic or written by an author that your partner likes.
- **Identify an annoying habit and try to stop it.** For example, stop leaving the toilet seat up or using all the hot water when you take a shower.
- **Show that you pay attention.** Even a small gesture, such as taking the telephone off the hook when your partner says "let's talk," will show how much you care.

I second that emotion

Sharing emotions can be intensely romantic, especially if you do not normally reveal how you feel. Allowing your partner to peer down into your inner self, making yourself somewhat vulnerable, definitely pulls at the heartstrings.

There are limits to what you should reveal when you are trying to build romance. If, for example, you're a man who secretly likes to wear ladies undergarments, revealing this to your partner may make her swoon, but not from romantic fervor. Sexual fantasies are often better left in your imagination. If you are considering opening up to your partner, consider what the reaction may be. I'm not saying that you must keep every secret, but I am advising that if you want to create an aura of romance, some secrets are best left until another time.

If the shoe is on the other foot — if your partner is telling you something that is important to him or her — being a good listener is romantic. Listening doesn't necessarily mean piping in. Some people are looking for a sounding board so they can test their ideas, but more often than not, when it comes to sharing emotions, the person doing the listening doesn't need to comment. Your job in that situation is to use whatever body language or words possible to convey that you are paying attention.

Climbing out of your rut

Doing something unexpected can be romantic. Following the same routine can become boring, and boredom is definitely not romantic. If you do something to take your partner by surprise, like suggesting a walk in the pouring rain — without an umbrella or shoes — you will definitely grab his or her attention. By putting yourself in a new light, your partner will see you differently, and that creates a positive impression.

There are some caveats to this advice, however. Not every surprise is a pleasant one. Practical jokes, for example, are quite unromantic. Your partner wants and needs to be able to trust you completely. If you keep him or her constantly on edge by pulling various stunts, then your surprises will only arouse anger. You also don't want to pull a good-intentioned surprise that is going to get a negative response. For example, if you're a blonde and your partner loves your golden tresses, dying your hair dark brown may not be favorably received.

Establishing relationship rituals

While some repetitive behavior can be boring, reenacting relationship rituals will have the opposite effect. A second honeymoon to the same place you took your first one is very romantic. But a relationship ritual doesn't have to be quite that elaborate or expensive. Kissing each other hello and goodbye is such a ritual; when one party skips this peck, it can be sorely missed. Going out to dinner on a certain night of the week may be a romantic ritual. Even doing the grocery shopping together could inspire closeness. *Together* is the operative word here; whatever the ritual is, if it involves the two of you and is done regularly, then it can strengthen the bond that exists between you. That will give a boost to your romance.

Putting your best foot forward

Like it or not, what you look like does play a role in setting a romantic tone. If you live with your partner, you obviously can't look your best every second of the day. But you can't always look your worst and expect that to have no effect on your relationship. Everybody likes to dress comfortably while at home, but clothes can be comfortable without looking ratty. And while our bodies do change as we get older, a little effort can go a long way towards minimizing those changes.

Your appearance also counts outside your four walls. If you like other people to admire your partner, then you also have to take into account that your partner may have the same desire. Maybe you'd like to give your face a rest from shaving on weekends, but unless your partner likes the scruffy look, those rough cheeks won't make her feel much like nuzzling. At the other end of the spectrum, some women put too much emphasis on hair and makeup, failing to recognize that their partners may prefer the natural look from time to time.

Creating a pleasing environment

The appearance of your environment is also important to romance. I'm not saying that you have to put every single thing in your home away, but if you're so messy that you can't even find a place to lay down together . . . well, that's not going to encourage romance, is it?

Many people particularly enjoy having candles or flowers around to decorate and add a scent to the room. Not every person has the same appreciation of these sensations, but even if these accoutrements do nothing for your feelings of romance, don't dampen your partner's spirits by belittling these touches. In fact, you should provide the flowers on occasion, if they bring your partner pleasure.

On the other hand, don't go overboard when it comes to decorating a home. Each partner should have his or her own space that feels comfortable, but if your partner has only one such room in the house, then the two of you probably won't be spending much time together. Ideally, home decorating should be done with both people in mind so that every room is conducive to a get-together.

Tickling your partner's funny bone

While those romance novels may make it seem like a person in love has to be dark and brooding, laughter lifts the spirits and can help make any relationship more romantic. You can't always be silly, and I'm the first one to admit that half of the jokes my late husband used to tell went right over my head. But the guffaws don't drive romance — good spirits do. So while you don't need to keep your partner doubled over with laughter, do make an effort to keep a smile on both your faces.

Becoming great friends

It is definitely a plus if the two of you are great friends, which means you enjoy being together and doing things as a couple. I wouldn't necessarily go as far as to say you should be best friends; that implies that you do everything together. While living in such a cocoon may seem idyllic for a short time, eventually the two of you have to grow and act individually. If you do everything together, when one or both of you start to change, you may get the impression that a rift is growing between you.

If each of you has a life outside of the relationship, then when you are together, you always have something to talk about and ideas to exchange. If you are always together, then you don't get that outside stimulation and you really have to work at keeping the relationship from becoming stagnant. That's not to say that there aren't couples who live and work together and have a very romantic relationship. Many couples at least share the same hobbies, so that when they are together, their interests are identical. Such relationships can work well, but they shouldn't be looked at as the ideal, because I don't believe they'd work for most people. Romance requires a little mystery, and if you're constantly joined at the hip like Siamese twins, then there are no dark corners where that sense of mystery can lurk.

The truth will set you free

It's very difficult to be romantic if one or both of you is living a life full of lies. Don't get me wrong: I am all for the little white lie that prevents hurting a loved one's feelings. If an old flame calls you up, begs to meet you, and then hits you up for $100, there's no need to tell your mate. You may have been a sucker, but that meeting probably confirmed your reasons for having separated and, therefore, was well worth the money. If your partner found out about the meeting, he or she might get very jealous. Why put a loved one through that for no reason?

White lies are told to protect the other person. If you're telling lies to protect yourself, or if your partner is being dishonest, then that's a serious matter. Romance can only thrive in an atmosphere of trust. That's why it's so difficult for couples to get back together if one of them has been caught cheating. (And please don't think that lying about cheating is one of those harmless white lies. Yes, lying in this situation protects the other person, but mostly it allows the cheating to take place.) If one party has been hurt by the other, there's going to be some psychological scar tissue that covers that wound, which acts as a barrier to the tender feelings of romance.

Liars are rarely as good as they think they are. Even if your partner can't prove your tales to be false, suspicion is never conducive to romance. Often the very reason for the lie is to cover up for some inconsistency — getting home late, for example — which is what gets the partner's antennae up in the first place.

If the only glue holding a relationship together is a string of lies, it's not going to last very long. Tell the truth and see what happens. In the end, the truth will be the only hope the relationship has.

The inner game of romance

There was a book out some years ago called *The Inner Game of Tennis*. The concept was that if you tried too hard to hit the ball, you'd distract yourself and wouldn't play as well. The same concept works with romance. If you start thinking "should I do this" or "should I do that," then it's very difficult to be romantic. Romance is a feeling, and you have to allow it to envelop you. It's almost impossible to force yourself to feel romantic. So in order to rekindle your romance, the two of you should learn to luxuriate in each other's presence, drifting off into that tunnel of love.

Kissing can be one means of accomplishing this. Make sure that you both close your eyes and just allow yourself to sink into the kiss. It may be better not to get your tongues involved, as that might be too stimulating. The point is to *feel* love, not necessarily *make* love — at least not at that moment.

Ego stroking

In order to love someone else, you first have to be able to love yourself. That's sometimes easier said than done, so any help that a partner can give in that department will be well worth it. Both partners should be supportive of each other, exchanging compliments whenever appropriate. Try to keep track of your partner's mood. If it seems that he or she is feeling low, then make a point of coming to the rescue with some well chosen ego boosting.

Conversely, sarcasm will almost always reduce the level of romance. If one spouse is always worried that a mistake will provoke a barb from the other, then that fear will overwhelm any romantic inclinations. Constructive criticism is allowed, but if you are doing the criticizing, wait a few beats before opening your mouth to make certain that what you have to say is really constructive and not just a put-down.

Controlling your temper

Even more damaging to romance than criticism is the fear of provoking anger. Saying that you can't control your temper is not a good excuse. If the car in front of you cuts you off dangerously, you're entitled to a few choice words. But if your partner makes an unintentional mistake, any words said in anger can destroy all romantic feelings for quite some time. And if this goes on continually, then your romance will take a permanent vacation.

If your partner does have a temper, be careful not to take personally every cloud of steam that's vented. If your partner is screaming at the burned toast, maybe the toaster should be cringing, but not you. It may be more difficult to live with a volcano, but if you're committed to one, don't assume that every eruption is going to bury you in hot ashes and lava.

Don't be a dishrag

The opposite of the person with a temper is the one who never speaks his or her mind. Romance needs stimulation, and for that to happen, both partners have to share their thoughts. If communication is a one-way street, then romance will take the first bus in the other direction. Our minds are always going; we all have something to say. Don't be afraid to speak up.

How to Be Romantic 365 Days a Year

I want each of you to dedicate a few minutes each day to thinking about how to increase your romance. It could be while you're taking your morning shower or walking to the train or doing your crunches or waiting for your computer to boot up. Just picture your partner and try to think of what you could do to add a touch of romance to his or her day. Maybe you noticed that she was looking for a paper clip that morning, so you bring home a handful from the office. Maybe on your lunch hour you buy him some vitamins. Maybe you think about what you might say during the day when you send her a quick e-mail.

The time spent thinking about romance reaps dividends, maybe not every day, but certainly in the long run. It also gets you in the habit of working to rekindle your romance every day, and there's no better way to keep those flames burning brightly than to give them daily attention.

Chapter 6

Taking Commitment to a Higher Level

*T*o be loved is more than natural; it is absolutely essential to every person's development. If children don't receive sufficient love, they grow up having severe emotional problems. Sadly, the process doesn't always go perfectly, and that causes some people to be afraid of committing to a relationship.

Such fears can be created by a variety of circumstances:

✔ Some people do not experience love as children, either because they don't have parents or because their parents have problems of their own. These individuals do not learn how to properly give or receive love.

✔ Other people have parents who go through a divorce, which makes them feel that no relationship can last. They eventually assume, "Why bother making that commitment in the first place?"

✔ Still other people experience painful relationships themselves and opt to avoid any commitments so they do not have to go through such a difficult process again.

Because you're reading this book, I am going to assume that you are in a relationship that does have an element of commitment to it, perhaps even the permanent commitment of marriage. At some point, both you and your partner agreed that you were in love and no longer wished to go outside of the relationship for either romantic love or sex. I hope that at some time, you were both so in love that you were on that proverbial cloud nine. Now some time has passed, and the feelings are not quite the same. What should you do? In this chapter, I show you how to move past any ruts that your relationship may be in so you can improve your level of commitment to your partner and reap the benefits that commitment brings.

After the Fire

I want to make one thing very clear — the intense feelings that two people have for each other when they first meet do not last forever. If you are seeking those intense feelings, then you will be condemned to go through life leaping from one relationship to another in a never ending search to recapture the rapture of new love, leaving each partner as soon as the emotional level starts to taper off.

Perhaps you are thinking, "Maybe that's a good idea. Maybe we should all go bouncing around from one person to the next as if we live in a pinball machine. That way we could experience the most intense ecstasy of love over and over again." Ah, but there's a catch. After you've gone through this process a couple of times, your heart begins to harden, and that intensity can never be quite as strong as it was before. Soon there comes a time when you can't recapture anything like those first feelings no matter how hard you try. At that point, you may never kindle a love strong enough to melt your heart so you can become one with another person. While we are all entitled to make a few mistakes, to adopt a lifestyle of permanently bouncing from lover to lover will never leave anyone satisfied.

So where do you find the satisfaction you're looking for? In a relationship that is well cared for. In the next section, I show you how to make the love you have for your partner grow and blossom.

The Garden of Love

Just because we may never recapture the intensity of a new love doesn't mean we have to put up with a love that has become pale and wan. While love changes over time, it can develop new strengths and different intensities, but only if you put some effort into making that happen. You could make the analogy that romance is the garden of love; in order to reap a crop, you have to till the soil, plant fresh seeds, add fertilizer, irrigate it, and pull out any weeds that may sneak in. If you have a next door neighbor who likes to parade around in a bikini, then you might also have to build a higher fence to keep out the varmints.

Tilling the soil

As I say in Chapter 5, boredom is one of the biggest dangers you face in a relationship. If the two of you follow the same routine day after day, if you can predict what your mate is going to do and say (maybe even exactly when he or she is going to do or say it), then romance is going to have a very hard time surviving on your little acre of land.

The only cure for boredom is to stir things up — in other words, till the soil. I realize that you can't turn your lives upside down on a continual basis. If no one followed a routine in the morning, your household would be chaotic and nobody would get to work or school on time. But what would happen if now and then you set the alarm 15 minutes earlier and the two of you just hugged each other for that time? And what do you think would happen if you pulled the plug from the TV for an evening? Would you really fall apart if you didn't watch the late news? I once scolded Johnny Carson on the *Tonight Show* because couples were listening to his monologue instead of making love. I'm not saying you should never watch late night TV, just that you shouldn't do it every night.

And don't make these changes with a heavy heart. Make a commitment to livening things up, and I bet you'll have a happier life. Forget about the romantic quotient for a moment; any time you're in a rut, you're not living up to your potential. So start stirring things up, and do it enthusiastically.

Here are some ideas to get you started:

- ✔ Surprise your spouse with breakfast in bed — on a weekday.
- ✔ Order a sexy gift, like a teddy from Victoria's Secret or boxers with hearts on them, and have it delivered to your spouse's office.
- ✔ Leave work a few minutes early and meet your spouse outside his or her office. (Check with a secretary or co-worker first to make sure he or she won't be working late.)
- ✔ Have a picnic on the living room floor.
- ✔ Suggest a game of strip poker.
- ✔ Celebrate your half-anniversary or the anniversary of your first date.
- ✔ Give your partner a foot massage.

Planting the seeds

The seeds of love are the words and gestures that we use to express how we feel about each other. You may love your partner, but how is he or she going to know it if you don't express it in words and deeds? Say you're sitting in your office, and you look over at the picture of your spouse and feel a little twinge of love in your heart. That's great, but your spouse won't know your thoughts unless you express them. You can send an e-mail or call your partner, or you can just whisper it in his or her ear when you see each other that night. But if you let the thought slip away and never communicate those feelings, then it's like spilling seeds on cement.

Keep in mind that there are various ways of planting seeds. You can do it casually, just flinging handfuls of them onto the ground, or you can get down on your knees, poke a hole in the dirt, and carefully lay some seeds in the hole. The same holds true for romance. You can merely say "I love you," or you can take your partner into your arms, squeeze him or her tight, and whisper those words slowly. Your approach makes a difference; your words will have quite a different effect if you make that extra effort.

What might make you take the second, more amorous approach? Commitment to your mate and to the relationship. I admit that such romantic gestures could be interpreted as being silly. In fact, some people only make them while pretending to be silly, to cover up their embarrassment. But while you may feel silly at first, if your partner responds positively, that silliness is going to be replaced by some deeper emotions. Those feelings of love will start to grow and intertwine around your hearts. By the time you're through, you should both be feeling quite marvelous.

Annette and Warren

It seemed that every time Annette was busy in the kitchen, Warren would come up behind her, put his arms around her, and start to cuddle her. He even put his hands on some delicate places, like her breasts and her buttocks. Annette considered herself a good cook, and getting each part of the meal done at the same time required concentration. Having Warren putting his hands all over her was a distraction that she didn't need, but when she asked him to stop, he would put on a long face.

Seeing Annette in the kitchen always made Warren grateful that he was going to get such a good meal, especially after spending five years living as a bachelor and eating a lot of peanut butter sandwiches. He wanted to show his gratitude, and because he worked long hours, it was not unusual for him to find Annette in the kitchen when he walked into the house.

Farmers know that there are seasons when it is time to plant and others when the fields should lay fallow. While it's wonderful that any partner should want to express his or her love, you do have to respect your partner's needs. In the case of Warren and Annette, where a quick squeeze might have been appropriate, the more aggressive fondling was not. If Warren really wanted to show how much he loved his wife, he could have helped with the dinner preparations by setting the table and maybe uncorking a bottle of wine.

Fertilizing and irrigating

It is very easy for two people to take each other for granted, especially if the years that you've been together are really starting to add up. You sleep in the same bed every night, see each other every morning, and have dinner together most evenings. After a while, you each become part of the furniture. Okay, that's an exaggeration, but if you're not careful, the relationship could become closer to the one you have with the family dog.

How do you prevent that from happening? You have to fertilize and irrigate. I may be getting carried away with these farming images, but there are two basic ways of keeping a relationship from becoming stunted:

- Consciously say what you feel.
- Consciously show what you feel.

The reason I say *consciously* is that it's not enough to give your spouse a goodbye kiss while your brain is on automatic pilot. Of course, some mornings when you're on the way to an important meeting, that's fine. But other mornings, you have to stop and say to yourself, "This is the person I love," and put some of those feelings into that kiss. While you've got your thinking cap on, instead of kissing your partner on the forehead (the way you've done for the past 5/10/20 years), try some variety. One morning, rub noses. Another, lick an ear. Another, go down on your knees and propose. In other words (getting back to my earlier advice), stir things up. It's not essential every day, but do it enough times so that the dogs of boredom get chased away.

Weeding

I promise that this is the end of my agricultural phase, but again, I think the description is fitting. One or two weeds in a field won't harm the crops, but weeds have a way of multiplying. Before you know it, there's no room for the plants that are being cultivated because the weeds take over. Similarly, in a relationship, small dissatisfactions can start to pile up until they dominate the love that you are striving to cultivate.

The big difference between a weed and these peeves is that while weeds need to be picked by someone else, for the most part a peeve has to be self-eradicated. Let's take a simple pet peeve that is so often mentioned that it has become an emblem for these types of differences: leaving the top off the toothpaste tube. Is this really a big deal? No. But if you love your partner, and this habit annoys him or her, is it any more of a big deal to screw the top back on?

Some of these pet peeves become very petty indeed. A couple can begin to interact with each other the way a parent does with a teenager, and to some degree this behavior is an outgrowth of that relationship. Teens do things to rebel because they have to cut the apron strings. You certainly don't want them to demonstrate their independence by taking drugs, drinking too much alcohol, or getting failing grades, so parents put up with other harmless signs of rebellion like a messy room or loud music. Now if one half of a couple starts acting like a parent, harping on keeping the house neat, for example, then the other may start to rebel against this by consciously leaving clothes lying around. In my experience, men are more likely to behave rebelliously, because they start to associate their wives with their mothers. And unless a truce is called, this can escalate to the point of launching major battles.

Both partners have to actively prioritize. Whenever an irritating situation arises that has the potential to lead to a scuffle, ask yourself this: Which is more important, your love for each other or a petty grievance? In theory, this seems like an easy choice to make. But one difficulty many couples have is deciding who makes the first concession. If two people have been having these petty fights for some time, putting the top back on the toothpaste can have weighty implications; it's a little like waving a white flag. But your relationship isn't supposed to be about winning, is it? The two of you are lovers, so you both should be willing to compromise. You must talk these issues out and let each other know that there are no winners or losers; you either win together or lose together.

In some situations, one partner may be justified in feeling right about a certain issue. For example, it may seem obvious that a toothpaste top belongs on the tube to keep the contents from drying out; the party who complains about it being left off is going to feel that he or she is right. That person may feel less willing to compromise as a result. But each battle has to be put in context. If a toothpaste cap were the only weed growing in your field, then neither of you would really care about it. Weeds only become a problem when they multiply, and the same is true with these petty peeves. One important way to prove your commitment to your partner is to make a serious effort to eradicate the source of each other's pet peeves. And don't think of it as "giving in" — instead, look at it as making your relationship stronger.

Committing to Your Partner's Personality

Your partner came into your relationship with a set of characteristics and habits. Chances are that some of those characteristics and habits drive you a little nuts sometimes, but if you are committed to your relationship, you must learn to accept the whole person you're in love with. This section offers advice for how to do just that.

Accepting the absentminded professor

Some people are absentminded types who truly can't remember to put the top back on the toothpaste. They're not rebelling, it's just that while they may have a lot of brain power, they lack common sense. They're not trying to annoy their mates, but once they start brushing their teeth, their minds move on to something else and the toothpaste tube top becomes invisible.

Such people do exist, and if your mate is one of them, then you have to adopt a different philosophy. You are not going to get your partner to change dramatically, and if you allow his or her bad habits to bother you, you'll be driven to distraction. You have to look at this aspect of his or her personality as you would any other trait. If your partner is short, there's no point in trying to get him to be tall because you can't.

A behavior pattern can be almost like a physical trait. I say *almost,* because anyone can make some changes. Now let's say that your lover forgets to call when he or she is going to be late. I don't put that into the category of pet peeve. The person sitting at home waiting is understandably going to get very worried. Why put anyone through that if there is no need? I think it's reasonable to demand that the forgetful person remember at least one or two important things, and that includes calling if he or she is not going to be home on time. If someone is capable of holding down a job and bearing other responsibilities, then that same someone is capable of remembering to make a phone call.

Bridging the gap between the grasshopper and the ant

You may be familiar with the story of the grasshopper and the ant. The ant spent all summer working hard to gather and store food while the grasshopper enjoyed herself. Then, when winter came, the grasshopper came begging for food. The ant didn't want to part with any of her supplies, because she had warned the grasshopper about the coming cold season.

It's very easy to play the role of the ant with a partner who keeps making the same, or similar, mistakes over and over again. For example, you tell him to put gas in the car, he doesn't do it, and then he begs to take your car because he's late for an appointment. As a result, you're stuck going out of your way to put gas in his car. If something like this happens over and over again, it can become very difficult for the "ant," the person who is always prepared, to forgive the "grasshopper." Love, and a person's patience, can be stretched only so thin.

But the ant and the grasshopper weren't lovers. If they had been, then maybe the ant would have been attracted to the grasshopper's playfulness. Maybe the ant needed somebody to drag her out dancing or for a swim in the lake. It's easy to get angry; something your partner has done upsets you, adrenaline is released into your bloodstream, and when it hits your brain, your temper flares. But while you may not be able to control that first burst of anger, you do have to learn not to hold a grudge. That's part of the commitment you have made to each other, especially if you are married. You must remember the "for better or worse" part.

If you want this relationship to work, you have to forgive your partner's faults. If you allow yourself to become bitter, you're ruining your life as well as your relationship. You have to look at your partner and actively remember why you fell in love with him or her in the first place. I'm not saying that it won't take some effort, but if you don't make that effort — if you allow your anger to simmer — you're going to damage the relationship beyond repair.

But, of course, it takes two to tango, and the person who is playing the role of grasshopper has to make some compromises as well. Maybe you feel that you can never live up to the standards your partner has set. In that case, you have to bend over backwards in other ways. If you know you're driving your spouse crazy, then you should go out of your way to bring home presents to show that you are thinking of him or her. Or take your partner out to do something enjoyable, or spring some other pleasant surprise. If the "grasshopper" does nothing but take, take, take, then eventually the other person's well of love is going to run dry and the relationship is going to end.

The Limits of Commitment

You're probably familiar with at least the first line of Elizabeth Barrett Browning's poem that begins, "How do I love thee? Let me count the ways." Here's a little homework assignment: Find and read the entire poem (from *Sonnets from the Portuguese*), and ask yourself if you really love your partner to that extent. We sometimes say the words (though probably not quite as eloquently), and we may even mean them in the first few months of a relationship. But we humans are selfish by nature, and not many of us really put our love on such a high plane. Do we make sacrifices for each other? Of course we do. But at some point we start to say "enough." We may be willing to give up our life for our partner in a moment of danger, but how willing are we to give up a ball game or a day of shopping at the mall?

When God called down to Abraham and told him to sacrifice his son, Abraham was willing to obey — at least that's what the Bible tells us. But few of us are as strong as Abraham, and so it is difficult to make complete sacrifices for each other. Our level of commitment is not endless, and we shouldn't expect it to be. Reality does have a place in a relationship. But it can be difficult to decide where the cutoff point lies.

Living on the edge

Some people go through life constantly testing their mates' devotion. They practically torture their spouses in order to feel more certain of their commitment. This is obviously not healthy for either party.

Elizabeth and Alan

Elizabeth's father left her and her mother when she was six. He moved out of town, and she never saw him again. Because of her father's abandonment, Elizabeth never felt totally secure in any relationship. There was always this subconscious fear in the back of her mind that any man she was with would leave her.

Alan truly loved Elizabeth and had the potential to be an ideal mate. But Elizabeth wasn't content with having a man who made simple compromises for her. She would push any man to the brink, over and over again, to test the level of his commitment to her. She would purposefully come in very late and not offer any excuses. She would buy an expensive dress and then refuse to wear it. She'd promise to meet Alan somewhere and then not show up, or she would show up at his office when she knew that he had an important assignment to finish.

Elizabeth did love Alan, and most of the time she was absolutely wonderful to him. Her behavior left Alan feeling very confused. He didn't understand why she would suddenly do something out of the clear blue sky that was absolutely unreasonable. At times he was completely devoted to her, and at times he came close to leaving her.

You're not supposed to drag total commitment out of your partner; he or she is supposed to offer it to you willingly. Occasionally, a relationship like Elizabeth and Alan's may last forever, but because such relationships are inherently unstable, many crash and burn. These relationships really need the help of a therapist, who can talk to each partner and analyze the situation in order to derive the reason for one partner's erratic behavior. A therapist can offer suggestions for ways to change that pattern of behavior and can make it more bearable by explaining its origins.

Seeking a soul mate

Love is composed of a single soul inhabiting two bodies.

— Aristotle

I don't know if the term *soul mates* heralds from the time of Aristotle, but I do know that many people today are seeking soul mates: partners meant for them and no one else. Not surprisingly, many couples can't quite live up to such a high expectation, and they end up not staying together. Feeling required to live a perfect life is too much pressure. You need to fight once in a while to let off steam, or there could be a volcanic eruption somewhere down the line. Since none of us is perfect, you have to recognize your partner's faults as well as your own. It's wonderful to strive for a lofty goal, but you also have to appreciate that no couple achieves that summit every day of their lives. Most of us fall short in many ways, and that includes our ability to commit.

One hundred percent commitment in a relationship would mean wanting to spend every possible second staring into each other's eyes. I don't believe that's possible or even desirable. Each of you has to retain your individualism so you can retain the qualities that attracted you to each other in the first place.

But just because I have declared it impossible to achieve an absolutely total commitment to your partner does not mean that you should not do your best to make the relationship work. Think of it as an exciting challenge; if there were never any risk of failure, life would be utterly boring.

The existence of temptation gives value to commitment, and I don't mean only the temptation to cheat with another person. Commitment is making choices that put the relationship in the proper priority. That's why I include the temptation to watch TV instead of having a deep conversation, the temptation to please the boss by working a little late rather than heading home to share dinner with your spouse, and the temptation to call your sister for the second time today instead of joining your partner in the den for a cup of coffee.

I encourage you to strive for the highest possible level of commitment that you can attain without deeming yourself a failure if you don't reach the pinnacle. What steps can you take to prove (and improve) your commitment to your mate? The next section offers some concrete suggestions.

Shaking Yourselves Out of a Rut

> *I feel like Zsa Zsa Gabor's sixth husband. I know what I'm supposed to do, but I don't know how to make it interesting.*
>
> — Milton Berle

I have to admit that from my chair I have a slightly skewed view of the world. Couples who enjoy a great relationship do not call me to make an appointment. I see only people who are experiencing problems. Because you're reading this book, I must assume that you fit into that latter category to some degree (hopefully to a mild degree).

From my office chair, I see many couples whose biggest problem is boredom. Their relationship has gone stale, and they can't seem to make the change by themselves. Change can be frightening, but not changing can be deadly (at least to a relationship), so you've got to give it a try.

My best advice? Be daring. I am not necessarily advising that you go sky diving or bungee jumping. All I'm suggesting is that you do whatever it takes to drag yourselves out of your rut. It could be as simple as watching a different TV show than you always do or as elaborate as going to the airport and buying two seats on the first available flight, no matter where it is going, and taking off for the weekend. Following are some suggestions that fall somewhere in between these two extremes:

- ✔ If you've always had long hair, cut it off. And if you've always been clean shaven, grow a mustache or a full beard.

- ✔ Even if you both like rock music, the next time you have some extra money for a concert, buy two tickets to see an opera or a philharmonic orchestra.

- ✔ Rearrange the furniture in your living room.

- ✔ Hire a limo to drive you to a family picnic.

- ✔ Wear a see-through blouse without a bra when you go out to dinner.

- ✔ Cover yourself with washable tattoos before going to the beach or a pool party.

- ✔ Dress in your fanciest clothes, bring along a candle and some matches, and have dinner at McDonald's.

Setting aside time for each other

Obviously, people have to earn a living, and these days it's common for both partners to hold down jobs outside the home. As a result, the amount of time a couple spends together has become more limited than ever before. Back when most people lived on farms, a couple would eat every meal together, and in the winter months they might be together 24 hours a day. Today, with so many people living in the suburbs and driving downtown to work, you may spend more time in your automobile than with your partner (if you don't count the time you spend sleeping by each other's side). I discuss these challenges in detail in Chapter 16.

When a resource is scarce, you have to allocate it carefully. Rather than just hope that your schedules will change someday so you can spend some time together, make that time a part of your schedule. Make plans in the morning to go for a walk after dinner that night. Sign up for weekly dancing lessons and make sure that you both attend every week. Plan in advance to go antiquing the next weekend. And give these appointments a very high priority. Don't just cancel them the minute a work-related or other commitment appears on the horizon. To show how committed you are to each other, cancel something else on your schedule instead. And if you do have to change plans, reschedule that appointment with your lover right away.

Sharing a hobby

Typically, men do certain activities — say, watching sports on TV and woodworking — and women take up others — following soap operas and taking yoga classes, for example. Now ask yourself this question: What do we do together? You sleep together, have sex once in a while, eat most meals together, perhaps attend a religious service once a week, and maybe watch TV together. But shouldn't there be something else in this mix? Something that is not necessary (like sleeping and eating) — something fun and intellectually stimulating?

I suggest that each of you make a list of activities that might interest you and see if any of your interests match your partner's. What might be on that list? Here are just a few examples to get you started:

- Antiquing
- Cooking
- Gardening
- Going to the theater (or opera or concerts)
- Hiking
- Playing tennis
- Raising pedigreed animals
- Remodeling a room (or the entire house)
- Skiing
- Snorkeling
- Traveling
- Volunteering for a charity or at a hospital
- Working for a political candidate

The possibilities are limitless. You can actually make an interesting project choosing what the two of you might like to do together. You could spend hours searching the Internet together for ideas; it would give you lots to discuss. If you know other people who pursue a particular hobby that interests you, invite them over for dinner (which you could make together), and talk about it to learn more.

Ideally, when you find the right hobby and start pursuing it, you will no longer say, "Darn, I have to do this activity instead of watching this game or that soap." Instead, you'll both be excited to do whatever pastime you have chosen together.

Putting some life back into your conversations

The best way to connect with a loved one is to share ideas. When the two of you first started dating, you probably had plenty of ideas to share and, therefore, plenty of things to discuss. But as time has passed, chances are that your discussions are no longer as animated as they used to be. At times, you may even feel that you have nothing new to say to your partner.

If this is the case, make a conscious effort to find new things to talk about and new ideas about topics that interest both of you. I suggest that you carefully look through newspapers, magazines, and Web sites for interesting articles that you can both read and then discuss. You should steer clear of subjects that you know you both strongly disagree about, because that's more likely to cause a debate instead of a discussion. I'm not saying that you have to agree on everything, but to further the relationship, pursue discussions where you know you have some common ground.

Need some ideas for how to start an interesting conversation? Try asking your partner some questions like these:

- ✔ When we retire, should we live where we do now or move to warmer climes? At what age do we want to retire?
- ✔ Which local politicians are doing a good job? Which ones have proved to be a disappointment?
- ✔ Which cuisine is the best — French, Italian, Chinese, or American?
- ✔ Is it better to live in the city, the suburbs, or the country?
- ✔ Should sex education be taught in our classrooms?
- ✔ Should there be a death penalty?

Making new friends

Here's some great news: You and your partner can get help as you search for new ways to stimulate your conversations. If you've been a couple for a decade or more, you may feel that you've exhausted certain areas of discussion. In addition to generating new ideas by reading articles, you can also generate them by bringing new friends into your life.

Now there's nothing wrong with your old friends, but sometimes old friends yield to old patterns. Let's say that you invite over a certain couple who you've both known for years. They come to your house, and the same thing happens that has happened a hundred times before — the guys talk about one subject and the women about another. If it's hard enough for the two of you to rekindle your romance by making changes, it's going to be that much harder to get this other couple to join you. So while I'm not saying that you should stop seeing your old friends, you're likely to find some added stimulation if you try to make new ones.

Where do you find new friends? You could invite one of your co-workers and his or her spouse to go out one evening. Maybe there's a couple that you regularly say hi to at church or synagogue; ask them over for dinner. Do you have neighbors who you know only in passing? Or maybe parents of some of your kids' classmates?

You may find some of these couples more boring than staring at your four walls would have been, but if you keep trying (and eventually narrow your search), I'm sure that you can begin adding to your list of friends so it becomes more varied.

Chapter 7

Renewing Your Marriage Vows

. . . .

In This Chapter

▶ Celebrating your years together

▶ Tailoring your vows

▶ Making renewal an active part of your life

. . . .

U p to this point I've been assuming that some of you are married and some of you are not. (These days it's quite common for a couple to spend years together without being married, perhaps living under the same roof or perhaps not.)

I believe that a romance is a romance is a romance, and they all can be rekindled with or without a license from any governmental agency. However, this chapter is aimed at those of you who have taken that dramatic (hopefully once-in-a-lifetime) walk down the aisle together.

Reasons for Saying "I Do" Times Two

I was married by a judge. I should have asked for a jury.

— Groucho Marx

Whether your wedding was a lavish affair in front of a large crowd or merely the two of you standing in front of a justice of the peace and a couple of witnesses, you've already agreed to spend your lives together "'til death do us part." So what's the point, you might ask, of renewing those vows? Your vows came with a lifetime guarantee (and no small print), right? What are we asking you to do here, commit bigamy with your own spouse?

One reason that you might consider renewing your wedding vows is a simple statistic. The national divorce rate stands at around 50 percent, and while that statistic is somewhat skewed by the fact that some people go through the process many times while others never separate, it still throws a pall over the institution of marriage. We've all heard that love is blind, but sometimes after a few years those blinders fall off, and when the two individuals get a closer look at each other they decide to head for the hills. If the vast majority of marriages never came apart at the seams, then married couples would have less reason to worry about their own marriage. Since that's not the case, it can be reassuring to agree to go through the process again.

But because you and your partner are unique individuals, and the combination of your two lives is even more unique, there should be no comparison between your marriage and anyone else's, should there? The only thing that should matter is that your marriage is working; if neither of you is in the habit of breaking promises, what others do shouldn't cause you any concern.

That's definitely true, but while you could look at a renewal as merely a further commitment to your original vows, I think you should also look at it as a chance to celebrate your marriage. If your marriage is working well, why not celebrate? If you've gotten passed all the bumps on the road of life so far, I'm all for congratulating yourselves with a public renewal of vows. We all can use a pat on the back for a job well done, and there's no better way to offer congratulations to each other than to renew your promises.

I do have to issue one warning at this point. If your marriage is not working well — if the two of you have issues to deal with — a marriage renewal is probably not the answer. It may mask the cracks for a short time, but eventually those cracks will reappear. So don't look at a marriage renewal as a quick fix. If your marriage needs repairs, take care of them first. Let some time go by, and if it looks like the marriage is going to hold up, then celebrate with some sort of renewal of your vows.

Strengthening a second (or third) marriage

But there are many other reasons to go through this process besides the desire to have a party. For example, not every marriage is a first marriage. If one or both of you have gone through a divorce (maybe even multiple times), then the extra reassurance provided by a renewal of vows might be very appreciated. In such marriages, you might not want to wait for the tenth or twentieth anniversary to renew your vows. I'm not saying that your marriage is necessarily shakier because of past mishaps, but any added signs of commitment couldn't hurt. Plus, a renewal will show those people who warned that you shouldn't get married again that they didn't know what they were talking about.

Recognizing that your job is not done

Another reason for renewing vows is that the job of a husband or wife isn't done until one of you goes to that great wedding hall of fame in the sky. Openly renewing your marriage vows can give you additional strength to continue to remain faithful to each other. Any promise loses its power over time; it becomes easier to make excuses to be weak. You could say to yourself, "I've been faithful for 20 years, so if I weigh cheating just this one time against 20 years of holding myself back, how bad could it be?" But if you've recently renewed your vows, that process will definitely strengthen your backbone to continue to resist whatever temptations come your way for the next 20 years.

And if you outlive your partner, after your better half is gone you'll be thankful that you did renew those vows. You'll know that you took at least that particular opportunity to tell him or her, once again, how important he or she was to you.

Embracing a lifetime of change

Keep your eyes wide open before marriage, and half shut afterwards.

— Benjamin Franklin

If the two of you have been married for quite some time, you've both gone through many changes physically, intellectually, and emotionally. These changes have been gradual, so they may be hard for you to see. But if you look back at your wedding pictures and try to remember your emotional and intellectual selves back then, I'm sure the changes will become quite apparent. If you love each other despite the changes you've both gone through, that's another reason to recommit.

Many middle-aged and senior women worry that their husbands may not find them attractive any more. And males, with their bulging bellies and receding (perhaps receded) hair lines might be concerned that they're not the studs they once were either. So by reaffirming your marriage vows, you're giving each other the message that whatever the ravages of time, you're still hanging in there.

Setting an example for the younger generation

The example that you set definitely affects your children. The more often they can witness the two of you demonstrating your love for each other, the more likely that they'll imitate you and try their hardest to stick with their spouses. I certainly recommend making sure that your kids see you hugging and kissing and holding hands. (Although I also recommend the lock on the bedroom door to protect more intimate signs of affection.) And because your kids probably weren't at your wedding (unless this is a second marriage for either or both of you), then a renewal of vows is a chance for them to witness the commitments that you and your spouse have made to each other.

Your kids may even want to take part in the renewal ceremony. They could write something to recite, or (if they're old enough) each of them could get up and say a few words about your relationship. Just remember that this is your day, so don't give them total control but only a supporting role.

Bringing years of experience to your vows

> *Immature love says: "I love you because I need you." Mature love says: "I need you because I love you."*
>
> — Erich Fromm

The love that you have for your spouse now is inevitably different than it was when you got married. While the intensity may have waned over the years, the ties that bind you have added up through those same years. Chances are that you feel more tightly connected than you did when you first married.

After some years have passed — perhaps even a decade or two — you now know each other quite well. The fact that you still love each other actually means a whole lot more because of that. You don't just love your spouse superficially; your love extends down to the very depths of his or her heart and soul that you've had all this time to explore. When you say "I do" a second time, those two little words are backed up by years of experience and carry even more weight than they did when you uttered them the first time. (And this time, speak up so those of us in the back can hear you!)

Sticking together through life's speed bumps

If you've been together for a long time, then there's no doubt that you've hit some of life's little speed bumps. Actually, you may have even met some rather large bumps. For example, each of you may have lost one or both of your parents. This is to be expected if you stay together long enough, but there's no getting around the fact that your spouse takes on greater importance when you no longer have your parents to fall back on. So while you may not have understood fully what your wedding vows meant the first time around, they'll have a much deeper meaning for the two of you now.

And while parents' deaths are inevitable, life can also throw lots of other curves your way. I'm not going to go down a laundry list of possible calamities, because I could never cover them all and don't want to make you feel paranoid. But they exist, and if you've gone through some, then you know that living through such experiences can bring you and your spouse closer together.

And you also know that the future holds more of these, including the likelihood that one of you is going to have to live through the loss of the other. So if the sun happens to be shining on your lives right now, why not say "thank you" to each other (and the powers that be) by renewing your vows?

Celebrating shared memories

If you're both 50 and you've been married for 25 years, then you've spent half of your lives together. Even if you haven't been together quite so long, you still have quite a bank of shared memories stored up. And if you have children, then there have been even more special moments that only the two of you can appreciate.

Let me tell you, looking at old photographs of your kids when they were younger is a very different experience if there's nobody to share those memories with you. In a divorce, the assets get divided, but that memory bank can't be split up. When you lose the person who was with you every important step of the way, you lose quite a lot of yourself. You've made a big investment in this person, and renewing your vows can be a very good insurance policy to protect that investment.

Making sex part of your celebration

A few years back, I was asked to speak on The Love Boat. There were 800 couples on board for this Valentine's Day cruise, and they all renewed their marriage vows. When it was my turn to speak, I gave them all a homework assignment. In response, the captain asked that they not all go to their cabins at the same time or the rocking of the boat might have tipped us over!

The point of this story is that you should put any ceremony that includes renewing your marriage vows into the proper context. This isn't a business. More than anything, this is a celebration of your love for one another, and as a married couple, having sexual relations is definitely one way that you've been expressing that love. I go into more details on this particular topic in Part III of this book, but I didn't want any of you to think I'd forgotten my roots.

But that's for the more private part of the day. In the public arena, however you choose to renew your vows, whether among many others on a cruise or in front of family and friends, make sure that you don't get bogged down in the details and forget about each other. When you first got married, the bride's parents probably handled a lot of the load. This ceremony is going to be something that you plan together. Just don't make it all so complex that you expend all of your energies taking care of your guests, leaving nothing left over for each other. You're not as young as you used to be, so plan the day carefully. You don't want to be so worn out afterward that all you can manage to do when you crawl into bed is fall asleep.

Taking a trip down memory lane

A natural part of the process of renewing your vows is thinking back on all those memories that the two of you have accumulated over the years. I suggest that you make a conscious decision about how this is going to occur. If you do it in a piecemeal fashion, it won't have the same impact. Try to set aside a block of time when you and your spouse can look over old pictures, movies, and videos, leaf through diaries, and just talk about the "good old days."

You may want to include others in this trip down memory lane, or you may prefer that just the two of you take part. As close as you may be to your children, there are certainly some moments in your lives that they don't know about. So while it's fun to take a field trip through the past with your children, the two of you may feel a greater closeness if you just do it together. In fact, you may want to pack up all your memorabilia in a box, throw it in the car, and spend an evening at a motel so that you can be totally alone without any distractions. That way you can laugh, cry, and even make love without worrying about who is around. If you can't afford to reenact your honeymoon or take some other vacation as part of the occasion, this evening could be a nice substitute.

There were probably a few times when you were at each other's throats during your journey through life together. I suggest that you be diplomatic and not bring those particular days or nights up. It's best to have a selective memory when it comes to your spouse, and let's face it, I'm sure that you would benefit from your spouse's partial amnesia as well.

Even if you do take a private voyage into the past, you could also create a more public trip down memory lane, making a point of including those people (like brothers and sisters) who were there for much of the time. Each person probably remembers a certain incident that the others may have forgotten. If you videotape this session, then you'll have a more complete picture saved for posterity. And if any family member is particularly adept at making such memories amusing, then it will be a very entertaining tape as well.

Making Your Vows More Meaningful

Your first marriage vows were probably not very specific because the two of you didn't know each other very well yet. This time around, you've got X number of years as husband and wife under your belt. You know each other a lot better, and now that you're older, you know yourself a lot better too. So whatever ceremony you plan this time, you can be a little more specific with your vows.

I'm not suggesting that you vow to become a saint. We all have our faults; I'm hanging on to some of mine with both hands, and I give you permission to do the same. But that said, chances are that a few of your bad habits even annoy you. If not, I'm certain that you know which of them annoy your spouse. So why not pick one or two and include them in your vows as traits that you're going to try to change? I can't predict whether or not you'll be successful, but your spouse will definitely appreciate that you made the offer.

Certain vows become more meaningful as time passes, even though the words may not need to change for your renewal ceremony. For example, in your first vows, the phrase "in sickness and in health" was probably something you said but didn't think much about. As you get older, however, these words develop greater meaning. You're both going to undergo some physical changes that affect your relationship, if this hasn't already happened. Let's take one unavoidable change: menopause. Do you both know what changes menopause creates, especially in your sex life? This would be a good time to talk about them, especially if menopause hasn't set in yet to the female half of your dynamic duo. By talking about such issues, you'll help to assure your spouse that if something serious comes along, the two of you can work together to handle that, too.

Sustaining the Celebration

Make an effort to let the good feelings from your renewal ceremony have more than a 24-hour life span. If you've made some specific promises to your spouse, try to live up to them. The next time you feel a little angry at your spouse, in the spirit of these new vows, release that anger and give him or her a hug instead.

And if you find the renewal process effective, then why not make it a regular part of your marriage? I'm not saying that you should make a big deal about it once a year. But you could have a small private ceremony, just between the two of you, every year on your wedding anniversary. When you make that toast to each other, say a few words that will fill in for a full renewal of your marriage vows. Rituals are a good way of acting out our feelings constructively.

Planning Your Ceremony

Weddings now represent a $40 billion industry. While the money spent on marriage renewal celebrations represents a small fraction of that huge sum, the size of the entire industry means that many potential sources of services and information are available to you. If you're looking for a caterer, a photographer, or a printer to handle the invitations, any business that services the wedding industry will be able to serve your needs.

Many tourist locales that cater to honeymooners make a point of trying to attract people looking to renew their vows. Some cruise lines offer special packages for people renewing their vows; you might find that you can join a whole boatload of couples doing the same thing, lending a communal effect that can make the experience even more rewarding.

While many wedding books and magazines focus on elaborate dresses and ceremony that include huge bridal parties (which you most likely won't have), the Internet offers some good resources for planning your renewal ceremony:

- ✔ WedNet, at www.wednet.com, offers useful planning information and also connects you to the top 100 wedding-related Web sites. About.com also has many links to appropriate sites.

- ✔ If you look at the home pages of other people who have already gone through the renewal procedure, you may get some ideas of ingredients you want to include in your ceremony.

- ✔ A site that suggests poems, quotations, and other readings appropriate for your ceremony is www.weddingguideUK.com.

- ✔ You can explore many Web rings on the subject of weddings; I found one that is linked to 1,310 sites, so you see there's lots to explore. Another Web ring I found is called Second Time Around Wedding Ring, which leads to a few interesting sites, one of which contains the full text of *Frankenstein* by Mary Shelley. I didn't quite get the connection, unless Shelley's book is meant to serve as a warning not to let this renewal ceremony get out of hand and turn into a monster.

Chapter 8

Getting Away from It All:
Romantic Getaways

When a man faces his Maker, he will have to account for the pleasures of life he failed to experience.

— Talmud

*W*hen I first came to the United States, I worked as a housemaid for $1 an hour, and on that princely sum I had to support both myself and my baby daughter. I give you this piece of information so you don't think I was born with a silver spoon in my mouth or that I believe that everyone can afford an expensive romantic vacation.

City parks have been called the poor man's vacation spot, and trust me I've used them that way. And you know what? They can be very romantic. Just take a walk through New York's Central Park on a sunny spring weekend, and you'll see hundreds of people holding hands, kissing, and being very romantic. Romance, after all, is a state of mind. If you're in the right mood, you can turn any place in the world into a place where romance can bloom.

But since having become Dr. Ruth and having increased my pay scale somewhat, I also know that travelling away from home creates wonderful opportunities for romance to spread her wings and envelope you in her unique aura. And the farther away you travel, the farther you'll be from the pressures that surround you on the home front. Being able to relax is most certainly a boon to creating true romance. So in this chapter we run the gamut from cheap romantic vacations (that may last only a couple of hours) to those higher up on the socioeconomic scale. Even if you can't afford the fancy ones, reading about them may help to rejuvenate your fantasy life.

Planning the Perfect Vacation

Never think of a romantic vacation as existing solely during the time you're actually out the door and on your way. To get the most out of any vacation, you have to include the time you spend planning your vacation in the equation. (By the way, this applies to unromantic vacations as well, such as those with small children and dogs.) Fantasy is an important part of sex and romance, and you can spend months fantasizing about a vacation and get a lot out of it, even if you end up not going. Just don't go so far off the deep end that the vacation itself can't compare with your fantasies. Throw the occasional rainy day and flat tire into those fantasies so that you don't wind up disappointed.

This process can start even before you've chosen where you want to go. Let's say you were trying to decide between going to Paris or going to Rome (lucky you). I would suggest that you go for a meal in an Italian restaurant and share a bottle of Soave, and the next week visit a French restaurant and sip some Beaujolais. The wine is optional, but the concept is a good one. If you've never been to either country, you'll get a small taste of each, and it might help you to make up your mind. And even if it doesn't, you'll have had two nice meals, which can be very romantic on their own.

But meals are just the tip of the iceberg. There are lots of ways to get yourself into the spirit of the vacation:

- ✔ Buy some books about the places you want to go and read them together.
- ✔ Go online and begin exploring any cities on your potential itinerary.
- ✔ Try to find restaurants online that give their menus so you can choose what you'll want to eat when you get there.
- ✔ Buy a map and plan out your route.
- ✔ If you're going to a country where the population speaks another language, get books or tapes so you can pick up some important vocabulary words and practice pronouncing them.
- ✔ If you're traveling out of the country, familiarize yourself with the currency so you'll know how much your purchases really cost.
- ✔ Shop for some appropriate clothing. (Maybe some new sexy clothes should be part of that "appropriate" wardrobe.)

✔ Exercise to get into shape if you're going to be doing a lot of walking, hiking, or skiing. (Doing those exercises together can also be romantic. Be sure to check out Chapter 11 for details.)

✔ If you are going to a tropical isle, you may want to take some scuba diving lessons; you need to be licensed in order to rent the equipment once you're there.

✔ If you'll need to rent a car, do some research into what model you might like to get.

Doing any one of these things, or all of them, will put you in a vacation mood, and that will put some romance into your everyday life.

Defining the ideal getaway

This planning stage is the time to speak up about your likes and dislikes. If he's putting in a lot of time planning a vacation around fishing, for example, and she hates everything about fishing, then there's not going to be a lot of romance on this particular trip. And if going to museums and art galleries is her cup of tea but it bores him to tears, then that poses a problem. Some compromises are okay, but if this is supposed to be a romantic vacation, you both have to buy into the heart of the trip or the romantic quotient is going to be very, very low. If you can't find a vacation destination that makes both of you happy, then I have some serious questions about your relationship.

I've been using the word *vacation* freely but haven't defined it. Almost everyone would agree that taking two weeks and renting a cabin by a lake constitutes a vacation. But what if you take those same two weeks and spend them at your mother-in-law's house sharing a bedroom with your kids and helping her paint? Is that a vacation? From my perspective, it doesn't sound very romantic.

Some people don't know how to relax. I, for one, could never spend a week at some resort sitting on the beach. I don't want to totally unwind because I wouldn't feel confident that afterwards I could put the pieces back together into my same energetic self. But I love to travel and see new things. I adore skiing and come back feeling invigorated from that type of trip. If your partner prefers an active vacation and you prefer a relaxing one (or vice versa), pick a place that offers a bit of both. But if you spend all day long on your cell phone, even when you're on "vacation," then your partner is not going to feel fulfilled regardless of what type of trip you take.

Certainly you have to be realistic. If your partner is the head of a company, perhaps the only way that he or she can take time off is to spend half of the day electronically linked to the office. Half a vacation can be better than none, as long as both parties head out with the same set of expectations. If you know that your spouse will spend a lot of time working, and you don't mind as long as you can sit by the pool with a good book, then it can work out fine. But if your partner pretends that he or she won't constantly be on the phone to the office, and then does it anyway, you're going to feel resentment.

So the first step of your vacation planning is to agree on a vacation description. If you can come up with a definition that you both can live with, then you'll be halfway to paradise. If you butt heads over this, then it may be wiser to take the money that you were going to spend on a vacation and put it into some marital therapy sessions.

Finding Romance with Kids in Tow

> *The most important thing a father can do for his children is to love their mother.*

> — Theodore Hesburgh

The ultimate romantic vacation is the honeymoon, because you should still be enveloped by the bliss of the wedding. Even if you have children from a previous marriage, they're not expected to accompany you on this particular trip. But on subsequent trips when kids are on the scene, is it possible to have a romantic vacation with them in tow? Kids make it more difficult to keep romance in the air, but if you plan your vacation properly, it can certainly have a strong romantic quotient.

You have to realize that a vacation is romantic because it gives you time to be together — time that you don't have when you're at home burdened with busy schedules. Having leisurely conversations, walking arm in arm, and cuddling for more than a few seconds at a time will restore some of the intimacy that everyday life takes away. As your intimacy level builds, you'll feel more romantic towards each other. Part of that will include increased sexual desire, but the romantic glow is something that you'll be able to bask in all day long.

During a vacation with children, you're not going to be able to concentrate your full attention on each other. However, you will still spend large chunks of time together, so having a romantic vacation doesn't have to be a lost cause. And because rekindling your romance is very important to your relationship, it's also very important to your children, whether they know it or not. So don't let this aspect of your family vacations slide. Make it a priority to include as much romance as possible, even if the kids don't like it.

Maximizing your living space

My first piece of advice has to do with your living arrangements. If you cram two kids and the two of you into one motel room, then any hope of being romantic is going to be squeezed right out the door. I suggest that instead of a hotel or motel, you reserve a larger living space. For not much more money (and in some cases less money), you can rent an apartment or townhouse where the kids will have their own bedrooms and you can have some privacy. If your own home isn't filled with delicate antiques and is located in an area people like to visit, you might even try house swapping with another couple, either people you know or people you meet through a house-swapping service.

Making use of sitters

Shop around for a babysitter before you get to wherever you're heading. It's not just that there may be competition for the few sitters there, but you may find out that there aren't any available at all. If having one or two romantic dinners is important to you, you may want to switch to a different locale.

Another possibility is to bring along your babysitter. Maybe a teenager who already babysits your kids, or a niece or nephew, would like to visit a new place. He or she would probably be willing to accompany you in exchange for you paying all expenses. Then you could eat out almost every night and maybe even read that book by the pool without constantly having to put your head up to see whether your kids were still afloat.

Some couples take one or more grandparents on a trip for the same purpose. While that can work out in some cases, the success of the trip depends on the personality of the grandparent. If grandpa adores being with the kids, then he'll be happy to see the two of you walk away so that he can have the grandchildren all to himself. He may even agree to share a room with the children so you get one all to yourselves. But not every grandparent is so easy to get along with, so think carefully before offering the invitation.

If one set of grandparents lives quite a distance away from you, you could pick their part of the country to visit. Then you two could go off on a side trip for a couple of days and leave your kids with their grandparents (with everyone's permission, of course).

You could also share a vacation with another couple that has children. Then you can exchange babysitting chores so that each adult couple can get whole blocks of time to themselves. And if there are other kids along for the trip, all the young ones tend to have a better time; they focus on each other more than on you.

Keeping your kids (and yourselves) happy

With younger children, if you can avoid revealing everything you have planned for them, that might give you some leverage. Let's say there's an amusement park nearby that you intend to take them to. Don't tell them about it in advance. When you arrive at your destination and the kids are crying because they don't want to go to a museum that the two of you are interested in, you can offer the amusement park as a bribe. (Of course, if you're heading for Orlando, it's going to be a little hard to hide Disney World from them.) I'm not encouraging you to regularly bribe your children, but in some instances it's quite alright.

And, of course, do make sure that there are activities the kids will like on the itinerary. If you can wear them out during the day, they're more likely to fall asleep early, and then you can have some private moments together. (For this to work, try to prevent them from taking naps in the afternoon, which could encourage them to stay up later than you would like.)

Some of you may be attracted to the types of resorts that take your children off your hands for a fun day filled with various activities. If you stay at one of these places, make sure that you spend your time together wisely (by which I mean leave some time for a little "afternoon delight").

If your children are in their teens, then it's going to be more difficult to find any privacy; they're likely to stay up later than you can. On the other hand, teens tend to sleep late, so look towards the early morning hours as time you can set aside for just for the two of you. And if your kids are old enough to stay at home by themselves, then in exchange for taking them on longer vacations, reserve some weekends during the rest of the year when the two of you can go off by yourselves to be alone.

But even if you have your kids with you 24 hours a day, it's still possible to find some time for romance. Let's say you're going for a hike in the forest. Kids like to run ahead and explore. As long as they don't get too far out of sight and they stick to the path, encourage them to show a little independence. Then you can put your arms around each other, talk about anything you like, and follow behind them. If you're at the beach and your kids are trustworthy, tell them to build a sandcastle while you go for a walk along the beach. If you're at a campsite, you might make an arrangement with another family to watch your children for a while and then do them the same favor.

And it is even possible to be romantic with the kids around, though it becomes more difficult if you never do anything romantic in front of them at home. There's nothing wrong with curling up against each other on the beach blanket in front of the kids, but if they never see you hug or kiss normally, then they're more likely to react negatively and perhaps try to separate you. So part of your vacation planning may include setting the right climate for your trip; show outward affection for each other during the months leading up to the vacation. If your kids get used to seeing you give each other loving attention at home, they'll be less bothered to see you share some romance on vacation.

Short and Sweet Escapes

While the word *vacation* connotes a week or two of idleness, Webster wasn't a travel agent — don't let his definition hem you in. As far as I'm concerned, a few hours spent at a nearby motel can also be considered a vacation. In the first place, the setting offers you privacy, which can be quite a luxury if you have kids, in-laws, or anyone else sharing your living quarters. And while sex would certainly be part of such a mini-vacation, don't hesitate to use the time to discuss some important points that you don't want to raise in front of the home crowd.

Being intimate means a lot more than just having sex together; any form of communications that you can share will keep you closer. If you're living with in-laws, for example, you may need the personal space to fight about something in order to clear the air. I know it may sound strange to qualify a couple of hours spent out of the house arguing as a vacation, but if you both come back feeling better about each other, then that type of quickie can do more for your romance than two weeks on a deserted island. Okay, maybe not two weeks on a deserted island, but you know what I mean.

If two hours out of the house qualifies as a vacation, then you can really start to appreciate the benefits that can be derived from an entire weekend. If you leave Friday night and don't spend too much time travelling, then you'll be left with almost two full days of time together. In that amount of time, you can get some serious rekindling going.

How to ruin a perfectly good vacation

Don't count on sex to fill your entire vacation, even if it's only a weekend. Naturally, I expect you to spend some of this time making love. I am Dr. Ruth, after all. But as I've said a thousand times, your most important sex organ is your brain. If you spend the time in between making love staring at the TV in your room, your senses will get dulled and so will the romantic element. Eating isn't the best occupation to fill in the time between having sex either. You can't be a great lover if you're bloated. And drinking, if it knocks you for a loop, is even worse.

How to make every second count

What you need to do is get out and exercise your body and your mind. I like museums, but they're not everybody's favorite way of passing time. Some other possibilities:

- Visit some quaint town and just walk down Main Street looking at the shops.
- Put two bikes on top of your car and go for a spin wherever you wind up.
- Bring two sketch pads, go for a walk, and stop every once in a while to draw a tree or a pretty view.
- Go to a beach community; even if it's not warm out, you could still dig a hole to China or make a giant sandcastle.
- Have a picnic and read poetry to each other.
- If you like the theater, go to a town that has a local production company and take in a show.
- If there are some movies that you've been meaning to see, go out to the cinema or rent a couple and watch them from inside your room. (Notice that I said movies *you've been meaning to see,* not just anything that happens to catch your eye as you channel surf. And when the movies are over, shut the TV off and go for a walk.)

As far as sex is concerned, there's a whole section coming up on that. I won't go into detail here except to say that you should use this time to experiment a little. You don't have to go off the deep end, but if you're having sex more often than when you're not on vacation (which I certainly hope is the case), then it makes sense to add a little variety to the mix.

Long weekends

While one can accomplish a lot towards rekindling a romance during a two-day weekend, adding a day on both ends can make such a vacation a lot more rewarding, provided you don't decide to head off overseas. If you're spending those two extra days up in the air traveling in an airplane, then you won't have gained very much. Lunch in Paris sounds like a wonderful idea, but you may wind up more exhausted than when you left.

But a four-day weekend at some nearby resort gives you the opportunity to lose many of those everyday tensions. You can take time to sit in a hot tub or get a massage, which will leave you feeling relaxed and more susceptible to romantic inclinations.

If possible, I would recommend getting a suite of some sort rather than just a simple room. If you're going to spend four days someplace, you want to be able to sit on a couch in a room that's not filled with suitcases and other paraphernalia. You might even find one that offers the use of a fireplace.

Firing up your romance

I know it sounds cliché, but there are good reasons why a spot in front of a fireplace is an ideal location for romance. In the days before central heating, this was the warmest place in the house and maybe the only area where you'd be willing to remove your clothing in winter. Even if the ambient temperature is being moderated by some other heating system, there could still be a chill that would keep you under the covers. But if you've got the added warmth of a fireplace next to you, then you can take your clothes off without the risk of goose bumps. If you turn off all the other lights in the room, you can still see each other, but in the glow of a fire, your faults, whatever they may be, will seem less prominent. Watching a fire is always fascinating, but it's not so distracting that your partner will think you've forgotten about him or her (as can happen while watching a flickering TV set). So if it won't break the bank to get a room with a fireplace, I say go for it.

Making each moment linger

Hot baths and massages are exactly the types of activities that you should engage in on a long weekend. Just as you've stretched out the weekend, you want to stretch out each of your activities together. If you give each other massages, make sure that you give plenty of attention to each part of your partner's body. If you kiss, do it slowly and linger over every sensation. You can brush each other's hair. Scratch each other's backs. And especially make sure that you make your sexual unions as extended as possible. Whatever time you normally spend on foreplay, stretch it out. When you're starting to feel very aroused, slow down and allow yourself to come back down for a while. And after you've had your orgasms, do the same with afterplay as you did with foreplay; keep it going. You probably don't have the luxury of that kind of extra time under normal circumstances, so make the best use of it when you do.

But because you can't make love every minute of the day and night, make sure that you have prepared other things to do. Just as with a shorter weekend, you need to change your frame of reference and keep that brain of yours occupied. Here are some other activities that you could engage in, assuming the weather isn't conducive to outdoor activities:

- Do a Sunday crossword together.
- Put together a complicated jigsaw puzzle.
- Fill in a paint-by-number picture.
- Give each other a manicure and pedicure.
- Write a poem together.
- Sketch each other in the nude.

Mixing Business and Pleasure

Some vacations are tied to business meetings. If one of you has a convention to go to, for example, the other may tag along; at the end of each day you get to be together, and perhaps at the end of the business part of the trip, you can take a few extra days all to yourselves.

Be very explicit when planning such a vacation. If you will be working part of the time, be very clear about how much time will be devoted to business. I would even advise you to exaggerate how busy you'll be, so that if more time gets freed up, it seems like a bonus. The last thing you want is your vacationing spouse tugging at your sleeve like a child looking for attention. Not only could this spoil any hopes of having a romantic getaway, but it may even imperil your job.

Sometimes your coworkers' spouses may be along as well. If your spouse is already friendly with some of them, then they can spend time together while you're busy. But while it may seem appealing to sit by the pool alone all day reading a book, it can quickly get boring. So work out ahead of time what activities your spouse can engage in that won't leave him or her feeling like joining you on this trip was a big mistake.

Cruising in the Lap of Luxury

While some people cruise around the world for months at a time, most people take cruises that last about a week. Cruises are marketed as being romantic, and they most certainly can be, but if you're on a limited budget and get squeezed into a tiny cabin, all I can say is that it's a good thing that you're already intimate.

Most cruise ships have about as many staff members as passengers, so you do get pampered. And while you're on board, because there aren't too many places to escape to, you will spend a lot of time together. Most cruise ships stop at a different port of call every day, giving you new places to explore without the hassle of packing and unpacking. But probably the most romantic aspect about a cruise is that it's supposed to be romantic. Couples don't go on cruises to play sailor and see the world, or to play golf or go scuba diving, though these activities (and many more) are available. The basic aim is to spend as much time together as possible in a relaxed and comfy atmosphere renewing your relationship. For this purpose, cruises are ideal.

Millions of people take cruises and can't wait until they can go on the next one. But some people feel claustrophobic when locked on a boat, and you may not know which group you and your partner fall into until you've experienced this form of travel. Therefore, you may want to experiment with a short cruise first; many cruise lines offer cruises to nowhere that last only one or two days. If you enjoy a short cruise, then you'll be ready for a more extended one.

For much more information on cruises, including specific destinations, check out *Cruise Vacations For Dummies 2001* (IDG Books Worldwide, Inc.).

Camping: Roughing It Romantically

At the other end of the pampering spectrum is camping. Some "campers" travel in luxurious RVs, but these people tend to be retired couples who spend endless weeks travelling around the country. Now don't get me wrong: This can be a very romantic way to spend your time, and I'm all for it. But this is a pretty luxurious interpretation of camping.

For most people, camping implies an element of roughing it. Because I'm not a camper myself, I'm not here to tell you how to set up a tent or hook an RV up to the electric and water lines. For those instructions, I suggest you read *Camping For Dummies* (IDG Books Worldwide, Inc.). I'm only concerned about the romantic aspects of camping, which certainly exist.

To the extent that your camping experience pits the two of you against the elements, it will bring you closer together, and that's definitely romantic. On the other hand, if you're staying in a campground, you may lack privacy, which will dull the romantic element. If you have children who are sleeping in the same tent or RV as you, then cupid is going to have a hard time finding a place to settle in.

If you're experienced family campers, then perhaps you've discovered your own ways of making the experience romantic. But if you look back at your camping vacations and find that the two of you generated little or no romance, then you have to discuss the reasons why. I understand that for some families, camping is the only affordable way of getting away from home. And if you are both satisfied with the level of romance in your relationship, then it doesn't matter if much of your vacation isn't highly romantic.

But because you're reading this book, I assume that you are looking for more romance. And the one or two precious weeks of vacation allotted to you are the perfect opportunity to rekindle that romance. If you've found that camping distracts you from romance, then think seriously about doing something else with your time. Or plan carefully so that the two of you can find some private moments.

Camping without clothing

Man is the only animal that blushes — or needs to.

— Mark Twain

While most people don't associate nudist camps with camping, these places certainly bring you back to nature. The purpose of visiting a nudist camp is not to become sexually aroused, but nudists do benefit from a feeling of freedom that could certainly be a romantic enhancement. The idea of having nothing to hide should bring the two of you closer, though I wouldn't say that visiting one of these camps is a must for couples looking to rekindle their romance. Nudist camps are just a possible way to experience something different that will take you out of your shell.

For those hardy couples who go off into the woods where they won't see anyone for days, camping is certainly an ideal romantic getaway. You get total privacy, few distractions, and lots of togetherness. As long as you bring plenty of mosquito repellent and keep clear of the poison ivy, you should be fine. There's always the risk of hitting a stretch of bad weather, but it's a good excuse for some extended time together in the tent.

Finding Relaxation and Romance at the Beach

I'm not a beach person, but there's no doubt that a week or two at the beach can be romantic. The beach offers total relaxation. You can sit there all day soaking up the sun, listening to the waves, and letting go of all your tension. Throw in a rum drink, and you're going to be as mellow as you can possibly be. If your normal life is a hectic one and the pace has been keeping the two of you from spending a lot of quality time together, then a week or two at a beach can be an ideal way to link up your psyches. Not to mention that you're lying around half dressed, languidly applying suntan lotion to each other — all that heat can definitely put a charge into your sexual batteries. It's no wonder that so many honeymooners head for a tropical isle.

The most important advice I can give you is to watch out for sunburn. If either or both of you are lobster red, then all you'll be thinking about is how to put out the fire; rekindling will be the last thing on your minds. Also be careful not to imbibe too much alcohol. Remember that your brain is your most important sexual organ, and you can't do much rekindling if your brain is constantly befuddled.

What should you do while at the beach? First, because you'll have so much bare skin showing, touch each other a lot. A caress can express your feelings in ways words can't, so stay in close contact as much as possible. But a beach is also a great place to talk. The sounds of the crashing surf make a great "white noise," so if you park your beach chairs close to the shoreline, you'll be able to speak to each other without people on nearby blankets being able to make out what you are saying. Even if you have kids who are digging a few feet away, you'll have privacy as long as you don't raise your voice. So while a beach is a great place to read a book, don't forget to use some of those moments to let each other know how you feel.

Though I'm not a beach person, I did some research so I could recommend a few beaches. For lots more suggestions, you may want to check out *Caribbean For Dummies,* 1st Edition (IDG Books Worldwide, Inc.).

- **The Hamptons (New York):** While you probably won't spot any celebrities tanning themselves on a Hampton beach that's easily visible to the public eye, you can drive around, or better yet rent a boat, and see some of the fabulous homes that the rich and famous occupy. You'll also find a wide variety of exotic foods and wonderful shopping, which you might expect given how wealthy this area is. On the other hand, finding an affordable place to stay is going to be tough. If your budget doesn't fit actually staying in the Hamptons, you can probably find a motel not too far away that will be affordable and yet not force you to drive too far to get to the beach.

- **Young Island (Caribbean):** There are scads of great resorts in the Caribbean, and the only reason I've chosen this one to highlight is that's where my co-author, Pierre Lehu, went on his honeymoon. Young Island is a small island resort not far from St. Vincent island in the British West Indies. Guests are housed in cabins scattered all over the island, many of which are private enough that they have outside showers. It's a private paradise. And if you can't find romance in a private paradise, well . . . .

- **Venice Beach (California):** While the beach itself is no different than most, a few yards from the shore is a scene that lets you know you're not in Kansas anymore. In-line skaters, jugglers, and bodybuilders form part of a crazy cast that could only be assembled in Los Angeles. So go early, soak up some sun, and then spend the afternoon gazing and mingling.

Taking an Active Role in Your Vacation

My preferred vacation spot is one that allows you to get out and move around. That could include partaking in your favorite sport (which in my case means skiing) or visiting assorted sites. If you can get your blood moving during the day, then I guarantee you that when you're back in your room at night, you'll both have the spirit and energy for romance. Plus, if you've been staring at each other all day in skimpy bathing attire, think about how exciting it's going to be when you take your clothes off later. On the flip side, if you're dressed all day in cold weather attire, you'll get a great surprise when you remember how great your partner looks in the buff.

Following are just a handful of recommendations for active vacations. Be sure to flip to Chapter 22 for more. You and your partner can do your own research if these possibilities don't appeal to you (or your wallets).

Hitting the slopes

My favorite ski resort is the Lodge at Vail (Colorado). Everything about the place is so convenient. Since they opened Eagle Airport, which is a snow board's throw away from the city of Vail, it has become extremely convenient to get there. And from the Lodge, you can walk to the nearest chairlift. They have great instructors, and when you ski with an instructor, you never have to wait on a lift line. My favorite slopes are the China Bowl slopes; they are so wide that you never have to worry about someone skiing into you (a major source of accidents). Vail also offers many other things to do when you're not skiing, like square dancing and cultural activities, so the evenings are never boring. I've been treated so well in Vail that I really feel that I advanced to a higher level of skiing. And because I'm known for saying that skiers make better lovers, better skiers make even better lovers.

What makes a skier such a good lover? Skiers are active people who enjoy the thrill of flying down a mountainside. They see a few flakes coming out of the sky and they get an adrenaline rush. With that type of personality, they usually don't just lie back in bed; they are active thrill-seekers under the covers as well.

Recharging in Rio de Janeiro

Rio is not a city where people have many inhibitions to begin with. To prove that to yourself, you only have to visit one of their famous beaches, like Ipanema. But at Carnival time, whatever inhibitions they do have are completely discarded. If the atmosphere during Carnival doesn't recharge your sexual batteries to full, then I don't know what will.

Carnival, otherwise known as Mardi Gras (Fat Tuesday), takes place right before Ash Wednesday and the start of Lent. Because Lenten observers are supposed to endure 40 days of fasting and praying, Mardi Gras gives them a last bout of merry making, which in Rio means taking part in the giant parade of floats and dancing and general mayhem that turns the entire city into one big party.

Getting to your destination

I posed for a photo that appeared in *USA Today* aboard a Singapore Airlines jet in one of their SkySuites — special seats that fold down to make a bed. Because I'm only 4'7", I usually manage to fall asleep in normal airplane seats. But I certainly recommend that you arrive as rested as possible if you are taking a long flight, so an amenity like a SkySuite may be well worth it. On the other hand, I don't recommend that you use this little bed to join the so-called Mile High Club. I believe that sex should remain private, and I also think that the risk of getting caught isn't going to make this type of sex better; it will act as a distraction. Sex should never just be a notch on your bed board. You should put in the extra effort necessary to keep your sex life from getting bogged down in a boring routine, but that doesn't mean that you need to go to the other extreme either.

Stepping out in New York City

Because I live in New York, I suppose I'm a bit prejudiced, but New York offers so many forms of stimulation that you're bound to feel some of it yourself. New York is one place where I would advise you to be well prepared for your visit. For example, if you want to go to the theater, you should book your tickets in advance so that you're not disappointed. And many of the top restaurants also book up way in advance. But even if you plan on coming on a shoestring, there's so much to see and do that you won't be disappointed even if all you do is walk up and down the streets. And if you see me, don't forget to wave.

Packing Tips for the Romantically Inclined

I'm not going to remind you to pack your toothbrush and toothpaste, because while it's true that a fresh mouth is a good thing to bring to bed with you, I trust that you have the basics of packing down. I would like to make a few suggestions of nonessential items that you might find useful, or at least fun:

✔ **A lubricant.** I don't want to put any pressure on you to have lots of sex on vacation, but I think it's a possibility that you've been considering on your own. After women have been having intercourse for a while, they sometimes run out of natural lubricants before they run out of desire; that can mean that a woman's vagina gets irritated. Not only might that put a crimp in your style during that particular sexual episode, but it might make you put off the next one for longer than you'd like. Plenty of lubricants are available on the market, and the only thing you have to remember is that any lubricants made out of petroleum (such as Vaseline) can eat a hole in latex; if you're using condoms, those are not for you. (If you're using condoms, make sure that you have some lubricated ones along.)

✔ **A deck of cards.** Card games can be a better way to while away some time than reading because you're both involved. And if you add a little betting on the side, particularly of articles of clothing, a card game can be a whole lot more interactive than a book.

✔ **Candles.** Some couples have a running struggle about whether to leave the lights on or off. Candles make a good compromise, offering some light but not so much that every flaw is plainly visible. Just be careful to keep the flames safely contained and to blow them out before you fall asleep.

✔ **Body paints.** These are washable colors that you can use to decorate yourselves with, possibly while taking a bath. They're a good way to have some added fun.

✔ **Sexy underwear.** Buy some for each other and model it while you're away. Just knowing what your partner is wearing under his or her clothes will give an added tweak to any sightseeing you may do during the day.

Making Love and Memories

I said in the beginning of this chapter that you should think of the time spent planning your vacation as being part of the actual vacation. Certainly anticipation is a great turn on. But you should try to stretch the value of each vacation out at the other end as well by making some memories that you can enjoy for the rest of your lives.

I am very wary of two people sharing their personal fantasies, especially their sexual ones. But on the other hand, you may allow yourselves to experiment a bit during a vacation, with the knowledge that you can always say that it was a one-time-only event. My advice, as regards any experimentation, is that it be kept within the bounds of your relationship. If you've never invited a third party to share your bed (a practice that I am entirely against), then don't bring up the subject during a romantic vacation because it might spoil the entire stay. Likewise, if one partner has a secret fetish, it should remain a secret. What might be in bounds? Following are some suggestions:

✔ **Role playing.** If you each have a favorite movie star, you could pretend to be that person. Maybe wear the clothing that he or she wore in a movie, or put on a wig of that person's hair color. You might even memorize some dialogue from a film. Or you can just pretend that you are certain characters — she may play a maid who ends up sleeping with her master, or he may play a butler who has a torrid affair with his mistress. Or you could pretend that you are two castaways on a desert island. Or Tarzan and Jane lost in the jungle. Or Napoleon and Josephine. Or Marc Antony and Cleopatra. I think you get the idea. If you plan this out ahead of time, you may be able to bring along some sort of costumes that make the fantasy more authentic.

✔ **Sex toys.** Again, if one of you has secret sadomasochistic tendencies, I wouldn't bring them out in the open during a vacation, especially one where you're rekindling your romance. But you may want to bring some sex toys with you: some short strands of rope, a feather, two masks, or a vibrator, for example. And if one partner decides that he or she is uncomfortable with their use, then the other must accept that decision.

✔ **Changing scenery.** For years I've been telling people that they shouldn't just make love in the bedroom; they should try it on the dining room table and the kitchen floor. That advice certainly applies on vacation, but be careful not to do it someplace where you might get arrested.

✔ **Different strokes.** Obviously, you don't need to be on vacation to try different sexual positions. But if time is short while you're balancing work and play, you'll be less likely to experiment. On vacation, you have a lot more time on your hands. If one position doesn't work for the two of you, don't worry about it; there are plenty of others to choose from. You could bring a copy of the *Kama Sutra* or the *Joy of Sex* if you want some ideas. Just be careful not to sprain anything or throw out your back, because that could ruin the rest of the vacation, both sexually and in every other way.

Part III
Heating Up Your Sex Life

The 5th Wave   By Rich Tennant

"JUST TO SPICE THINGS UP, I THOUGHT I'D WEAR THE FRENCH TICKLER INSIDE OUT THIS TIME TO ADD TO MY EXCITEMENT."

In this part . . .

For many couples, a romantic cooldown goes hand in hand with boredom in the bedroom. Maybe you've been together for years and assume that your sex life will remain the way it's always been. This part can help you change that outlook by recognizing the positive effects of keeping your love life sizzling.

The first step toward creating this kind of heat is recognizing the need to explore your partner's body and discover ways to create excitement that you never knew before. Chapter 9 walks you through some activities the two of you can do to accomplish just that. Chapter 10 stresses the importance of improving the way you envision yourself and your partner, both inside and out. In Chapter 11, I suggest stretching and strengthening exercises you can do together to improve your physical stamina as well as your sense of intimacy. And Chapter 12 helps you understand the changes to expect as your bodies get older, so you can find ways to enjoy each other sexually well into those golden years.

Chapter 9

Rethinking Your Approach to Sex

*O*n one hand, sex is a very selfish activity. Your main goal is to satisfy your sexual needs, and the sensations brought on by your orgasm can be felt only by you. But because you know how great an orgasm feels, you want your lover to share in these sensations as well. Therefore, sex is also an unselfish activity because the other part of sex involves the giving of pleasure.

How the giving and receiving of pleasures link is key to your sexual relationship. Any improvements you make in the area of giving and receiving sexual pleasures may contribute significantly to rekindling that romance of yours.

In this chapter, I show you truly pleasurable exercises that the two of you may do to create a greater sense of intimacy in the bedroom. I also discuss common sexual problems that couples face and offer solutions for you to overcome these problems together.

Rediscovering Each Other

When you are with the same partner for a long time, you naturally slip into patterns, especially in the bedroom. To spark your romantic feelings for each other, you must break those patterns from time to time. This section describes two terrific exercises for doing just that and offers suggestions for other ways to give and receive the types of intimate attentions you deserve.

Giving and receiving sexual pleasures

When you make love with your partner, you're of two minds. Part of you wants to give pleasure, and part of you wants to receive those special sensations that lead to arousal and orgasm. When doing two things at the same time, most of us find giving our attention to both difficult. As you become more and more aroused, your desire for the release that comes from having an orgasm grows stronger and stronger. You're going to experience difficulty concentrating on your partner's needs.

Of course a *synergistic effect* takes place during sex, which simply means that seeing your partner become aroused makes you aroused. This effect is why most people find that terrific sex occurs only when two people are involved instead of just one.

Nevertheless, there's something to be said for experiencing sex with your partner when one of you is the focus of all the activity. When you are the receiver, you can fully concentrate on all the sensations provoked by your partner. And as the giver, you can fully concentrate on creating the most intense pleasure possible for your partner.

The person doing all the touching and caressing may feel aroused as well, but he or she may not experience an orgasm. Keep in mind that no one ever dies from not having an orgasm. If you climb the walls in frustration an hour after the experience, your partner may help you out. But the rule of this game is that only one person is going to achieve sexual satisfaction from the exercise.

You may create this type of sexual experience in two distinct ways. One way is for you to give the pleasure by taking complete control, while your partner lays back and concentrates on the sensations you are provoking. The other way is for your partner to direct you, telling you exactly where to touch and how. In both cases, the idea is to make the session last as long as possible. If you concentrate some attention on your partner's genital area, be sure to also pay attention to some other body parts. When you shift your attention to different areas, you delay your partner's orgasmic response due to the continued rise and fall of arousals. When your partner does experience an orgasm, it should feel very strong.

These exercises offer different advantages depending on who is in control. If you are on the receiving end of the pleasure and your partner is calling the shots, you may just float along without engaging your mind; you may really lose yourself in the various sensations. (A woman who sometimes has difficulties attaining an orgasm because her mind wanders may particularly benefit from this variation of the exercise.) On the other hand, if you are giving your partner directions, you may need to concentrate to communicate to your partner what pleases you the most. Your requests educate your partner about what makes you happiest. He or she undoubtedly will take mental notes of your requests and then use some of those same pointers when you make love in the future.

Mapping your bodies

In the exercise I just described, sexual pleasure was definitely part of the equation, even if it was only for one half of the couple. Sexual release isn't always the goal of a romantic session between the two of you. Yes, sexual release may be a part of the romantic equation, but the intimacy you share during lovemaking also brings tremendous pleasure.

To create a greater sense of intimacy, you should sometimes explore each other's bodies without giving any thought to arousal. One or both of you may become aroused, but the goal of this exercise is to discover all you can about your partner's body — not to turn your partner on.

During these explorations, you should touch your partner the way he or she wants — not necessarily the way that creates the greatest amount of arousal. Of course, your partner may let you know when he or she derives some extra pleasure out of a certain touch, but don't let that information distract you from your purpose.

If you allow your partner to explore every inch of your body and you do the same to your partner, the two of you have nothing to physically hide from each other. This exercise may help you feel less inhibited about telling your partner which parts of your body give you the most pleasure. When that information is integrated into your lovemaking, you should definitely notice an improvement.

Can sex for one be romantic?

Is it okay for you to pleasure your partner without having an orgasm yourself? Is the experience romantic for both of you? The answer to these questions is yes! The outcome of your sexual experience depends on your attitudes. Consider another situation for a moment: Say that your partner works on some project in the hot sun, comes inside after completing the task, and collapses on a chair in the kitchen. Would you gain satisfaction from pouring a tall glass of ice cold lemonade to quench your partner's thirst? Of course. So is the feeling any different when you give your partner the sexual release he or she needs? Granted, your contribution becomes a little more complicated than pouring a glass of lemonade, but bringing your partner to orgasm is most definitely an expression of your love.

While body mapping may be a one-time exercise, I recommend that you body map on a regular basis. I'm not saying you should perform this exercise once a week or even once a month (though it certainly wouldn't hurt your relationship), but the intimacy created by this exercise may wear off over time. If you body map, say, twice a year, you rediscover your partner's body and counter whatever shyness may creep back into your relationship.

Extending your pleasure

With both the exercises I describe here, you should take your time and make your partner's pleasure last. Why do I want you to prolong these sessions? Because by doing so, you may learn to prolong your normal lovemaking. Of course, the time may come when you're both in the mood for a quickie (and there's nothing wrong with that), but if you can spare the time, why not extend your lovemaking time? After completing these two exercises, you know exactly how to give your partner the most pleasure for the longest period of time.

Work on extending your lovemaking time in other ways. You may actually start teasing each other, both verbally and physically, hours before you start to go at it. This playful teasing is especially important to women, who may take much longer than men to become aroused. The more of these early arousal signals you give each other, the better your lovemaking when the time comes.

Making time for afterplay

Whether or not you stretch out your foreplay into an experience like the ones I describe above, you must definitely make time for afterplay. Just as women take longer to become aroused, they also take longer to come down from their fully aroused state. Many men are able to fall asleep or watch the second half of the ball game immediately after orgasm, but a woman needs a longer period of time to get back to her "normal" state. While she descends back to earth, she needs to be held, caressed, stroked, and whispered sweet words of love.

Afterplay doesn't have to go on for hours, but a few minutes of afterplay does wonders for your relationship. In fact, afterplay can act as part of foreplay for your next lovemaking session — be it later that day, the next day, or even the next week. Her lovemaking experience is colored by how it went right up until the very end; the better her experience, the more eager she is to start the next lovemaking session.

I know some men say they feel a very strong urge to fall asleep right after they experience an orgasm. While I know that sex helps to relieve the day's tensions and creates a relaxed atmosphere, sex is not a sleeping pill. You're allowed to feel drowsy, but not so drowsy that you don't cuddle your partner. Remember, attention to afterplay helps your overall love life, so it's well worth staying up for another five minutes.

Resolving Common Sexual Problems

I want to offer a few words of advice about common problems that couples face in the bedroom. The discussion of sex can get pretty complex — in fact, I wrote an entire book on the subject: *Sex For Dummies,* 2nd Edition (IDG Books Worldwide, Inc.). I can't cover every detail from that book here, but I want to share some of my well-researched pointers. (For more detailed discussions of sexual issues, pick up a copy of *Sex For Dummies,* 2nd Edition — it's a good read, if I do say so myself!)

A man's challenges

Men typically face problems of two extremes in the bedroom: Either they reach orgasm too quickly, or they fail to become aroused.

Climaxing too quickly

The main sexual problem that impacts males is *premature ejaculation,* which occurs when a man ejaculates earlier than he wants to. Premature ejaculation is, to put it simply, a learning difficulty. With practice, any man may recognize *premonitory sensations* — the feelings that come just before he has an orgasm. If he calms himself down when those feelings arise, he may resume intercourse without ejaculating.

 A man should practice combating premature ejaculation with his partner. I don't want to make this problem seem simple; sometimes premature ejaculation can be complicated. If a man can't figure out how to calm himself down on his own, he should definitely read more information about premature ejaculation. If he still can't solve his problem, he should consult a sex therapist.

Failing to perform

Even the most macho male may experience performance problems. Most of the time these failures are one-time-only events. Maybe he had a really bad day at work and can't focus on sex. Maybe he drank a little too much or ate too much and his digestive system kicks up, interrupting his concentration.

Whatever the cause, no permanent damage is done unless he becomes too concerned about the problem. If, the next time he has sex, he is actively worried that he's going to have a problem either obtaining or maintaining an erection, those worries may actually cause the feared result. His fears may become a self-fulfilling prophecy, and this cycle may be difficult to break.

The best way to avoid getting caught in this cycle is for you to be up front about the cause the first time you experience the problem. If you drank too many beers, for example, admit this openly. Then, the next time you partake in sex, make certain that you're stone cold sober — and the problem resolves itself. If you develop performance problems that are psychological and not physical, you and your partner should consult a sex therapist.

A woman's woes

> *One cardinal rule of marriage should never be forgotten: "Give little, give seldom, and above all, give grudgingly." Otherwise, what could have been a proper marriage could become an orgy of sexual lust.*
>
> — Ruth Smythers, *The Young Bride's Handbook,* 1894

Women rarely have problems with the mechanics of having sex, because they don't really need to do very much to participate. However, women may develop difficulties enjoying sex, especially enjoying orgasms.

Despite all that has been learned about women's orgasms and written about them, many women still cannot have an orgasm. In the Victorian era, a woman's orgasm was something to be frowned upon, and still today, in some African societies, clitoridectomies are performed on young women so that they can never enjoy sex. Eventually, western society came to appreciate that women should enjoy sex, and then women who couldn't reach a climax were labeled *frigid.* Now we know better and call them *pre-orgasmic,* because the vast majority can learn to become orgasmic. (Only those who have some sort of medical problem, like severe diabetes, cannot make the leap.)

Another issue that has recently been brought to light has to do with what we call "receptivity." Many women don't think about or fantasize about sex as much as men do. But once they've begun a sexual encounter, they may be quite receptive to it. These women may think they have a problem because sex doesn't cross their minds every few minutes. Many women shy away from sex as a result, not realizing that they could enjoy it if they gave themselves half a chance. Other women are motivated to engage in sexual stimulation in order to have the non-sexual stimuli they seek, like hugging and kissing. Then, once they've started, they do become aroused and want to continue.

Faking it

Faking an orgasm once in a while is not wrong. If faking orgasms becomes routine, the woman has a problem. Admitting to the faked orgasms becomes a difficult task for her because she has put off telling her partner for some time; she fears hurting her partner with her confession. A woman needs to nip this problem in the bud.

If you are having trouble coming to a climax, let your partner know as early as possible. Together, the two of you can explore why this problem occurs and what, if anything, you can do to alleviate it. If you can't resolve the situation on your own, visit a sex therapist for consultation.

Pleasuring yourself

The basic solution for this problem is to teach yourself how to have an orgasm. No matter how hard a man may try to help, his presence is distracting. After you learn how to give yourself an orgasm, you can give your partner a lesson.

If you can't give yourself an orgasm using your fingers, I recommend that you use a vibrator. The sensations caused by a vibrator may be much stronger than those you create yourself; you need the vibrations to be strong enough to cause you to climax. Your next step is to figure out how to achieve orgasm without a vibrator, and the final step is to teach your partner how to bring you to climax. If using a vibrator is the only method that works for you, you and your partner may learn to integrate its use into your love life. Using a vibrator is certainly preferable to not deriving any sexual satisfaction at all.

Heating Up Your Sex Life

Even if you and your partner enjoy a satisfactory sex life, that doesn't mean you can't improve upon what you're doing, especially in ways that heighten your sense of romance.

Boredom is one of the main foes of romance and, as you may expect, boredom in the bedroom may dissolve your romantic relationship. If the two of you partake in sex the same way — day after day, year after year — you simply aren't experiencing all of the potential pleasures sex can bring to your relationship. Variety truly is the spice of life, and you need to make every effort to spice up your lives between the sheets.

But I must add a cautionary note before I continue: While you may suggest a new position or the use of a sex toy, you should never pressure your partner into trying a particular sex act. If your partner refuses to try any variations that you suggest, perhaps the two of you need to consult a sex therapist. A professional sex therapist may help you determine why your partner is so hesitant to try a particular sex act. But remember, you and your partner are entitled to your likes and dislikes; if certain positions or acts do not appeal to your partner, don't push the issue.

I also want to put one of my pet peeves on the table, which has to do with the word *normal*. People always write to me asking if this or that position or sex act is *normal*. In my opinion, *normal* is a word that you should erase from your sexual dictionary. While most human behavior falls along a bell curve, that bell curve has little or no bearing on your own behavior. For example, the majority of people are not homosexuals, yet homosexuals don't have power over their sexual orientation. A homosexual can't become heterosexual just because most people are heterosexual, any more than someone who is 4'7" (like me) can grow in height just because most people are taller than 5'.

My point is this: If you and your partner want to have sex while hanging from the chandelier (not something that most people would find *normal*), don't worry about what your neighbors may think. Just make sure the blinds are closed and that you place a thick mattress underneath.

Making the most of your mouth

Oral sex has been in the media spotlight for some time now, and you and your partner may consider this variation. If you adopt oral sex into your sexual repertoire, you join a growing number of couples that find this act an acceptable way of exchanging pleasures.

If, however, one of you likes to engage in oral sex and the other resists, I do have a few words of advice to offer.

Let me start by saying that you may enjoy a perfectly good sex life and never engage in oral sex. The main point of sex is to have an orgasm, and if you and your partner find fulfillment, exactly how the orgasms occur is not important. But many people are attracted to oral sex. If you or your partner are hesitant to try oral sex but not adamantly against it, I can offer some tips:

- ✔ **Keep it clean.** I'm not accusing anyone of being dirty, but some people are turned off by oral sex because of a fear that the genital area is contaminated in some way. My suggestion is to share in the cleansing process as part of your foreplay. You may take a bath or shower together, making certain to thoroughly clean your partner's genital area, or you may simply clean each other using washcloths.

- ✔ **Practice.** If you are a woman, you may be concerned that you don't know how to perform oral sex. If that is your concern, I suggest that you pretend his penis is an ice cream cone. You may even practice on a real ice cream cone if you like, imagining that you are licking a penis and not a scoop of Cherry Garcia. As far as performing the *deep throat* technique —

> which involves deep penetration of his penis into your mouth — that act is something that you may either do at some later time (if you choose) or not at all. Don't worry about doing the perfect imitation of a porn queen if you are just beginning to explore oral sex.
>
> ✔ **Do what feels comfortable.** The other issue that concerns many women is whether or not to swallow the ejaculate. If this act doesn't appeal to you, don't do it. If at some later point you overcome your resistance to this part of oral sex, go ahead and swallow.

One cautionary note: Oral sex is not safe sex. Obviously, you cannot get pregnant from oral sex, but sexually transmitted diseases (STDs) can be passed back and forth. Saliva does act as a sort of defense mechanism, but saliva is not a foolproof defense. If there is any risk that your partner is infected with an STD, you should avoid performing oral sex. If you need more information about STDs and safe sex practices, pick up a copy of *Sex For Dummies,* 2nd Edition.

Finding the right position

In *Sex For Dummies,* 2nd Edition, I offer detailed descriptions and illustrations of a variety of sexual positions. Here, I touch on some of the most popular positions and mention their pros and cons.

Mastering the missionary

The male superior, or *missionary,* position is one of the most popular sexual positions. But you should be aware that the missionary position does have drawbacks. Because the man must hold himself up while in this position, he cannot use his hands for anything else. That means he cannot stimulate his partner's clitoris and, therefore, many women cannot have an orgasm in this position.

Putting her on top

If the woman is on top during intercourse, the man may stimulate her clitoris. The same is true if both partners are lying side-by-side. In fact, most other positions (besides the missionary position) allow for this type of stimulus. Don't get me wrong: When the woman has her orgasm — either before or after intercourse — does not matter. But if she likes to have an orgasm during intercourse and doesn't get enough stimulation from his penis, the only way she can experience her orgasm is if he stimulates her clitoris manually.

Backing your way in

Anal sex, like oral sex, eliminates the risk of pregnancy. But as the AIDS epidemic has proven, anal sex is most definitely not a form of safe sex, especially when performed without a condom. With that said, some people do enjoy anal sex. Whether or not you and your partner want to engage in this type of sex is up to both of you.

Having intercourse "doggle style" — the man enters the woman's vagina from the rear — simulates anal sex and may be a good alternative. If the man reaches around and stimulates his partner's clitoris with his fingers at the same time, both partners derive pleasure from this position.

Seeking the sexual holy grail

We've all seen movies and television shows that show both partners having orgasms at the exact same time. Simultaneous orgasms are an ideal that many couples try to attain and, admittedly, they're worth a shot. But don't ruin your enjoyment of sex by slavishly imitating the fictional people you see on screen. If the two of you are caught up in this search for the sexual holy grail every time you have sex and don't experience simultaneous orgasms, you're going to be disappointed.

Whispering (and screaming) words of love

To speak, or not to speak, that is the question. And you know what? I don't have the answer. I can't say that one way is better than the other. Although whispering sweet nothings (or shouting passionate somethings) may add to one person's pleasure, these vocalizations may be a distraction to another. I receive letters from people who stand on both sides of this issue: Some people complain about how verbal their partners are, and others desperately wish that their partners would emit some sounds to communicate that they are enjoying sex.

You may discover other issues involved with this subject. For example, volume may be a problem; if you worry that the neighbors may hear your partner screaming, you don't fully enjoy the sexual experience. And although you may enjoy a little verbal interplay, exactly what is said may be an issue. Should you use four-letter words? Some people find profanity a real turn on, while others cringe. How can you be passionate about what you are saying if you edit yourself at the same time? How can your partner enjoy the moment when he or she is turned off by your words?

The two of you need to discuss this issue outside of the bedroom. Talk about your likes and dislikes and decide on some vocabulary ground rules. Once again, don't assume that the dialogue in your bedroom has to sound like the dialogue you hear in the movies. Decide on what's acceptable based on your own likes and dislikes.

Speaking up about your needs

When the discussion of sexual needs comes up, my advice is for you to communicate your desires to your partner outside the bedroom. In fact, discuss any sexual problems you are concerned about *before* you engage in sex.

The best place for this type of discussion is somewhere without distractions. Take a walk along the beach or a drive down a country lane, and make sure that your cell phones and beepers are turned off. Because your discussion regards very private matters, make sure you're out of the listening range of nosey neighbors; you should feel free to say what is on your mind without the fear of prying ears hearing your conversation.

 I want to remind you that just because this discussion takes place in private doesn't mean that you should say the first words that pop into your head. Don't allow your emotions to get out of control. Weigh very carefully what you say and how you say it, because sometimes the content of these discussions comes back to haunt you. Sex is a sensitive issue; you and your partner may feel vulnerable and emotional during discussions about sex. To ensure that you don't have any regrets later, take a step-by-step plan of negotiations. The goal is to share your thoughts, not to get angry at each other. For example, if you feel neglected by your partner, try to explain this concern calmly without going on the attack. If you ask questions and wait for answers, you learn a lot more than if you make accusations and jump to conclusions.

Another topic you may discuss *outside* the bedroom is how to communicate your likes and dislikes *inside* the bedroom. For instance, you may agree to use hand signals to let your partner know where you want to be touched during lovemaking. Using hand signals means you don't have to announce your desire while you are engaged in an already emotionally charged moment. A woman may guide a man's hand to indicate where she wants to be touched and how strongly. He may not feel that his lovemaking abilities are being called to the test using this method, and she isn't distracted by having to verbalize her feelings.

Communication is essential to ensure healthy, fulfilling sex lives. Never expect your partner to read your mind when it comes to sexual matters. You and your partner need to discuss any concerns, problems, or fears before you jump into bed. And your discussions may lead you into new sexual experiences and refresh your sexual outlooks.

Getting Off the Fence

Q. I know my husband would like me to perform oral sex on him. I want to give him oral pleasure, but I can't seem to get up the courage. He has given up asking me, but on some days I think that if he'd ask again I'd say yes and just get it over with. But to offer oral sex on my own, well, I always chicken out.

A. You use the words "get it over with," and these words give me pause. Apparently, performing oral sex does not appeal to you. I think that you should fantasize about performing oral sex on your husband. Think about the pleasure oral sex is going to give him, and pretend that you're really getting into it. If you can't fantasize about giving your husband oral sex — if that picture turns your stomach — don't even think about doing it when you're in bed together. You want to avoid starting, feeling disgusted, and stopping the act. Not following through on oral sex once you begin is worse than never having oral sex at all.

Many people write to me and say that they like to please their mates by doing certain sexual acts, but they just can't bring themselves to perform oral sex. Sometimes they just aren't confident about their abilities or they have an innate distaste for the act. If this description fits your view of oral sex, don't force yourself to try it, because the results won't be positive.

Other people avoid experimenting because they believe that if they try oral sex once, their partners will expect oral pleasure from them over and over again. If you have this fear, you may easily overcome it. You merely inform your partner that you're going to try something new this one time, but that doesn't mean you'll try it again. Your partner must promise that he or she won't exert pressure on you to perform oral sex again because of this one experiment.

Avoiding resentment

You know the expression — "practice makes perfect." Therefore, you may argue that just because a new sexual position or technique doesn't work the first time doesn't mean that it can't work the second time. Although this rule holds true for certain human endeavors, it does not apply to every situation. When it comes to sex, your imperfect performance may boil down to your dislike of a position.

If you let yourself be pressured into doing something uncomfortable, you may easily start to feel resentment for your partner. Although you shouldn't allow fear to prevent you from trying a new position or technique, you also shouldn't allow yourself to be pressured into doing something that you know you'll never find acceptable.

Keeping it light

If you decide to try something new in the bedroom that you've never tried before (or maybe something that you tried once but feel you didn't give a fair shake), your best bet is to approach the situation with a bit of humor. Remember to relax and not take yourselves too seriously. If the "something new" works, great. If it doesn't, don't get upset — laugh about it.

Sex is supposed to be fun and give pleasure. If your attitudes are too serious, you're only going to run into problems. You can't force yourself to have a good time, but you can allow yourself to have a good time — and humor acts as a tension reliever.

Facing failure together

What if your sexual experiment doesn't work? For example, you are both willing to try some new position but can't quite pull it off. I hope you realize the world has not ended. Don't put on a long face. Displaying your disappointment only ensures that the situation will worsen the next time. You and your partner need to make the attempt again. Laugh off your first attempt, don't assign blame to anyone, and proceed to try another position that has better prospects.

Ringing Your Partner's Bell

While reading this book, you may expect to come across specific suggestions on how to improve your sex life. Guess what? In this section, I offer you a dozen possibilities to explore as you and your partner work on igniting your sexual fires:

- ✔ **Share your past favorite sexual moments.** Do you ever sit back and daydream about past sexual escapades with your partner? Instead of just fantasizing about them alone, why not sit down next to your partner and share these recollections? If your timing is right, your reminiscing may lead to the creation of an additional memory for your sexy scrapbook.

- ✔ **Leave a surprise love note in the shower.** If you're in the shower and you know your lover is going in next, surprise your partner by scrawling a little love note on the shower wall with some lipstick.

- ✔ **Give up your favorite sexual position for a month.** Do the two of you enjoy a favorite sexual position? Try giving it up for 30 days. Not only may you discover a new position, but you also may find the old one seems fresher when you return to it.

- **Make love in the kitchen.** One advantage of this location is that you're a lot closer to a variety of flavorings: jams, honey, and whipped cream. Another advantage is your closeness to some interesting toys (turkey basters, spatulas, and so on) that may add some zest to your enjoyment of sex.

- **Peruse a sexy magazine together.** Do you ever wonder what he sees in *Playboy* or what she sees in *Cosmopolitan*? Spend an evening reading these (or similar) magazines together. Discuss the appeal of these publications; the conversation may turn out to be very enlightening.

- **Complete a task as a team.** A great way to bring the two of you closer is to accomplish some task as a team. Here's one idea: Write a poem together about your favorite sexual position. That activity should set the home fires burning.

- **Turn up the tunes.** Do you keep silent during sex because you're afraid the kids might hear you? The next time you have sex, turn on the radio loud enough so that any noises you make seem like part of the broadcast. Then feel free to let 'er rip.

- **Re-experience a childhood game.** Did you ever play doctor with someone of the opposite sex when you were a child? Why not try this game again with your spouse? As adults you can make the situation more realistic; one of you may even don some whites for the role of doctor. Using your imagination in this way may create new sexual roles for both of you to play.

- **Tie a few love knots.** As an exercise in intimacy, tie your wrists together using a ribbon and enjoy the experience of being Siamese twins for a few hours. For a variation, link your ankles instead.

- **Be spontaneous.** Many people worry about boredom in the bedroom. If you don't want to be boring in bed, don't allow yourself to be boring the rest of the day. Add a little spontaneity to your everyday life. Start a food fight with those grapes you're eating. Spray shaving cream at each other. Yank down his shorts at the barbecue. Toss a water balloon her way while she gardens. Spice up your everyday existence, and the excitement will spill over into your lovemaking.

- **Play hide-and-seek.** Take a trip into your childhood for a game of hide-and-seek and add an extra bit of excitement by creating adult rules. The seeker must buy each minute of time spent seeking with an article of clothing. If the hider has a good hiding place, the seeker may be bare by the time he finds what he's looking for.

- **Dress by request.** You may be married 20 years and still not know how your partner likes you to dress when you go out for a night on the town. The solution to this dilemma is to play dress-up. Dress each other from head to toe. Plan ahead so that you can shop for any special clothes your partner may not have in his or her wardrobe. Then go out for dinner to show off your new looks to the world.

Chapter 10

Feeling Attractive: Be Sexy, You're Worth It

*M*any single people have trouble getting dates, and these folks often blame at least part of the reason on their looks. Television, movies, and magazines emphasize appearance above all else, so we naturally assume that how we look determines how attracted someone feels toward us.

There are several problems with placing so much emphasis on physical appearance. For example, the way you feel about your appearance may not have anything to do with how you actually look. Even some top models are known to look in the mirror and think "Yuck!" Plus, if you assume that you aren't attractive simply because you aren't an exact replica of today's hottest movie star or model, then you may convince yourself that all of your wonderful qualities are worth nothing in the eyes of your partner.

If you and your partner haven't changed much since your romance began, perhaps you don't have any concerns about how he or she feels about your appearance. But if you and your partner have been together many years, your appearances have likely undergone some subtle — or not-so-subtle — changes. (This is especially true for women who have given birth.) In this chapter, I discuss how to feel better about your own appearance, how to make your partner feel better about his or her appearance, and how to improve your relationship by letting yourself feel truly attractive.

Vanity, Thy Name Is You

Love looks not with the eyes, but with the mind; And therefore is winged Cupid painted blind.

— William Shakespeare, *A Midsummer Night's Dream*

While I can't totally agree with the great Bard, I do believe that we are often *first* attracted to each other because of looks. But after two people fall in love, looks greatly fall from their place of importance. On your first date, you may not know much about this person except that he has a wonderful smile. But after you've known him for 5, 10, or 25 years, that smile is only one of hundreds of reasons that you find him attractive.

Strangely, we don't always believe our own ears when it comes to our appearance. I get many letters from women who say that they don't want to undress in front of their husbands because they've put on weight, even though their spouses actually like the way they look. And then there are men who worry excessively about going bald while their partners don't even notice how little hair they have left. What do these examples tell us? Concerns about how you look often do not originate in your partner's view of your appearance; instead, they stem from your own vanity.

With Madison Avenue telling us over and over again how important our appearance is, it's not surprising that people fall into such traps. And that's exactly what vanity is, a trap. No relationship can survive on looks alone, and the more importance that a person puts on his or her appearance and the appearance of his or her partner, the shallower the romance will be.

Of course, some people do have legitimate reasons to feel concerned about the impact their appearance is having on their relationship. Some people simply let themselves go after getting into a committed relationship; they not only put on weight, but they also won't bother with their hair or their clothing, almost wallowing in their slovenliness. Will such behavior turn off a partner? Probably. But keep in mind that the disinterest doesn't just stem from the change in appearance but from the alteration in that person's spirit.

Someone who loves you may be willing to overlook physical faults but may have greater difficulty ignoring a change in attitude. If you act as if you don't care what you look like, your partner may adopt the same attitude, and that may put quite a strain on your relationship. So no matter what changes Father Time graces you with, don't give up the fight. If you're trying your hardest to overcome the ravages of time, your partner will almost certainly be more willing to overlook them.

So what can you do if you find yourself feeling ashamed of the way you look or uncertain about your partner's feelings for your body as it looks now? Read on.

Take a long look at yourself

How do you learn to accept the way your body looks? The first step is to actually look at yourself. You may be surprised at how many people have never examined themselves naked in front of a full-length mirror. I'm not talking about just walking by and glancing sideways at your reflection; I'm talking about actually spending some time staring at yourself from every angle. You shouldn't be doing this scan to search for flaws but instead to see the sexy side of yourself. As you're looking, first figure out what you consider your best assets. Next, flaunt whatever part you think looks good and try to get a mental picture of what your partner sees when you're naked in front of him or her.

A man should do one additional exercise while he is in front of that mirror, and that is to give himself an erection. Under normal circumstances, a man always looks down at his penis. Because of the optical effect called *foreshortening*, his penis appears smaller to him than it does to someone else. By looking at himself in a full-length mirror, a man can see what his partner sees, and in most cases he is favorably impressed.

A woman doesn't need a long mirror to see her genitals, but a hand mirror and a flashlight are necessary. If she has never done this before, she should definitely have a good look around. A woman should spread her vaginal lips and investigate her labia, clitoris, and the inside of her vagina. Many different types of vaginas exist — particularly with regards to the size of the lips — yet all are beautiful. A woman should come to know and appreciate what she has.

Get active

Weight gain is a serious problem for many individuals and couples. While partners may be affected by any major changes in appearance, weight gain carries the added burden of supposedly being "voluntary." (I put this in quotation marks because weight gain is not always voluntary; physical conditions often play a big role in weight gain.)

I hear various versions of the same question many times from women and men alike.

Q. My husband and I have been married for 15 years. I admit that since our wedding day, I've put on an extra 30 pounds. I was a very thin 110 before we married. I don't consider myself fat now, but my husband is always carping about my weight, and his attitude bothers me. How should I handle this problem?

A. The first thing to keep in mind is that as you grow older, your metabolism slows down so that weight becomes easier to put on without a change in your eating habits. In this specific case, while I agree that you are not fat, perhaps your husband is worried that you may continue to put on weight as the years go by. If you can convince him that you are trying to at least maintain your present weight, he may be less likely to harp on this subject.

Another reason why weight gain can be such a sore subject is that it tends to go hand-in-hand with a change in lifestyle. If you are becoming larger as the years go by, chances are good that you are also becoming more sedentary. Even if your partner overlooks the physical changes you're experiencing, it's more difficult to shrug off a lifestyle change. For example, maybe when you first started dating you both enjoyed playing tennis or going for bike rides. If you've stopped doing those activities together because you're simply not as active anymore, then you've eliminated one very positive aspect of your relationship.

A little effort can make a huge difference in your partner's attitude toward your weight. The most important thing you can do is let your partner know that you care about your appearance and your health. This may simply mean that you get up a half hour earlier three days a week and go for a brisk walk before work. Or it may mean that you promise to spend an hour each weekend doing the physical activity such as playing tennis or riding a bike that you both used to enjoy together. These small positive steps can have a big impact on your relationship.

Wear a smile

I know it may sound simplistic, but your smile functions as your best outfit. Although I would not feel comfortable walking around in a nudist camp, I do admire nudists for baring all their physical faults — whatever their faults may be — and not worrying about them. And although I don't suggest that you join their ranks, I do advise that you adopt their attitudes. By looking at your body in a positive light, you help your partner do the same. If you're always complaining about your looks, eventually your partner is going to start sharing your attitude. So no matter what else you put on each morning, remember to think and act positive about your appearance.

This positive attitude is also very relevant when it comes to feeling sexy. To enjoy sex, you have to let go of your inhibitions. Letting go is very hard to do if you are constantly worrying about your weight or your wrinkles or anything else that you see as a flaw. If you're lying next to your lover worried about what he or she is seeing, how can you let yourself fully undergo the sexual experience? If your brain is working full time, your libido can't take over. If your libido is held in check, then sex won't be nearly as enjoyable as it could (and should) be.

The Importance of Paying Compliments

If you have been with your partner for many years, his or her appearance may have become so familiar to you that you don't think to offer a compliment now and then. Take a second look at your lover and see if you can't express a warm, admiring comment; you may find that it goes a long way toward warming the fires. One sincere compliment can transform an average evening into a romantic adventure. Most women soak up compliments like the desert takes in a spring shower, and despite what we tend to assume, men's needs aren't all that different. Letting your partners know that you do think they look good is essential to rekindling romance.

Of course, you don't have to comment on everything that you notice. You don't have to pretend to love the cellulite that dimples your partner's behind (unless, of course, you're a big fan of dimples). But if your companion has gone to the trouble to look nice — new clothes, a changed hairstyle — then you need to open your mouth.

What if you don't like the new hairstyle? Although saying you like the old hairstyle better is okay, you need to say something positive about the new one as well. Hopefully your partner will get the hint, and on the next visit to the stylist, he or she will ask for a different 'do. But until that happens, you don't want your lover feeling ugly, because that certainly won't help your love life.

Dealing with the strong silent type

Some people, mostly men, don't give compliments that easily. He may say something nice if you look particularly good, but even then his lips may stay sealed. Although silence may be better than the criticism some partners constantly receive (and, unfortunately, criticism is *all* some partners receive), it doesn't offer any of the encouragement that is so necessary to a strong romantic relationship.

How do you get your man to throw a few compliments your way? Here's the one thing not to do: Make a sarcastic remark when you do get a compliment. Some women are so surprised when their partner launches a compliment in their direction that instead of being happy, they react bitterly to all the compliments they wanted and never received. If a man comes to the conclusion that he's going to get attacked for making a compliment, then you can be sure he's going to be even more hesitant the next time around.

Another problem area arises when women fish for compliments. "How do you think this looks on me?" is a question that throws many men for a loop. Are they supposed to say how they really feel or toss out a compliment no matter what? Most men don't pay much attention to women's fashions, and most women probably won't listen to their mate's opinion anyway, so this exercise tends to be useless and only muddies the waters with regards to compliments.

Asking for what you need

So what should you do if you are feeling deprived of the compliments you need? Sit down and have a talk with your partner on the subject of compliments. Let your fella know how good compliments make you feel. Try to discover how he feels about the subject of flattery. Both of you may discover something new from these discussions, and maybe this newfound knowledge will enhance your romance.

Try to have this discussion at an appropriate time. For example, if your mate misses the perfect opportunity to give you a compliment, a little later in the day you could say something like, "You haven't commented on my new hair style. Don't you like it?" Then segue from that question into a more complete discussion about this area of your relationship. Don't try to make him feel guilty, but instead try to dig down to see how he feels. You may discover that he has never given much thought to giving compliments, so you'll be exploring new territory.

Because you'll be the instigator of this conversation, prepare yourself with some other examples that will help him to see the light. These could be compliments that he has given to you, compliments you've given to him, or compliments that he has heard other husbands give to their wives. You could also ask him a few questions, like "Do you feel comfortable when someone flatters you?" and "Do you think I give you enough compliments?"

Picking up nonverbal signals

Women may be looking for verbal compliments and not even realize that they have been receiving nonverbal compliments all along. A man is much quicker to give a friend a high five or a thumbs-up than a verbal compliment. Likewise, he may feel much more comfortable giving you nonverbal praise.

If your man is looking at you in a fond way, consider that look as a compliment. If he winks at you or even pats you on the behind, know that he is communicating his attraction. These nonverbal compliments may not be complete substitutes for some words of praise, but women must learn to place appropriate values on them. If a man gets some positive reinforcement for giving such compliments, saying something nice once in a while may be an easy next step.

Giving men compliments

Although men may not be as quick as women to give compliments, they enjoy receiving them. Some men may seem a bit embarrassed upon first hearing a compliment, but given the chance to go and glance in the mirror, they are quite happy to have been told they look good.

Men generally don't receive as many compliments as women do. Therefore, women should not overdo the flattery. If a woman is always complimenting her fella, then he's going to start to discount those compliments. She shouldn't be stingy with her remarks, but she doesn't want to give him so many compliments that he starts to take them for granted.

Why don't men give compliments?

One reason that men shy away from compliments stems from the years these fellas spend hanging out with other guys. As teenagers, it's customary for guys to pick on each other. Giving a compliment would require one guy to actually look at another guy in a positive light. If this happens, the young man giving the compliment might be perceived as having homosexual tendencies. (Guys do compliment each other when it has to do with sports — "nice hit," for example — and they admire each other's cars, but that's usually as far as the flattering goes.)

Of course that thinking is ridiculous, but teens do many ridiculous things. Young men certainly look at each other and copy each other, but the unwritten rule says that young men don't give compliments to each other.

Many of these same young men know that they're supposed to give compliments to women, but after spending so much time squashing any attempts to say something nice to their friends, suddenly switching gears is difficult. And even if male teenagers do manage to flatter their girlfriends for a brief time during courtship, some revert back to their old, silent ways when the relationship becomes steady.

Feeling Sexier

Whether you're being deluged with compliments or have given up on ever receiving a single one, you can do things for yourself that make you feel more sexy. If you love your partner and enjoy sex, you should not let external circumstances drag down your sexual spirits. You can make yourself feel sexier, and hence, lead a sexier life.

Programming your dreams

The first step toward feeling sexier has to do with what goes on inside your head during the time you are sleeping. You can't control your dreams, but you can influence them. The best examples of this process are the nightmares that may occur after you watch a scary movie. Some people experience those bad dreams for months.

But fear isn't the only emotion that you feel in your dreams; sexual arousal may certainly play a starring role. If you have sexy dreams, these flights of fancy may help you feel sexier when you're awake. So I suggest that you fall asleep thinking about some sexual fantasy and see what develops. Even if you don't remember what you dream about, chances are good that your libido still feels the effects.

Tickling your libido with fantasy

You have your worries — we all do — but if you allow them to constantly fill in the blanks of your mind, they clog up the pathways where sexy thoughts should be traveling. Women, especially, find ignoring their anxieties difficult. A man may be able to turn on his thoughts about sex like he turns on a faucet, but a woman's libido needs to trickle its way down from her brain to her feet (and every place in between). This process takes time. In order to lubricate the path, women should allow some sexy thoughts to make their way through their brain cells on a regular basis.

I suggest that you build up a library of sexual fantasies. I can't tell you what turns you on, so you have to choose your own sexual fantasies. Whether your sexual escapes are memories of sexual escapades (done either with your current partner or somebody else) or fantasies about total strangers (such as movie stars, your neighbors, or a whole football team) doesn't matter. Just don't tell your partner what got you "in the mood;" all he needs to know is that you are.

You can plug in one of these fantasies whenever you have a quiet moment, but these sexual daydreams may be even more useful as a means of pushing out negative thoughts. If your boss has got you going crazy and all you can think of are ways to do him in, take a deep breath, reach into your catalogue of fantasies, and escape for a few moments into a more pleasant place. You'll feel better, and that will help grease the way so that when you're with your partner you can fall into his arms instead of going off to sulk in a corner.

Triggering sexual memories

Memories are great, but little mementos may also help to bring these sexual thoughts back. Photos are the best reminders. You may not want to leave some types of photos lying around, either at your home or the office. Find someplace where you can tuck a few pictures of some memorable experiences away — where either children or fellow employees aren't likely to look — so that you can occasionally take a peek. Other types of mementos may include

- a matchbook cover from a hotel where you had a hot time.
- a love letter, card, or note.
- the boarding pass from a memorable trip.
- a ticket stub from a particularly enjoyable evening out.
- a leaf or a blade of grass that got stuck to the blanket you used while making love outdoors.

You may don some underwear or a top that reminds you of a particular time when you were very aroused. If you don't wear the same perfume every day, maybe a spritz of a particular scent might do the trick. And if you want to create an aural trigger, stick a portable tape recorder under your bed the next time you make love, then you can listen to the sounds the two of you made any time you want. (Well, almost any time; you may not want to bring this tape to your workplace.)

You can also create your own sexual triggers:

✔ **Pick a color that will remind you of sex.** For example, you may choose pink. Place some pink highlights around your home and office. The accents don't have to be much; even a box of pink tissues in your office will be enough. That box is a perfectly normal thing to have, yet every time you look over at those pink tissues, you'll remember the reason you placed them there.

✔ **Schedule time to think about your partner.** Put some marks on your calendar just to remind you to stop and think of how much you care for him or her.

✔ **Listen to meaningful music.** Create a collection of music for your car that includes songs that have a special meaning for you.

The point isn't *what* you do but that you do *something* that triggers the right cranial pathways that lead to where your libido sits. By signaling that part of your brain on a regular basis, you are sure to feel sexier.

Letting your body speak volumes

Several years ago, Madonna's song "Vogue" popularized a style of dance where people do a series of poses. Although you may not want to go so far as to pose all day long, you certainly feel better about yourself (and sexier, too) when you stick out your chest and walk like you own the world. Pick up your shoulders instead of letting them droop. While you're at it, suck in your stomach and throw your head back. Pretend the wind is blowing in your hair and there's a band parading alongside of you playing "Staying Alive" from *Saturday Night Fever.*

At work, don't slump over like you're carrying the world on your shoulders. Even if the weight of the entire office actually is your responsibility, stand up tall and take some deep breaths until you feel better about yourself. If need be, do some stretching exercises. When you get up and stroll over to the water cooler, don't slink over to it, but make the action seem as if you're doing something very important. And if you walk home from the train station with that attitude, I guarantee that when you walk through your front door, your partner is going to see a new, sexier you.

Keeping a sex diary

Whether or not you maintain some type of regular diary or journal, keeping a *sex* diary may help you in several ways. First of all, reading back over your sexual history should certainly serve as a turn on. Your sex diary proves to yourself that you are a sexual person, especially if you only write about the highlights. And your journal may help you to remember certain positions or movements the two of you did that you found particularly exciting, which could encourage you to try these positions again.

I want to make one cautionary note about your sex diary: Make sure it doesn't fall into the wrong hands. Hide it well. If you keep your journal as a file on your computer, be certain that it's not stored in a way that someone could just stumble upon it and discover your sex secrets.

Imagining a new you

No matter who you are or what you look like, you can always be someone else in your imagination. Maybe you can't picture yourself in a certain situation, but you can imagine yourself as someone else. You may choose to see yourself as a friend, a neighbor, a fictional character, an entertainer, someone you read about, a notable person from history, an author, or a movie star. You should imagine someone with a strong personality who is fearless, daring, and sexy. By putting yourself in their shoes, maybe you can make yourself act as sexy as you really want to be.

In order to help you put on this mantle of another person, wear clothes that he or she might be more likely to wear. You can more easily picture yourself as Marilyn Monroe if you have on a pair of high heels, for example. And there's nothing wrong with going over the top, at least in private. Following up on the Marilyn Monroe idea, you can put on a light dress, forget your underwear, and place a fan on the floor. I guarantee your mate won't ask you 20 questions to guess what celebrity you're imitating or what you are in the mood for.

Transforming Yourself Inside

Feeling sexy is obviously not only limited to how you look but also very much tied into your entire psychological makeup. You may look like the proverbial million dollars, but if you're depressed or angry or scared, you're not going to feel sexy. These emotions are powerful, and they will drown out your libido. And this condition affects both men and women equally. In this section, I help you figure out how to recognize the emotional problems that affect your sex life.

Letting go of anger

Strong emotions cannot just be pushed aside in an instant; you need time to absorb them. But for the sake of your relationship, you have to learn how to let go of anger and other negative emotions fairly quickly. For example, say your boss makes you particularly upset one day. Naturally, you want to vent to your spouse about your feelings when you first get home. But if you push your spouse aside later that night because you are still furious, how fair is that? After all, who is more important in your life, your boss or your partner?

If this episode happens occasionally, it's no big deal. But if you let your other emotions take over day after day, the romance in your relationship is going to be pushed into the back seat, and maybe right out the door.

Put a time limit on these emotions. When someone pushes your buttons, expect that your blood pressure is going to go up. If your work is criticized, of course you're going to feel blue. If your company loses a big account, it's natural to worry about the security of your job. But at some point you have to learn to shrug these emotions off. The intensity of the specific emotion determines, to some degree, how long you hang on to it. But remember that you're trying to focus on the positive. If your teapot is still boiling an hour after you've come home from a hard day at work, then purposefully take it off the flame by thinking about something positive.

Taking control of your emotions

Sometimes the psychological burdens that prevent you from enjoying sex are brought on by external factors that you *can* control. When, for example, you've got a boss who takes joy in driving his employees up the wall, you have to begin looking for a new job — not just for the sake of your relationship, but for your own sanity.

The root of the problem may lie in your own psychological makeup. If you can't shake the blues when there is no good cause for them, you should see a counselor or maybe even a doctor. I'm not in favor of going on medication at the drop of a hat, but some people cannot pull themselves out of a depressed state without taking medication. And even if the depression is not so deep, a counselor may help you make progress more quickly.

If you constantly blow your lid without real justification, you should look into taking some classes on anger management. An angry person almost always directs at least part of his or her wrath towards a spouse, and that's certainly not conducive to romance.

Jealousy is another strong emotion that can attack the foundation of a relationship. If one of you has given the other a reason to be jealous, that's one thing. But if feelings of jealousy rise spontaneously, and if the jealous partner's demands become a burden on his or her mate, then the two of you need to seek some sort of therapy if the relationship is going to hold together.

Be honest with yourself and admit if you have a problem, and get the help you need. After you start feeling better, your relationship will improve. Convince yourself that if you don't make an effort to change, your relationship may soon be on the rocks.

You need to recognize that your relationship can be an important anchor. If you can keep your relationship strong, your partner can help you get over any difficulty that is bothering you. If you push the relationship toward the back, not only will it be damaged, but you may crash right along with it.

Chapter 11

Let's Get Physical: Exercises to Improve Your Sex Life

I once interviewed a quadriplegic gentleman on my television show and learned that he and his wife enjoy a very satisfying sex life. The discussion affirmed my belief that you can have a fulfilling sex life no matter what your natural physical condition. Except for rare circumstances, you can find ways to work around any physical problems.

But while some people overcome great obstacles to enjoy a healthy sex life, most of us allow poor eating habits and lack of exercise to decrease our sexual enjoyment. Don't get me wrong: You don't have to be an Olympic athlete to have terrific sex, because the most important factor of a good sex life is a healthy psychological state (see Chapter 10). But any improvements you make to your physical condition can also improve your sex life. So, to the extent that you can get yourself into better shape, go for it.

As you read this chapter, you'll see that I don't stick to the traditional steps for getting in shape. Remember, I'm not a personal trainer. I'm not concerned about how well developed your muscles become or how low you get your resting heart rate. My goal is to improve your relationship, and that goal is always in focus as I present these particular activities.

Applauding Dr. Kegel

Perhaps you have never heard of Dr. Arnold Kegel, but in 1952, he developed exercises to help women regain control of their ability to urinate after giving birth. Women later discovered that these exercises help to increase the sensations they experience during intercourse. By using the muscle control she develops, a woman can make her partner experience more feeling from intercourse as well.

The pelvic floor muscles are designed to go in several directions. (As a result, they can sufficiently expand during childbirth.) To recognize these muscles, during urination a woman should stop the flow. The muscles she contracts to do so are the pelvic floor muscles. She can further identify these muscles by inserting her finger into her vagina and squeezing the muscles surrounding it. (This squeezing action can make sex more pleasurable for a man. The more developed the woman's ability to squeeze her vagina around his penis is, the more pleasure the man feels.)

The actual exercise that Dr. Kegel developed consists of squeezing these muscles and then releasing the contraction in a series of repetitions. You may start with half-a-dozen repetitions and build up to about 25. You can do these sets throughout the course of the day, and no one will know that you are doing them. If you perform at least three sets of these exercises a day, after about six weeks you should begin to feel the effects.

Kegel exercises are traditionally thought of as a woman's exercise, but they are also effective for men. Men can figure out which muscle to squeeze just the way women do — by stopping their flow of urine and identifying which muscle they are using. Men can practice the same sets of repetitions of squeezing and relaxing the muscle. A man who exercises these muscles may develop greater control over his ability to ejaculate and will increase his sexual pleasure.

Getting Limber

Under normal circumstances, sex doesn't require great strength. (Some positions do require the vigor of a strong male, but let me be honest: If you never have sex in the shower standing up, you can still live happily ever after.) However, sex does require some movement, and the more limber you are, the better. Not only are certain positions more easily accomplished if you're limber, but you're less likely to find yourself stiffening up (and I'm not referring to *that* part of the male anatomy) the next day.

While runners and other athletes stretch their muscles before they start their sport, most couples don't stretch before engaging in sex. Although you don't need to stretch prior to sex the same way you do prior to a game of tennis or a long run, the benefits of stretching before sex may be quite rewarding.

Prolonging your pleasure

As I point out many times in this book, rushing into sex, and through sex, only limits the enjoyment you experience. Face it. How much true enjoyment do you experience during the course of a day? Wouldn't you rather sip that cup of morning coffee than gulp it down? Wouldn't you prefer to squeeze every last taste out of your dinner than shovel it in your mouth as quickly as possible? Well, the same holds true for sex. I know each of you may be impatient to reach that orgasm you're seeking, and you may be afraid the phone will ring or the kids will wake up and spoil the mood. But by drawing out the length of your sexual episodes, you really derive more enjoyment from sex. And one way of achieving this goal is by stretching before you begin.

Stretching in tandem

The first thing you should know is that stretching isn't bouncing. Bouncing your muscles may cause injuries, but slow stretching is perfectly safe.

The second thing you should know is that stretches should be done in the nude, and your partner should watch you stretch. This routine should definitely be part of the pleasure! Seeing your lover's muscles get all taut should cause some tightening of the strings of your own heart.

You can assist each other with stretching exercises. For example, to stretch your hamstrings (the back of your thighs) you need to put one leg up and rest it on something. Although a piece of furniture or a step may serve the purpose, certainly a loop made by your partner's hands would be more interesting. Likewise, with one leg forward and the other back, you can push against a wall to stretch your calf muscles. But instead of a wall, you may want to push against your partner. You can stretch your arm and back muscles by pushing against a solid object or (you guessed it) your partner. While these stretches aren't sexual in and of themselves, done together in a state of undress, they will most definitely enhance the level of your arousal.

For those of you who want to turn these stretching routines into more of an exercise, take some classes in yoga. After you master the regular variety of yoga exercises, you can take some courses in tantric yoga. The techniques you learn in tantric yoga include some eastern ways of having sex that you may find quite enjoyable.

Feeling the Burn

This section describes several exercises you do together that can absolutely be described as sexy. You don't necessarily have to be nude, but the less clothing you wear, the sexier these exercises become. Many of these movements involve *resistance* — pushing or pulling against each other. There's a good chance that the male partner is going to be stronger than his female counterpart. If that's the case, he's going to have to hold back; the two of you need to be at close to equal strength in order for these exercises to work. Although these exercises may prove to be more of a workout for one partner than the other, the fun factor increases when you do them together.

The seesaw

Both of you sit on the floor with the soles of your feet planted up against each other. Grasp each other's hands. You go backward, and your partner keeps you from going back too far. Then your partner pulls you to an upright position. Now it's your partner's turn to go backward. If you have difficulty supporting the weight of your partner, let him or her know so that he or she maintains some muscle control while going backward.

Standing back-to-back

This exercise does not work if one partner is much heavier than the other, so please be careful. Stand back-to-back with your partner and link arms. Taking turns, one of you leans forward, raising the other off of the ground to whatever height is possible. Even if you can't lift your partner at all, just the effort is good exercise.

Sitting back-to-back

Sit back-to-back with your partner on the floor. Both of you try to get up while pushing against each other. This exercise utilizes your leg muscles. If one partner exerts too much force, the other is just going to be pushed forward and won't be able to rise. So cooperation is the key to making this exercise work properly. If you can both push with equal force, you should both be able to get up. In the beginning, you can "cheat" by using your hands to get started, but eventually you should be able to do this without using your hands at all.

The wheelbarrow

Lie face forward on the floor (preferably a carpeted one). Your partner picks up your legs from behind, grasping your ankles. Then lift yourself up using your arms and begin to "walk" while your partner walks and holds your legs. Switch positions. Count how many "steps" each of you can take.

Couple crunches

Both of you lie down on the floor, put your legs straight up, and place your butts against each other so that you look like an upside down T. Then do crunches (half sit-ups). How many crunches you accomplish depends on whether or not you routinely do crunches. Eventually, even amateurs should work up to doing three sets of ten crunches each.

Floor cycling

After doing couple crunches and while still lying on the floor, push yourselves apart a few feet, line your feet up against each other, and push against each other in a pedaling motion. Don't try to do this quickly. Instead, work to push against each other so that you create resistance and give each other a workout.

Hamstring burners

Exercises that work the backs of the thighs are hard to find, but not for couples that exercise as a team. Lay down on your stomach while your partner straddles you, facing your feet. Using his or her hands, your partner puts as much pressure on your ankles as needed to make it difficult for you to raise your legs. As time goes by and each of you grows stronger, the "pusher" can exert increasing amounts of pressure. These burners should be done in sets of ten.

Re-creating Recreation

While performing regular exercises can be more fun when done with a partner, especially if they're clothing optional, burning up calories can be more fun if it's entertaining as well as aerobic. Here are some suggestions for ways the two of you can get some exercise and have fun at the same time.

Wrestling

Wrestling has become a popular sport these days, although I'm not sure that you can call what you see on television a sport. And I'm certainly not advocating that you break chairs over your partner's head. But wrestling for the fun of it by just trying to push each other around a bit can be very invigorating. (You do have to be careful not to hurt each other. For instance, the man can't use all his strength.) I recommend giving wrestling a try — you can have a good time and get a great workout.

If you're wrestling in the nude, this grappling can become a highly arousing form of play. I must caution men, however, not to take the game too far, especially in a sexual sense, unless you both agree ahead of time that "to the winner goes the spoils."

Walking

One of the best forms of exercise is walking, and this form of exercise is one that you can definitely do together. Is walking sexy, you ask? You bet it is. You see, when you go for a walk, you're together — no distractions. (Leave your cell phones at home.)You have plenty of privacy for intimate conversations, because even if you encounter other people, the most they can hear are snippets of your tête-à-tête. If there's a weight you need to get off your chest or a serious topic you wish to discuss, there's no better time to do it than during a walk. You may choose to talk about how to improve your sex life or how much you love each other. If you can make a habit of taking an evening constitutional every night after supper, I can almost guarantee that you'll see an improvement in your relationship.

If your gaits are so different that you can't seem to walk at the same speed, you could walk on two adjacent treadmills at a health club. The drawback is that while this alternative may offer an efficient form of exercise, with all the noises from these machines, conversation may be negligible, and that won't be very sexy.

Skiing

You may not think of skiing as a sexy pastime, but skiing is my favorite sport, so I have to give it a strong recommendation. The downside (no pun intended) is that you may not be together as you ski, especially if you're not at identical skill levels. But after you're back at the lodge huddled around a fire with drinks in your hands, well, there's nothing sexier than that.

Splendor in the grass

What's the difference between hiking and walking? Mostly it's the terrain. Unless you're lucky enough to live alongside the Appalachian Trail, your nightly stroll is probably going to take place on a sidewalk. But on weekends, you can go someplace where you're in the woods and the territory is a bit hilly. Then you can get a very good aerobic workout. During your explorations, if you find a nice, isolated spot where you can lay down for some open-air lovemaking, you may come to regard hiking as one of your sexist forms of exercise. Just watch out for mosquitoes and poison ivy!

Sports on wheels

If you like to add a little quotient of speed to your aerobic workout, wheels can certainly do the trick. First, there are those wheels that you strap to your feet, in terms of skates or roller blades. I see people whizzing through the streets of New York on skates and blades and all I can think is that they're going to get killed. Hopefully you live somewhere with a few less cars on the roads.

I like to go for a spin on my bicycle, and I feel that a bike offers a safer ride. You can certainly ride farther on a bike and maybe pack a lunch. And if you want to make it a cozy ride, rent a *tandem* — a bicycle built for two. Just make sure that both of you are pedaling equally hard, or one half of the couple may end up doing all the work.

Kayaking

Boats provide wonderful opportunities for sharing some romance, and my favorite boat, by far, is the two-man kayak. Because I like to talk, a kayak built for two suits me just fine. (I don't have to shout "Ahoy!" just to get the attention of my boat mate.) Kayaking is great exercise. If you know the area, you may be able to pull up on some deserted land for some additional exercise. (If you know what I mean — and I think that you do!) For those of you into thrills and spills, take your kayak on a river that foams with some whitewater rapids, and you can have a really exciting time.

Tennis

Tennis is a sport that allows two people to play as a team. And mixed couple matches erase any advantages that some men have over women. A couple has to compete together, and teamwork is sexy. When no other couple is around for a match, you can enjoy playing against each other. Tennis is a great sport for a couple to adopt to inspire romance.

Competition is healthy in any sport. It's good to be competitive. But don't be *too* competitive. Pointing out mistakes your partner makes or arguing about bad calls is not sexy. Keep the competition friendly. Cutthroat matches may drive your heart rate up, but they won't inspire heartfelt romance.

Dancing

You've probably already thought of dancing as being sexy, but did you also think of dancing as a form of exercise? If you've ever been at some event where you danced up a storm and found yourself out of breath and sweaty, then you know what I'm saying. If you participate only in slow dancing, then perhaps you haven't experienced the full benefits of this activity. Advocates of hoofing want to make ballroom dancing an Olympic event. That alone should tell you that there is the potential for getting a really good athletic workout by cutting a rug on the dance floor.

Look in the entertainment section of your local paper to find centers or events that feature dance. In my town, the community center offers lessons in swing dancing. And studios cater to teaching all styles of dance — from the cha-cha to square dancing. If you're not sure which type of stepping most appeals to the two of you, have a whirl at a number of different dances. The waltz, tango, samba, rumba, Charleston, fox-trot, and polka — all offer a chance to move in step with your sweetheart. What could be more romantic?

You say you have two left feet and don't want to demonstrate your lack of rhythm in front of a crowd? I suggest that you rent a teach-yourself videotape and practice at home. You may get so good that you don't need any lessons. But even if you do decide to take a course in jitterbugging, at least you won't look like rank amateurs.

Bird-watching

Not everyone likes to exercise, and some folks have bodies that don't permit them to do anything too strenuous. For these two groups, I have a suggestion: bird-watching. You may not normally think of bird-watching as a sport, but it's an activity that you can do together. And at least this pastime gets you outdoors.

You can't be a bird-watcher without doing *some* walking, although it may only be a few steps from your car. And bird-watching has an advantage over most of the other exercises I mention: You can spend a lot of time studying birds in books even when you're not outdoors. As I say time and again, having a hobby that you enjoy together keeps the romance alive and thriving. If the only sport the two of you engage in is bird-watching, you're still sharing a great romantic venture.

Sex or arousing aerobics?

I want to point out that although it's true that you expend some calories when having sex, you don't want to think of sex as an exercise. People are always writing to me and asking me how many calories are burned during sex (as well as how many calories are in a man's ejaculate). I never answer those questions. Not that I can't find the answers, but I don't think these answers would be helpful pieces of information. What if your partner starts extending the duration of sex just to use up a few more calories? That objective forces you to delay your orgasm. Drawing out lovemaking for added pleasure is wonderful, but as a part of your partner's exercise routine it's just not fair. Sex is complicated enough without throwing in any added twists. My advice is not to think of sex as anything other than a way for the two of you to exchange your love for each other.

Chapter 12

Great Sex in Your Senior Years

. . . .

In This Chapter

▶ Getting to know your changing bodies

▶ Figuring out the male's private parts puzzle

▶ Dealing with menopause

▶ Being practical (but not boring)

▶ Relishing the familiar

. . . .

To many people who don't know any better, the idea of seniors enjoying great sex seems unbelievable. Certainly most young people don't think that older people have sex, particularly their parents. The fact is that couples can continue to enjoy sex until their nineties, and maybe beyond.

As you age, you may find that sex doesn't occur with the same intensity or frequency as when you were in your twenties, but it's a big mistake to look at older people and think that they're sexless. Sadly, some older folks see themselves as sexless and give up on lovemaking when there isn't any need to do so. After all, we recently entered a new era in medical history where drugs like Viagra can restore what once was lost.

In this chapter, I explain what to expect from your body as you reach your golden years and show you how to keep the fires burning.

Rolling with the Physical Changes

I want to begin with the facts of life for seniors before I move on to rekindling your romance. In order to make improvements in your sex life, you need to know some basic information regarding the physical changes that occur as you age. Otherwise, you may misunderstand your body's aging process.

Jill and Randy

Jill, with her fiftieth birthday a few weeks away, decided to spend an evening alone and devoted the time to some introspection. When she examined her sex life with her husband Randy, she came to the realization that their lovemaking had severely diminished. Randy was three years older, and it was hard for her to believe he had lost all interest in sex due to their ages. Because she had maintained her appearance, she didn't think that her looks were to blame for their nonexistent sex life. She drew the only conclusion she could think of — Randy was having an affair. Jill knew that he had hired a new young secretary about six months ago, and she decided that the two of them had hit it off.

That night, when Randy came home, she confronted him with her theory. He denied that he was having an affair. When she asked him why their sex life had dwindled away, Randy couldn't come up with a logical explanation. Jill ran to her room crying and locked Randy out for the rest of the night. She believed her own theory over his pitiful denial.

The names have been changed to protect the innocent, as they say, but I see couples like this in my office countless times. The sad cause of these fights is nothing more than sexual illiteracy. Although the signs of menopause are widely talked about, neither Jill nor Randy know what happens to a man as he ages.

Rising to the occasion: The male experience

Let me begin by defining a term: *refractory period* — the time it takes a man to have another erection after he has ejaculated. When a man ejaculates, his erection goes limp, as I'm sure you all know. A young man in his twenties may be able to get another erection within a few minutes so that the couple can have intercourse again. But as a man ages, it takes him longer and longer to get a new erection. The refractory period stretches into hours, days, and maybe even a whole week.

Another change that men go through is a weakening of their erections. In other words, their penises don't get as hard as they once did. As long as a man's penis is hard enough to penetrate a woman, there is no cause for concern. But if he loses the ability to get his penis firm enough for penetration, the couple may have a problem.

The intensity a man feels when he reaches his orgasm decreases over time. Some older men who can get erections cannot have an orgasm during intercourse at all.

What causes these problems? Erectile problems may develop because of *arteriosclerosis* — a narrowing of the arteries that can arise due to high blood pressure, high cholesterol, diabetes, or smoking. Sometimes the problem occurs because of a leak in the mechanism that traps the blood in the penis. And any changes in a man's level of testosterone can play a role. Because there may be medical help available, don't ignore such symptoms or feel too embarrassed to speak about them with a doctor. Make an appointment to see a urologist, who specializes in these concerns. If you have a medical problem and treatment is available, then that should be the first recourse.

Relying on the power of touch

A young man has *psychogenic erections*. That term means that if a young man thinks of something sexy, sees an erotic picture, or maybe only looks at the floor, he gets an erection — without touching his penis at all. In fact, some teenage boys have erections almost hourly, like Old Faithful. As a man ages, these psychogenic erections occur less frequently, and eventually they disappear altogether.

When men first learn that their frequent erections will someday diminish, they want to know when this dreadful moment is going to occur. The answer is different for every individual. For some men, the change may happen in their late forties or fifties. Other men may not experience the transition until their sixties or seventies. But eventually the change happens to every man.

This change does not mean that a man can't get an erection; it only means that he needs physical stimulation to get one. His penis must be stroked or licked to cause an erection.

Getting back to Jill and Randy — Randy's inability to have a psychogenic erection was at the root of their problem. Jill would take off her clothes in front of him, and after all those years of having his penis respond on its own to this visual stimuli, nothing would happen. Had she expected this change, she would have just gotten closer to him — reached out and touched him and voila! Randy would have had an erection, and they would have been having sex. Because Randy wasn't aware of what was happening to him and was ashamed that he couldn't have an erection, all those moments that could have led to sex wound up as dead ends, so to speak.

Randy would never have cheated on his wife, because he would have been too afraid that this embarrassing moment would occur with another woman, too. Then he'd really feel that his manhood had been crushed. Other men going through these changes sometimes erroneously think that they are no longer attracted to their wives and do run off to the arms of younger women. And maybe because of the added excitement of an affair, these men can regain their powers, at least temporarily.

Initiating foreplay

If husband and wife are on the same page, they realize that this natural occurrence is nothing to be ashamed of. As a man grows older, he needs more physical activity to become aroused. The inaction of the man's penis is easily dealt with by initiating some foreplay for him, just the way he has been initiating foreplay for her all these years. If a couple has a good relationship from the beginning, foreplay should not be a problem.

For the younger men out there, don't scrimp on the foreplay. You don't want your wives to feel that *you* aren't trying your best, because years down the road, you'll need *her* help getting your engines started.

Some men turn to masturbation at this time in their lives. While a man may be ashamed to ask for his wife's help in achieving an erection, he may be inclined to give himself an erection by touching his penis. Some men may have masturbated occasionally throughout their years of marriage, while others may turn to masturbation only as a last resort. The problem with relying on their own powers to find sexual satisfaction is that masturbation leaves their wives in the lurch — thinking that their husbands are giving at the office when they actually are not.

This particular stretch of road in a marriage can be a bit rocky. You can prepare for these more difficult times by keeping the lines of communication about sex open throughout the relationship.

Staying close during menopause: The female experience

Because I'm not a physician, I'm not going to discuss hot flashes and whether or not a woman should use estrogen replacement therapy. I want to address the main change that menopause causes in a woman with regards to sex, as well as a change that many women expect but certainly don't need to experience.

Adding lubricant to the mix

Menopause inhibits the amount of lubrication that is produced when a woman is aroused. Older women do not *feel* any less aroused, but their dry vaginas can cause them discomfort during intercourse. Luckily, the solution to this problem is easy — add some lubricant. Plenty of good lubricants are on the market, and as more baby-boomer women reach menopause, the pharmaceutical companies will probably develop improved lubricant products.

Does it spoil sex when you interrupt things to add some lubricant? Well maybe, if you leave the lubricant in the bathroom medicine cabinet — at the other end of the hallway, just past the rooms of your teenagers. Keep the lubricant and a towel handy near your bed and avoid making it a big deal.

Overcoming the loss of desire

Some women claim to lose the desire for sex when they go through "the change." I wonder if this loss isn't a self-fulfilling prophecy. If the vast majority of women lost their desire for sex after they went through menopause, then the safe conclusion would be that this loss of desire was part of menopause. But clinical observations don't bear this out. Although some women do lose some or all of their desire for sex, others don't feel any different, and still others experience an increased desire. Are those women who feel less desire undergoing unusual hormonal changes? Or are they just expecting to lose their desire and living up to that expectation?

If you feel that your desire for sex has disappeared since menopause, before seeking medical help I would suggest trying some home remedies. If these remedies don't work, go straight to your gynecologist.

The first home remedy requires sitting down with your partner and telling him what's wrong. Let him know that you're not feeling the same arousal levels as you used to; see if he can help. Maybe your partner needs to be a bit more attentive. Because men are usually shut out of discussions having to do with female problems, many spouses run the other way when the subject of menopause arises. The lack of sexual desire may make a wife feel like something is wrong with her. By discussing the problem with her husband, rationally, the couple may be better able to handle whatever changes do occur.

The second home remedy calls for you to engage in sexual relations even if you don't feel like it. Pressuring you to do something you don't want to do is not my style, but when it comes to sex, sometimes you need a gentle push. Hopefully, after hugging and cuddling with your husband in the buff, your sexual appetite will wake up. If you don't give yourself a chance, you're like Randy, who gave up on having sex with Jill because he couldn't have a psychogenic erection.

If this home remedy doesn't work the first time you try it, give it a few more chances. If this step still doesn't get your motor running, it's time to see a doctor.

The Viagra Dialogues

Science has been doing a good job of beating back old Father Time for the last few decades, but the sexual area was not impacted until recently. Then Pfizer came out with a little blue pill called Viagra, and the second sexual revolution of the century began (the first revolution being the advent of the Pill).

In addition to Viagra, I know of several other new drugs that are coming out on the market that aid men in obtaining and maintaining their erections.

Uprima, a drug marketed by a pharmaceutical company called TAP, works like Viagra and may help women as well.

These scientific breakthroughs are wonderful. Be it from advanced age or disease, why should men have to give up sexual intercourse? Other treatment options existed before these medications were introduced, but none of these remedies were very satisfactory. For example, a rod could be inserted in the penis. This process and others suffered from being complicated, expensive, and not always offering a pleasurable result.

Although taking a pill to get an erection is certainly a pleasing remedy for a man's sexual problems, you cannot assume that a pill is a cure-all for a couple's romance troubles. If he pops one of those pills and announces, "Honey, I took a pill, so take off your clothes and jump into bed," he is doing more harm than good. A couple needs to talk about how to integrate such pills into their love life to bring about sexual harmony. Then the pills can do wonders for their sex life.

As a society, it's going to take some time to integrate pills into our love relationships. No matter how this issue is studied and written about in the media, one overall game plan cannot be suggested. So many types of relationships exist that no one set of rules applies. Your doctors should not be giving you these pills without any instructions whatsoever. At the very least, your doctor should explain to you the impact that these pills may have on your relationship. In addition, you and your spouse need to discuss the bearing these pills may have on the frequency and timing of your sexual intercourse. If your relationship problems may be made worse by these pills, you and your wife may wish to consult with a sex therapist before beginning treatment.

Taking Viagra may present new problems to a couple with an established sexual routine. Some of the possible scenarios are as follows:

- The wife, who has not enjoyed sex for a few years, is happy that her husband can no longer perform.

- A couple's sexual problems stem from the relationship, not from the man's ability to achieve and maintain an erection.

- The husband is satisfied with having sex once a week, but now his wife is pressuring him to get a prescription and perform more frequently.

I don't want to paint a bleak picture. My point is that a pill that helps you obtain and keep an erection may introduce new problems in your relationship. These problems may be overcome with compromise or professional marriage counseling. I think that most couples will be able to integrate Viagra, or a similar drug, into their sex lives without too much difficulty. And the result could mean a rekindled romance.

Taking a Fresh Look at Your Romance

Enough with all the medical news. Let me switch gears and run through some of the good things that come with growing older. When you first started having sex, it was great. Then the natural result of sex came along — children — and sex may have taken a back seat. As your careers took off and your children became teenagers who stayed up late, sex may have tapered off even more.

Besides the physical changes that occur as you age, a number of other changes take place as well. For one, your children may go off to college or leave home to pursue other interests. Whether or not you missed the privacy you gave up when you had children, you should discover the joys of being able to walk around naked and have sex when the mood suits you.

You may start to slow down in your work life even before you retire. Some seniors find that they have accrued a considerable amount of vacation time over the years. Having seniority at your company may mean that you can extend your weekends. Or your seniority could mean you have fewer responsibilities and can get home at a reasonable hour. Extra time together definitely helps in rekindling your romance.

The new steps you need to perform before enjoying sex due to physical changes — playing with his penis, putting some lubricant in her vagina — may increase the intimacy between the two of you. Becoming closer is good for your sex life and your romance.

This time in your life represents a true crossroads for many couples. Some couples can't cope with the physical changes, and their marriages become sexless or their relationships don't survive. Others find ways to deepen their relationships because of the changes. You can choose the better direction when you approach that fork in the road, because you now know what physical changes to expect as you grow older.

Appreciating new sexual experiences

Sex is easy to take for granted when you are young. After all, when you are in your twenties, the orgasm you just had may be followed by another orgasm in an hour. As your sex life changes, you may find that you have a better appreciation for your sexual opportunities. Growing older means developing a maturity and a wisdom to appreciate life's pleasures — from watching a sunset to playing with grandchildren to enjoying sex.

Getting the most out of sex

You need to know how to make the best use of the sexual powers that remain vital as you age. Knowledge definitely helps you maximize the return you get from each sexual episode. Even if the opportunities occur less frequently, a little know-how may mean you'll be just as satisfied.

Seizing the (break of) day

Although a young couple may fancy having sex at any time, most couples tend to engage in sex at night. (For variety's sake, I encourage people to make love at different times.) But an older couple may find that morning sex is the most enjoyable.

Sex in the morning is more enjoyable for an older couple for two main reasons. The first reason is that they are well rested and energetic after a good night's sleep. Thus, they are better able to exert themselves. Older couples don't need to start having sex the moment they wake up. I recommend that the couple get out of bed, wash their faces, have a light breakfast, and then go back to bed and make love.

The second reason morning sex is more pleasurable for older couples is physiological. Testosterone, the male hormone, affects the man's ability to become aroused. This testosterone level goes up and down during the course of a day and is at its highest level in the morning. If a man has any trouble achieving an erection, morning sex makes it easier for him.

It's all in the timing

When both partners are easily aroused, it doesn't matter much who initiates sex, because soon both are fully stimulated. Older couples may find that they are both *not* easily aroused. For various reasons, an older couple may not always be in synch. A man may have an erection in the morning, but a woman may take several hours to warm up due to her arthritis. Until her swollen joints are warmed up, she may not be in the mood to have an orgasm.

Although fighting off the effects of age would be great, you may find that you sometimes have to accept the physical changes that occur over the years. The first compromise you may make to the aging process — which hits you usually in your 40s — is the need to use reading glasses. As the years advance, you have to adapt to all sorts of other aids and habits in order to make it through each day. Much the same way, you have to make some adaptations in your sex life.

An adaptation may mean that he wakes up on Monday morning feeling aroused, and so she helps him to get an erection and allows him to have intercourse. Then on Wednesday night, she's in the mood, so he caresses or licks her clitoris until she has an orgasm. At other times, they can kiss and cuddle — both knowing that it's not going to go any further than that. A schedule is far better than haggling over when to have sex together and winding up rarely having sex at all. You both have to be attuned to each other's needs and do your best to satisfy them.

Don't think of having scheduled sex — when partners are satisfied at different times — as being strange; think of it as being very intimate. If sex is more fulfilling when you have separate orgasms, don't allow "convention" to stop you. Do what is necessary to stay vital and sexually active. I think you will find that scheduled sex is worth the effort.

It's very important that each partner do his or her part with enthusiasm. If you act as if this schedule is a chore, you are taking away the pleasure from your partner. You shouldn't be counting orgasms. ("He asked me for an orgasm three times last week and I didn't get any.") You're not going to have desires at the same time. But if you give each other orgasms regularly, that is all that matters.

Sharing a slow and steady fire

Of course, sex is only one component of romance. You can't expect your spouse to give you an orgasm and ignore him or her the rest of the day. Finding other activities that bring you closer together like walking, dining, and reading to each other are essential. The process of rekindling your romance continues throughout the day.

The years bring on changes that require different approaches to keeping that romantic flame alive. For example, both partners are going to be sensitive about changes to their appearances. The physical changes may be subtle during the first few decades of the relationship and become more noticeable as the years add up. Gray hair, wrinkles, potbellies, loss of hair, and loss of muscle: All of these physical changes mean you have to assure each other that your love hasn't grown any dimmer because of the natural aging process. Give compliments to your partner and tell him how much you love him as often as you can; it's more important these days than ever.

Media misinformation

You may be aware that the lack of older people in the media affects how young people think of those of us over 50. But it may surprise you to learn that the image of senior citizens in the media also plays a role in your own thinking as well. I'm not going to try to con you into believing that a sign of aging, like age spots, is particularly attractive (or that Madison Avenue should be trying to sell products that create them). But age spots are a natural part of growing older. If you never see anyone on TV with them — except in commercials advertising products that remove them — you're going to find these spots even more unattractive. As an older adult, you have to make a special effort to use your love for your partner as a filter for sifting through what the media pronounces as beautiful or natural. Ignore those age spots or any other signs of growing older and relish each other as you are.

Tim and Harriet

Tim and Harriet, in their late sixties, were married for forty years. Harriet had put on some weight over the last decade. While Tim still loved her very much, he found that he wasn't attracted to her physically any more. His sexual urges had dwindled. Tim didn't want to leave his wife, but he had taken to masturbating while reading Playboy on the nights that she played cards with her friends. Harriet still had needs and she didn't want to masturbate; she wanted to make love with her husband.

Several things are going on here at the same time. I learned this because I interviewed each client separately, as I always do when I see couples. Although Tim was convinced that the change in his wife's appearance had reduced his appetite for sex, it was really his need for physical stimulation to obtain an erection that had made him turn to masturbation. The erotic images that he looked at helped the process but weren't the entire key to a solution. On the other hand, Harriet had sensed that something was wrong and decided that he no longer found her as appealing. As a result, she had become ashamed of her body and tried to keep it covered. Perhaps Tim would have at least started to feel aroused if he saw her naked, even if he did not get an erection. But Harriet had removed that stimulus from him.

Tim and Harriet need to start their love life over from scratch. They should develop new ways of making love that are much more deliberate and planned than in the past. By signaling their desire for each other with words and working together to help each other to orgasm, their sexual relationship can be re-ignited. I advised Tim to try fantasizing about one of those centerfolds when he has sex with his wife. I explained that fantasizing isn't cheating. In fact, the opposite is true, because thinking of centerfold models helps him to have sex with Harriet. I advised Tim not to tell his wife about these fantasies so that her feelings wouldn't be hurt.

This story illustrates the importance of communication. Growing older can be tough. Your body starts to undergo changes, but your mental outlook doesn't necessarily take the same steps. You still feel like the old you, but your body just won't respond the way it once did — and the way you'd like it to. You're not the only one who isn't sure of what is going on in your relationship. Your spouse is going through changes as well. Unless you explain to each other what is happening in your heads, you may end up veering off course and feeling isolated.

I understand the difficulty in admitting "my penis isn't working the way it once did," or "my vagina doesn't provide enough lubrication anymore." But if you don't talk about these subjects, you're likely to imagine other reasons for what is going on — which can cause even bigger problems. Swallow your pride and admit to your partner what is going on in your mind and with your body. If you talk it out, you can find workable solutions and continue to enjoy sex for a long, long time.

Part IV
Romancing Real Life

The 5th Wave   By Rich Tennant

"I couldn't find any rose petals, but I figured corn flakes make more sense in a milk bath anyway."

In this part . . .

Stress plays a huge role in the dampening of romance. Many couples respond to stress by turning against each other or living completely separate lives rather than depending on each other for support. This part identifies common stressors and reactions to them and offers suggestions for ways to work together to deal with life's pressures.

Chapter 13 shows you what to expect during pregnancy and immediately after birth so both new parents know how to help each other through a magical but very trying time. Chapter 14 details the challenges your romance may face with kids of any age in the house and suggest ways to carve out private time to ensure your romance survives childrearing. In Chapter 15, I discuss the emptiness many people face when the kids leave home and show you how to prevent that emptiness from rearing its ugly head in the first place.

Work consumes much of our time and energy, and Chapter 16 discusses how to carve time for romance out of your busy work schedules. For many couples, money is the source of bitter arguments, so Chapter 17 tackles the tough topic of how to approach financial decisions as a team and prevent them from undermining your relationship. Finally, Chapter 18 suggests ways to work through crisis situations with your romance intact, whether the two of you are coping with a chronic illness, the death of a loved one, or a natural disaster.

Chapter 13

Finding the Romance in Pregnancy

• •

In This Chapter

▶ Knowing what to expect with each trimester

▶ Adjusting your sex life

▶ Preparing for the stress of delivery

▶ Caring for each other after the birth

• •

*B*ecause pregnancy results from an act of love, the potential certainly exists for those nine months to be filled with romance. But having given birth to two children myself, I also know that you have to be realistic: There are times when a pregnant woman does not feel very romantically inclined at all.

While there are romantic pitfalls during pregnancy, if you know about them ahead of time, they're relatively easy to sidestep. This chapter fills you in on what to expect, so that when you look back on your pregnancy years later, you can recall it as a time of great romance.

Baby-Making Basics

The first thing you need to know is that pregnancy is a three-part event. (Four-part if you include the post-pregnancy period, which you must do if you're going to forge a stronger relationship from this experience.)

✔ In the first three months, the woman does not look very different, but she often feels tired and may have bouts of nausea.

✔ In the second trimester, she starts showing her new state of pregnancy and starts feeling better, possibly even euphoric.

✔ In the third trimester, she pretty much looks like the Goodyear Blimp, which can make her feel physically uncomfortable and have an impact on her emotional state as well.

Women have been undergoing this process since the beginning of time, so you should adopt a positive outlook about pregnancy. That outlook is an important first step in managing the emotional changes that occur. If you allow the physical and emotional changes that are taking place to overwhelm you, then there's no telling what the state of your relationship will be at the end of those nine months.

The first trimester

The first three months of pregnancy tend to go by quite quickly, especially because you may not even be aware that you are pregnant for the first month or more. But while you may walk around oblivious to the fact that you're pregnant for many weeks, odds are that you'll become quite aware of your new state when the nausea and tiredness kick in.

Sharing the news

The very first opportunity to make your pregnancy romantic occurs when you communicate the news to your partner. Timing is everything, and announcing the news at the wrong time, which could cause an unexpected reaction, can set you both off on the wrong foot. If you know that your partner is having a bad day at the office, don't announce your pregnancy the moment he steps through the door that night. Let him unwind, maybe give him a glass of wine, and make your announcement in a fun way. (Perhaps you can hint at it by stuffing a small pillow under your shirt and seeing if he notices.)

If you're not sure how you feel about being pregnant, then wait until your own thoughts have settled down before telling him. If he's usually home when you arrive at night, maybe you need to go to the park and gather yourself a bit before walking through your front door. Your life is not a movie with a script that has to be followed. Do things at your own pace so that you feel most comfortable.

Ernestine and Barry

Ernestine had always imagined that when she became pregnant, she and her husband would spend hours cuddling as they talked about the upcoming arrival of their baby. Her husband, Barry, had seemed excited when she first reported the news to him (which should not have come as a big surprise, because they had been trying to have a baby for six months). However, soon afterward he seemed to become totally cool to the idea. As far as Ernestine was concerned, she was not backing out of the pregnancy, so it concerned her greatly that the father of this child may not actually want it.

Ernestine expressed her concerns to Barry's sister, Becky, with whom she was very close. Becky took Barry out to lunch and asked him what was going on. He explained that Ernestine had seemed to change her mind about going back to work six weeks after the baby was born, and she had even talked about taking a whole year off. He was worried about being able to make ends meet. He hadn't discussed this with Ernestine because he didn't want to worry her, but he hadn't been able to disguise his concern.

Staying in touch

Whether or not your baby was planned, both of you are going to encounter bouts of self-doubt during the pregnancy, especially if this is your first child. Self-doubt is perfectly normal, because a child is going to bring a dramatic change to your lives. Practical issues need to be confronted, like how to live on one salary or find a good nanny or daycare provider when mom is ready to go back to work. You also have psychological issues, which present themselves as questions such as "Will I be a good parent?"

Rather than hide these doubts from each other, you must talk about them. If you're afraid of expressing this train of thought, then you're going to build a wall between the two of you. By sharing your emotions, you are able to give yourselves the support that can help carry you both through.

Sharing your doubts and fears is, believe it or not, romantic. If you close up like a clam, afraid that you may panic your partner by letting him or her know how you really feel for nine months, you may do a lot of damage to your relationship. Nine months is a long time to hold in your emotions, and it may not be any easier to speak up after the baby is born. To remain close, you must talk to each other about everything. There may be moments of elation and moments of fear, but as long as you share them all with each other, the end result will be a stronger relationship.

Negotiating nausea and fatigue

Don't be misled by the term *morning sickness,* because the hormones that launch the urge to worship the porcelain god can affect your body at almost any time of the day. Thankfully, most women don't suffer from morning sickness while they're sleeping. Scientists say that your body goes through this process of heaving back out almost everything that you put into your stomach (with the possibly exception of crackers) in order to protect the growing embryo from your predilection for eating foods that may cause it harm. If that's true, maybe we could get rid of the USDA and just let pregnant women decide what foods should make it to the grocery store shelves.

But as annoying as these bouts of nausea can be, they won't affect your relationship as much as the waves of fatigue that overcome her. Most women work these days, and few start their pregnancy leave during the first trimester.

That means that chances are you'll be saving whatever energy you can muster for pleasing your boss. You may not have very much energy left over for pleasing your man, who more often than not will see you with your head on a pillow.

Because most men don't pay attention to the effects of pregnancy before they become personally acquainted with this condition, many fathers-to-be are surprised by how tired their spouses become. Maybe your husband won't mind your constant state of unconsciousness (perhaps feeling that it will give him more time to watch sports without feeling guilty!), but he may miss having you around.

The most important thing the husband of a pregnant woman can do is to read a book on pregnancy. (I recommend *Dr. Ruth's Pregnancy Guide for Couples,* because that's the only one I know of that spends more than a paragraph on sex. My co-author and I, a gynecologist, go into the romantic aspects of pregnancy in great detail, and you can even find a new position named after the two of us!) Some men take the changes their wives go through personally. If your husband does this, he must become educated regarding the reasons you are acting the way you do. And reading about the positive changes that are likely to take place in the second trimester should give him the incentive to show some patience while you play the part of Sleeping Beauty for two months.

The second trimester

In the second trimester, your body starts to stabilize. The baby is growing inside of you, your belly is growing right along with it, and your emotional state strengthens also. I suppose this is nature's way of getting you to bond with this baby so that you're ready for the final (and more difficult) months of pregnancy.

Heating up

Many women feel very aroused during this trimester, some reporting that they have the strongest orgasms they've ever experienced. Perhaps this new sexual superwoman arises from feeling so fertile, the way nature intended you to be. Or maybe it's a new combination of hormones coursing through your bloodstream. Whatever the reason, definitely take advantage of it, and make love as often and as wantonly as possible.

Some men eagerly jump on board and go along for this highly sexed ride. But there are those men for whom your growing belly has a negative effect. Some are afraid that they may damage the baby with their penis. Others start to think of you as a mother, identify you with their mother, and get turned off.

The first group of scaredy-cats can be easily convinced of the error of their ways by giving them the facts. Your baby is well protected inside your womb, and the penis cannot do it any harm. As your belly grows, you may want to switch to other positions besides the missionary position, where he is resting on top of the womb, but that variety should only strengthen your sex life, not weaken it. For more information on what positions work best, see *Sex For Dummies,* 2nd Edition (IDG Books Worldwide, Inc.).

Reminding him of mother

If your man is exhibiting signs that your status as a mother inhibits him, you must nip that situation in the bud. If he feels this way now, with the baby still inside of you, what's going to happen to his libido when there's an actual child in your arms?

Chances are that he won't even be aware of the reason that he's turned off. All he knows is that when he looks at your pregnant body, his vision turns upside down: Instead of thinking WoW, he remembers MoM.

In most cases, all you have to do is talk this situation through. Let him know that you're still the same woman he married and was very attracted to, and don't be shy about it. Prance around naked. Put your arms around him. Touch him all over, especially "down there." If you become aware of his hesitation early enough, you can make him see that there is a clear difference between you and his image of a mother. By getting him excited and having sex, especially the wild sex you may be craving, you should be able to convince his subconscious that you're going to remain a red-hot momma, not turn into his mommy.

If for some reason you're not able to make him see your sexual side, then I suggest that the two of you go for counseling. Don't say to yourself, "He'll change once I'm no longer pregnant." Your baby is going to make you appear even more motherly, not less. And babies distract all couples from sex to some extent, which only gives him more excuses to avoid you.

If the months between sexual encounters begin to pile up, the process of rekindling your romance becomes even more difficult. And when the baby is around, finding opportunities to go for counseling can be difficult. While you're pregnant, the baby is perfectly portable and won't start crying in the middle of a session. So while you may be tempted to look at this as a temporary condition that can disappear on its own, I encourage you to be proactive about resolving it early.

Taking matters into your own hands

Some women get so turned on during this trimester that their men may not be able to keep up. If this happens to you, don't be afraid to masturbate at those times when sex is not available. This not only relieves the sexual tension but also helps to convince you that motherhood and sex do mix, something that you may have more difficulty believing when that baby makes its first appearance. If you don't masturbate, you may be tempted to get angry at your partner. What you have to remember is that his hormone levels aren't changing along with yours, so while he may be willing to increase the number of times the two of you have sex, that still may not be sufficient to satisfy your needs.

The third trimester

As you enter the third trimester, you can't hide that you are pregnant. You can only fit into maternity clothes, and even they may seem tight. Before you were ever pregnant, you may have worried about what you would look like when you hit this stage. But concern for your appearance quickly becomes displaced by the discomforts arising from having two people sharing one body.

Because this is not a book about pregnancy, I'm not going to enumerate all the various problems that you may face in your third trimester, except to the extent that they impact your romance. Overall, I do believe that this is a romantic period in a couple's life. You may not have sex as frequently as you do during the second trimester — perhaps you won't have intercourse at all. But by sharing in the wonder of having your baby moving and kicking around, as well as selecting names and going to Lamaze classes, you are sure to bond.

During the third trimester, the man has to pick up the slack. Many chores are no longer possible and others simply aren't comfortable for a very pregnant woman. While he may not view doing these chores as particularly romantic, she definitely does. Of course, if he's a boor and doesn't pitch in, his inaction can have the opposite effect.

Preparing for a changing sex life

Q. My wife is in her seventh month of pregnancy. We've been having sex up until now, but she just decided that she doesn't want to risk hurting the baby by having intercourse any more. I've read that we can't hurt the baby by having sex, and I even had her ask her doctor, who concurred, but she's still not willing to change her mind. She says she felt some contractions the last time we had intercourse and refuses to have sex until after the baby is born. She masturbates me, but it's not the same. What can I do to get her to listen to reason?

A. Some women do experience contractions as a result of having intercourse, and we don't know exactly why this happens. One theory is that when a woman has an orgasm, she experiences a variety of contractions in addition to the ones in her genitals; for example her toes may curl. The uterus may be contracting as a result. It's also known that substances called *prostaglandins* in the ejaculate can trigger contractions, though we don't know if there is enough of this substance in a man's ejaculate to actually make this occur.

My first suggestion is to ask your wife if she will agree to have intercourse in a manner that would resolve these two aspects of sex that could lead to contractions: You would wear a condom, and she would not have an orgasm. Ask her whether she would be willing to try this once to see what happens. If she refuses, you musn't put any more pressure on her. As long as she is giving you satisfaction through masturbation, you just have to accept the situation as it stands. Being pregnant is not easy, and by showing your concern for her feelings, you are helping to cement your relationship for the future.

Your sex life undoubtedly changes as the pregnancy advances. If having intercourse in the missionary (male superior) position doesn't become impossible during the second trimester, it most definitely does in the third. Some couples fear that having vaginal intercourse may endanger the baby in some way. Some women find that sex triggers some contractions, called *braxton hicks contractions*. But if your baby is not ready to be born, these contractions won't start labor, so there really is no danger from engaging in intercourse using other positions. Side-by-side, rear entry, and even female superior positions may work for you.

But just because intercourse may be safe does not mean that it must take place during the final months of pregnancy. Intercourse should be pleasurable, and if one of you is very much in fear of causing labor to begin early, that can certainly remove any pleasure from the experience. In fact, it could make intercourse terrifying. You never want to color sex with such negative characteristics, which can carry over even after the baby is born. It's better to postpone intercourse and satisfy each other in other ways.

Keeping abreast of your changing body

Whether or not you decide to breast feed, during the latter stages of your pregnancy your breasts are going to be a lot bigger than they've ever been. Your new breasts are definitely going to attract the attention of your husband. The only problem is that all this swelling is likely to also make your breasts tender, so that the last thing you want are his ministrations towards them. This can be a source of conflict.

To avoid this, make sure that you prepare him for the worst. Tell your husband as soon as you start noticing increased sensitivity that your breasts may soon be off limits. If he doesn't get his hopes up, it's easier for him to contain his frustration at this situation. You may also find that you can satisfy both your circumstances. If he can learn to be very gentle, you can allow him to cup them, look at them, and maybe kiss them gently, which can give him satisfaction without causing you any added discomfort.

Overcoming shyness

Some women don't like helping their partners achieve sexual satisfaction if they aren't making love as a couple. During pregnancy, you need to overcome that hesitation. You have a long period of time when you either cannot or won't want to have intercourse, but your husband still needs sexual satisfaction.

The good news is that pregnant women tend not to be as shy as they were before they became pregnant. In the delivery room, you're naked with your legs spread open in stirrups as all sorts of people wander in and out of the room. Believe me when I tell you that you don't care. Part of that bravado comes from the very strong need to rid yourself of the internal pressures caused by having what is by now a very large baby inside of you. But part of it also comes from feeling a little like a fertility goddess. It's not that

you want to flaunt your body, but suddenly all those parts that previously only had a sexual purpose, like your breasts and genitals, now serve a very utilitarian purpose.

Chances are good that you may start to feel this way before you actually give birth. So when I advise you to let your husband have sex with you or to masturbate him, you may feel much more open to this during the last few weeks as you approach your due date. You may experience moments when you're tired of the whole deal and very cranky, but you may also have times when you feel absolutely in awe of what is happening and more in control of your life. When you experience the high that comes from bringing life into the world, you may find yourself more inclined to want to give special pleasure to the person who helped create it.

Avoiding hubby neglect

With all the distractions that come from having a baby moving inside of you, you may be one of those women who just doesn't feel the need to have an orgasm during the late stages of pregnancy. If that's the case, you shouldn't feel badly about it, but that doesn't necessarily give you the right to ignore your husband's sexual needs.

Keep in mind that the two of you will not have intercourse during the first six weeks or so after the baby is born. If you also don't have sex for a month or two before the birth, that is a long period of enforced celibacy. It won't kill your husband to live without intercourse, and he can masturbate to relieve the sexual tension, but it would be better for your relationship not to spend such a long time without being physically intimate. I suggest that even if you do not feel like having an orgasm, you should either allow him to have intercourse in a comfortable position, masturbate him, or perform oral sex.

Making the Birthing Process Romantic

Most delivery rooms are sterile-looking places because, in fact, they have to be germ-free. But that doesn't mean that you can't do something to enhance the atmosphere while you're delivering your baby. You won't be allowed to light candles in a hospital, but you can tape some photos to the wall, bring a boom box to play some background music, and even spray a favorite scent into the air. By placing your mark on your surroundings, both of you feel more in control of the situation. While the delivery room may never be what you would call a romantic setting, you can enhance the romantic aura with a little preplanning.

Playing it safe

In the attempt to create a greater sense of intimacy during the birthing process, some couples choose to have their babies at home. I need to pull out my soapbox for a moment and come down rather heavily against this decision. Because of my profession, I know a lot of gynecologists, and I have heard a lot of horror stories.

If something does go wrong during the birthing process — and it can — you want to be as close to an operating room as possible. If you can be quickly wheeled into the operating room, most of the time doctors can right whatever goes wrong. But if you have to wait for an ambulance and then drive to the hospital, it may be too late.

So by all means try to make the birthing procedure as natural and romantic as you can, but don't go overboard by placing both you and the baby in jeopardy. Certainly, billions of babies have been born under primitive situations in human history, but millions of mothers and babies have also died under those conditions. Please don't take such a needless risk.

Because many couples would prefer a more homey setting, some hospitals do have labor rooms that are decorated to look just like a bedroom. Of course if an emergency develops, the operating room is just around the corner, so they offer the comforts of a home delivery with the safety of a hospital. If you want this type of experience, see whether your doctor is affiliated with a hospital that has such rooms. Be forewarned that even if this is a possibility, if a lot of mothers give birth on the same day, you may end up in a normal delivery room in any case.

Enduring labor day

You can't predict how long labor will last. Some women give birth in a few hours; others take a few days. The longer the process takes, the more uncomfortable you are going to be. And as the hours of discomfort continue to mount up, you're going to become crankier, also. You can't take your frustration and pain out on your doctor or the nurses, so who's likely to bear the brunt? Your husband.

To lessen the impact this stressful time can have on your relationship, you have to talk about what to expect ahead of time. If you're both aware that labor may be long, grueling, and tense, he'll have an easier time shrugging off your bad mood, and you'll be more likely to recognize the cause of your griping and apologize before doing it again.

One of the reasons this can be such a frustrating experience for both partners is that most men are natural fixer-uppers. If you tell a man there's a problem, chances are that he's going to look for a solution. But in this case, there's nothing he can do other than to give you some ice chips and tell you to breathe properly. When you scream at him "Make this stop!" he's going to want to do exactly that, even though you are only venting your own frustrations. And if this behavior has been going on for hours, you're both going to be tired and your tempers will fray.

In the "good old days," men were left to pace in the waiting room, and such interaction between husband and wife didn't occur. Prior to that, husbands waited outside the house while midwives ministered to their wives. While I think it's great that the father-to-be is now the birthing coach, you mustn't forget that right after the delivery you go back to being husband and wife, so do your best to forgive and forget.

Postpartum Romance

To be honest with you, the postpartum period is not going to be immediately filled with romance. In the first place, you are going to feel a certain amount of discomfort from having given birth. You're going to be tired, need rest, and have a newborn on your hands doing his or her best to keep you sleep-deprived. Plus, you've heard about those infamous postpartum blues.

Beating the blues

I don't say that postpartum blues don't exist. In fact, I know that some women are not just blue but actually clinically depressed after giving birth. For those women, professional help may be necessary.

But for women who are not clinically depressed — who perhaps feel lethargic or even a little lonely after having given birth — my philosophy is not to let such feelings overcome your natural enthusiasm. If you give in to the blues, or any emotional letdown you encounter in your life, it only seems worse. If, instead, after five minutes of feeling sad you say to yourself "Enough!," put your baby in the carriage, and go for a walk, I guarantee you'll feel better. So don't allow any expectations of being blue to become a reality. Fight back against the blues by being active.

Here are some practical things you can do to beat the blues:

- ✔ Invite some friends over for tea.

- ✔ Go for a massage.

- ✔ Take a yoga class.

- ✔ Join a new mother's group.

For fathers: Practicing patience

And what about all you new fathers out there? What is your role? You get to play knight in shining armor, protecting your wife from the onslaught of family and friends who want to see the new baby. Your wife needs to rest, and somebody has to be the bad guy. You're elected!

But apart from that, the weeks immediately after birth are not going to be easy for you. Even if your wife takes up most of the burden of nighttime feedings because she's breast-feeding, you will be awakened during the night as well, which may cut down on your efficiency at work. And in addition to being tired, new mothers are very focused on their babies. Intercourse is off-limits for at least six weeks until the new mother heals, so the father takes on an auxiliary role, which can be difficult to accept. I'm not saying that you're not going to love your baby completely, but you may feel some jealousy as the baby hogs center stage for such a long period.

What you need during this period is patience, and lots of it. Don't hesitate to masturbate if you're feeling sexually frustrated; you don't need any added reasons to be stressed out. And most of all, do all you can to set the stage for romance to blossom once again. Fathers these days are a lot more involved in taking care of the baby than ever before, and that's great. But just as a new mother may ignore her husband because of the baby, you may end up doing the same thing. It's going to take a while (like two decades), but that baby is eventually going to grow up and leave the nest. The two of you want to have as strong a relationship as possible during those years and the years that follow. If a small rift opens up between you, over time it can grow into a deep valley. So use the power of romance to make certain this doesn't happen.

What, specifically, can you do during the weeks immediately after the birth?

- ✔ **Take paternity leave.** If your company allows you to, take some time off after the birth of your baby. If that option is not available, try to arrange to leave the office early at least one or two days each week.

- ✔ **Let your wife escape once in a while.** Make an appointment for your wife to go to the beauty parlor, and take care of the baby while she's there.

✔ **Schedule a quiet dinner out.** If you can find a babysitter you trust (perhaps a relative or very close friend), go out for a long, quiet dinner.

✔ **Have a romantic dinner at home.** If you can't find a babysitter you trust to handle a newborn, then order in some nice food, set the table with your good china, light a candle, and have a romantic dinner. If the baby interrupts, put the dinner on hold until he or she is back asleep.

✔ **Bring home some fresh flowers.**

✔ **Encourage your wife to go for walks.** The exercise can lift her spirits, and the baby will probably sleep while in the carriage, so the two of you can spend some time talking and being intimate.

✔ **Make a point of calling her several times a day.** Don't just ask how the baby's doing, but check on her spirits.

✔ **Take charge of the housekeeping.** Chances are that she's going to be worried about it, and by handling it yourself, you can ease this concern. If you're too busy to do it all, then perhaps you could hire a housekeeper, even for just a few hours a week.

✔ **Take over the baby's night feeding.** If your wife is nursing, have her express some milk so that you can feed the baby at night occasionally. One good night's rest will do wonders for the new mother.

Chapter 14

Managing Romance with Parenthood: From Infants to Teens

*A*t some point little babies begin to sleep through the night, new moms heal, and your sex lives are supposed to return to normal. Notice that I said *supposed*. In most cases you do resume your normal sex life but you may find that it's not as easy as it sounds, particularly after having your first child. A new mom's body has just gone through some significant changes, both parents are tired and possibly feeling stressed, and distractions are plentiful.

If you're lucky enough to re-ignite your romance after giving birth, you may still encounter some challenges as your little ones grow up. Maintaining some privacy for the two of you when you share your house with kids isn't easy. In addition, many parents struggle with showing their affection for each other when they have an audience.

In this chapter, I show you how to keep the home fires burning from the day you bring junior home from the hospital until the day his little sister heads off to college.

Nestling with a Newborn

For the first six weeks after your baby is born, don't expect to have sexual intercourse. Doctors recommend a waiting period of six weeks for two reasons. The first reason is obvious: A new mom's genitalia needs physical recovery time before she feels comfortable having intercourse. The second reason relates to a new mom's overall state of mental health. Doctors know that mental fatigue is as important an issue as the physical recovery from childbirth. The result: Most new moms simply don't have the physical or mental desire for sexual intercourse during these first six weeks.

When I was writing *Dr. Ruth's Pregnancy Guide for Couples,* I interviewed a midwife with years of experience counseling new mothers. Her advice to these women was to not let those first few months with their babies get them down. She told these new moms not to believe all the rumors about how tired they would be and how much work was involved in taking care of a newborn. Then she had her first child, and she sang a different tune. This midwife couldn't believe how totally exhausted she felt or how much time and energy her little bundle of joy required.

Of course, each child is different. My co-author's second child, Gabrielle, slept through the night from day one (which was handy because his wife was still in law school). But many babies wake up several times a night and in turn wake up their mothers; the sleep deprivation causes new mothers to feel like limp rags.

And babies do more than sap a woman's physical strength. A new mother may become so attached to her child that the flood of emotions leaves little or no room for her libido to function properly. Most women find that a six-week break from sex is necessary; the time enables new mothers to prepare themselves emotionally to reconnect with their husbands in the most intimate way.

Honing in on hormones

Many women assume that their hormones, which go on a roller-coaster ride during and immediately after pregnancy, are to blame for their lagging libidos. Hormones do play a role in some women's lack of desire. However, most women respond to behavioral treatment for libido problems after pregnancy. For this reason, I don't think hormones should be blamed for most instances of low libidos.

I'm not saying that hormonal problems never occur; they do. I just don't want any woman assuming that she's going to have difficulties becoming aroused after childbirth because of the natural changes her body goes through. Instead, I'd like to see every woman try to restore her libido naturally. If, after following the advice in this chapter, a woman really can't become aroused, she should consult a doctor.

Raring to go

I don't want to create a self-fulfilling prophecy, so let me say very clearly that the vast majority of new mothers do restart their sex lives without any difficulties. A woman may be chomping at the bit before her doctor gives her the okay to proceed. If you're feeling strong sexual urges several weeks after birth, you shouldn't hesitate to bring this up with your doctor. If you had a caesarian, for example, your genitalia were not affected by the birth. If the wounds from the C-section are well on their way to being healed, you may receive your doctor's approval to have intercourse. And some people heal faster than others, so some mothers who have vaginal births may also start making love before the recommended six-week wait elapses.

Although the six-week waiting period is a good rule to follow, doctors pad this period slightly so that women don't feel pressure to have sex while they are exhausted and dealing with so many changes. Your doctor's intention may be good, but if you don't feel you need the full six weeks to recover, schedule an appointment for an early examination. On the other hand, if your genitals heal but you're still exhausted, use the six-week waiting period to your advantage. Six weeks without sex never killed anybody and the break may give you the rest you need.

Stretching Out the Celibacy

Let's say the six-week period is up and you still don't feel like making love with your husband. What's the next step? Can you stretch it out to seven or eight weeks? And what are the consequences if you do? I'm going to assume that you are physically healed. Obviously if you're not, intercourse is going to be out of the question until the doctor gives you the all clear.

Remember that intercourse isn't the only way of satisfying each other. Even before the six-week mark, you can masturbate or give oral sex to each other. Many new mothers choose not to partake in oral sex because they need time for some psychic healing as well. A new mom may focus so intently on her newborn that she doesn't think about sex; this natural consequence is generally accepted by the new mother's partner. But to stretch the celibacy much beyond the six-week mark can become unhealthy.

Your relationship with your partner should differ from your relationship with your children, and these relationships can't substitute for each other. Adding sex to your new mother lifestyle may seem difficult, but it's necessary. The long-run effects of neglecting your sex life may be dangerous to your relationship with all your family members. On the other hand, you do not have to have an orgasm in order to have a good sexual experience. So if you do have sex and don't have an orgasm, but you feel satisfied with the overall lovemaking experience, don't give it a second thought. This shouldn't continue *ad infinitum;* if it occurs for a week or two, then you needn't be concerned.

Building up steam

Perhaps you didn't think much about your husband's sexual needs during the last months of your pregnancy and immediately after the birth. You were probably too uncomfortable to have sex at the end of your pregnancy and too tired after giving birth. But while you suffered through those last difficult days before giving birth, your partner was perfectly healthy and continued to have the same perfectly healthy sexual responses. He had erections and thoughts about sex and maybe even experienced a case of blue balls (which occurs when a man has not had any sexual release for a while and an actual pain develops in his testicles).

Did he just suffer in silence during this time? Some men do. Some men have *wet dreams* — they have orgasms while they sleep; orgasms that are not in their control. And many other men turn to masturbation.

Some couples are open about such matters, and some men even masturbate in front of their wives. But in most cases, a man masturbates out of view, particularly if a baby is in the house and he uses some erotic materials to help the process along. Although he shouldn't feel guilty about masturbating while his sex partner is out of commission, most men try to keep this activity private. If his wife doesn't get back into the swing of things within a reasonable amount of time, he may begin to rely on masturbation so much that he may not really care if their sex life ever resumes (especially if he gets hooked on the erotica he uses).

Giving in to temptation

Another possibility is that he turns to someone else for sexual release. Maybe a woman at his office has been flirting with him for years and he has resisted her temptations, but now he hasn't had any sexual release in weeks — even months. On top of that, he's angry at his wife because she doesn't seem to want to start up their sex life again. The possibility exists that he may turn to another woman for both sexual release and revenge.

My purpose is not to underestimate your husband's character or to scare you into resuming your sex life. Fear is never a good motivator. My presumption is that you loved each other and had a good sex life before that baby was born. I can't give any reason why those conditions shouldn't prevail once again after the birth. But if a new mother becomes lazy about sex — if she chooses what seems like the path of least resistance — she must be aware of the potential serious consequences.

Coping with His Turnoffs

Certainly, the woman is not the only partner at fault if a couple's sex life fizzles after the birth of a baby. While she may be willing and able to resume intercourse at or before the six-week mark, he may be resistant.

Reminding him of dear old mom

Just as the husband of a pregnant woman may start to think of his wife as too "motherly" to be a sex object (see Chapter 13), so may a new father share that vision of his wife after she gives birth. The sight of a baby in his wife's arms may make him think of his own mother and repress any sexual feelings he has for his wife.

Sweating about finances

Some new fathers look at their helpless infants and start to worry about supporting these little ones. New fathers see money flying out the window in the form of baby carriages, playpens, and disposable diapers. These men ponder future expenses (especially college), start to calculate how much money their wives *aren't* earning right now, and begin to get very anxious. If the new mom begins saying things like "Maybe I won't go back to work" or "I can't leave this baby with a nanny after only three months," he really starts to sweat.

Many men who worry about their abilities to provide for their families wind up with diminished libidos. I sometimes see cases of reduced libidos in men who lose their jobs; new babies may provoke similar reactions.

Sporting a new physique

Some men assume that their wives get their girlish figures back the minute the baby and its assorted accoutrements slide out of the birth canal. When weeks pass and her tummy is still expanded, her breasts are still swollen, and those extra pounds are still clinging to her thighs and arms, he may have problems getting turned on. No woman can make those pounds disappear instantaneously, but she can begin taking positive steps towards getting back in shape almost immediately after the birth. The results of her fitness regime may not be immediately recorded by her bathroom scale, but letting her spouse know that she's not intending to remain this size forever may give him a psychological lift.

Reconnecting at Every Level

A young couple may really be thrown by the number of environmental changes that come with the arrival of their newborn. The stress isn't conducive to restoring good sexual functioning; the two parents may begin to drift away from each other outside the bedroom as well. The husband, who goes off to work each day, sometimes can't believe that his wife can't handle taking care of such a tiny creature. He may resent coming home and never finding dinner on the table or never finding a freshly ironed shirt when he needs to get dressed. The new mom may be jealous of her husband, who gets to leave the baby every day. She can love her child completely, but the constant attention her baby requires frays her nerves.

Bernie and Laura

Bernie was ecstatic with his new little boy, and every night he rushed home from work in order to spend as much time with his son as possible. Like any newborn, little Jeremy woke up several times a night in order to be nursed, so both parents were always fatigued. Laura's mother spent the first two weeks after her grandchild's birth sleeping on Laura and Bernie's sofa. Bernie didn't mind the intrusion because he knew that Laura needed the help. He pitched in more after his mother-in-law left, but so much work was left to do. He assumed that Laura stayed home from work to do most of the shopping, cooking, and cleaning, but Laura never seemed to have enough time to complete all the tasks necessary for their household to run smoothly.

At first Bernie looked forward to the weekends; then these two days began not to live up to his expectations. First, the baby made sure that catching up on the sleep he missed during the week wasn't on the agenda. And the visiting hordes needed attention. His parents and siblings, Laura's family, and assorted friends constantly dropped by to see the baby — Bernie hosted as well as cooked and bottle-washed. During these weekends, Bernie began to long for the peace and quiet of the office.

Five weeks after Jeremy came home, Bernie was asked to go on a short business trip. He wanted to say yes; the trip would mean a couple of nights of undisturbed sleep. When he asked Laura, who'd been suffering from a mild case of the blues, she burst into tears. He begged off from the assignment, a move that didn't do wonders for his career.

One day when Jeremy started crying, Bernie screamed at him. He knew his screaming wouldn't do his son any good, but Bernie's frustrations at being a new father had gotten the better of him.

The first piece of advice I give new parents in need of rekindling their romances is to get out of the house and away from that baby, even if it's only for a few hours. If your family members or close friends agree to take the baby off of your hands for a bit, take advantage of their offers. Because your home has all the equipment, your sitter may prefer to come to your house to handle this assignment. That situation shouldn't spoil your plans. You may begin your rekindling by going for a cup of coffee at a quiet cafe. Hopefully, your conversation over a cup of joe leads to the need to move to a more private location; most motels don't require reservations. You don't need to tell anyone where you're going — you can leave your cell phone number or an emergency number where you may be reached without giving the name of the motel.

Taking a day away

You did it — arranged for a sitter, checked into a motel, and placed your cell phone on the nightstand. Now, the two of you need to connect emotionally, the way you connected before parenthood descended upon you. So, here's the first rule for the time you spend away from home: No talking about the baby. You see, the two of you need to start the process of rekindling that romance of yours and in order to make any progress, you need to talk about something besides the teeny tyke. If this session is to reinitiate your sex life, you need to compress the entire courtship procedure into a few hours. Even if the husband is ready for sex the second he closes the motel room door, the wife often needs some tender loving care before her arousal kicks in.

Fostering foreplay

Remember what I say about foreplay: It's not just touching a woman here and there for a few seconds. Foreplay may start as early as the afterplay of the last lovemaking session. But if that last session was two months ago, the effect is not going to be very potent. In order to make a new mother focus on her own sexuality, her husband has to nurture her lovingly.

Expect to spend the first hour cuddling, stroking, kissing, and listening to her. If she's really at the end of her rope, she may even have a crying jag or two, so bring some tissues with you. She may need to let a lot of emotions flow out of her until there is room for her libido to blossom. But even during these emotional moments, keep the focus away from the baby as much as possible; encourage her to consider herself and what she's feeling instead of considering the baby during this time. Assure her that it's okay for her to say she's frustrated and tired and depressed and edgy. What she shouldn't do is go through a litany of what the baby did to make her feel that way.

Preventing another pregnancy

I'm assuming that with all that you're going through with this newborn, you're not ready to have another one in nine months. If that's true, you can't assume that your first act of intercourse after birth is safe. Your menstrual cycle may not have begun yet, but remember, the menstrual flow occurs *after* you release your monthly egg. So no signal tells you whether or not you are fertile. The only way you know that you are ready to make a baby is when you have sex and become pregnant again.

Nursing generally delays the onset of a new mother's menstrual cycle, but that delay is not guaranteed, and nursing doesn't delay menstruation for as long as you are nursing.

The significance of all this information is obvious: If you don't want to make another baby, use a contraceptive. You need to visit your doctor for an examination in order to get the all clear to have intercourse; ask your doctor which contraceptive is the best for you at this moment, particularly if you are nursing.

After all that venting, she may not feel turned on. She may truly enjoy the time you spend together but still not want to have an orgasm. I recommend that she try to make love, but of course she must not be forced into it.

Bring some lubricant to this encounter. If she's not aroused, lubricant helps make intercourse comfortable. And even if she is excited and does lubricate naturally, her genitals are still recuperating so you want to make sure that the area is extra slippery to avoid any possibility of pain.

Once the lovemaking begins, her libido may awaken and she may get very involved. But even if she only becomes somewhat aroused, that arousal is an important first step toward feeling sexual.

Basking in the afterglow

Afterplay is always important and especially important after your first lovemaking session since the baby was born. Whether or not your wife has an orgasm, chances are good that she feels very emotional. She requires as much tenderness as you can offer, so don't hold back. I know that after a few hours away you both may start to worry about the baby — rushing at this time is a big mistake. Assume that because your sitter hasn't called your emergency number or cell phone that the baby is perfectly okay. Bask in that afterglow for as long as possible.

Learning to become orgasmic again

If everything goes perfectly in that motel room, you have intercourse and you both have orgasms. You jumped that hurdle. Now you're ready to resume your love life on the home front.

But what if our new mom didn't have an orgasm? She may feel quite content with making love without getting turned on, but that feeling can't last forever. If she was orgasmic before the baby, she needs to regain that ability after she gives birth. If she doesn't, both parties feel frustration.

If a woman has orgasms before she has a baby, any difficulty achieving orgasm after giving birth is probably not due to a physical problem. Chances are good that she's not allowing herself to have an orgasm.

Letting arguments prevent orgasms

One potential psychological cause for her inability to achieve orgasm may be due to some issues that the two of you need to deal with as a couple. For example, the new mother wants to go back to work. She is worrying that she can't get her old job back or that her skills are losing their value in the mar-ketplace. As rewarding as being home with her child is, she also craves being around adults. But her husband balks. He decides that she should raise their child, not a nanny. The couple argues about this issue for several months and she resents his attitude.

The new parents may have argued from time to time before the arrival of their baby and these arguments didn't stop them from having orgasms. But now, all the changes in their lives make achieving orgasms difficult. A running argument may be enough to prevent either parent from becoming aroused.

Some disagreements can easily be resolved. If he needs to do more work around the house, the couple should be able to work out an agreement. But if the couple philosophically debates about childcare, they can't expect to resolve this issue instantaneously. The couple also doesn't want the disagree-ment to continue to get in the way of their relationship.

Devoting a weekend to reconnecting

New parents may need to spend an entire weekend developing the closeness needed in order for her to become orgasmic once again. Of course, if the couple spends the entire weekend arguing, they're not going to ignite roman-tic feelings. My advice is to call a truce. Agreeing to a truce doesn't mean that either party has changed their minds, only that for this short period of time they're going to talk about other subjects.

Plan some activities for the weekend that enable the two of you to discuss other topics of conversation. For example:

- **Attend a play or see a movie.** Pick one that has got some intellectual content and is not pure fluff.

- **Visit an art museum.** Peruse your local museum and choose your favorite artist; later, you may decide to pick up a book about the artist so you may relive the experience at home.

- ✔ **Take in a lecture.** Pick an interesting topic that you both can enjoy.

- ✔ **Visit car dealers.** Test drive that new car you both have your eyes on.

- ✔ **Read a book on nutrition.** A new baby may leave little time for planning nutritious meals; see if the two of you can devise a new diet that is healthy and appealing.

- ✔ **Skim through magazines on redecorating.** You completed the nursery together and this activity sparked your desires to work on another room in your home as a team; pick out some new color schemes, fabrics, and furniture for your dream room.

You get the idea.

I'm not suggesting that you spend an entire weekend in bed. Quite the contrary, I want you to go out and stimulate yourselves in all sorts of other ways before you dive into the sack. Be very clear about this before you head out the door. If he expects one long romp in the hay, he's not going to be in the proper mood for strolling among some statues of naked people and studying the artistry in their forms. For true romance to bloom, you need to become reacquainted with yourselves. Only then can your sex lives be equally satisfying to both of you.

Seeking medical help

Although most women respond to the behavioral techniques I suggest in this chapter, some don't. I'm not a medical doctor, so I'm not going to discuss the subject of hormone imbalances in detail. If a woman's lack of arousal continues despite her best efforts, she should explain the situation to her doctor. After undergoing some tests, she may find out whether she has a physical problem or not.

If her libido problem is physical, the doctor should be able to help correct it. If the tests don't indicate any physical problem, the couple should consult a sex therapist. Sex is an important ingredient for holding a couple together, and she shouldn't let her lack of desire go untreated.

Resuming Your Romance at Home

After you devote a day, a weekend, or however much time is necessary to ensure that both of you are able to truly enjoy intercourse again, you're ready to turn your attention to making your home life as romantic as possible.

Making love with a crib in sight

For at least the first few months after the birth of your child, your baby may sleep in a crib in your room. Does making love in the same room cause any psychological damage to your child? Absolutely not. Having your child in your room may intimidate you somewhat, but at this stage the baby is not going to understand or care what is going on, especially if he or she is sleeping.

If having the baby in the room bothers you a great deal, you must make a choice between carrying that crib elsewhere or making love in other parts of the house. Whatever you do, don't use the child's presence as an excuse to skip making love. That child is going to be living under your roof for the next 20 years or more; you must figure out how to have sex during this time. Figure out how to enjoy your sex life now that you're a family.

Establishing a solid routine

I realize that you can't go to a motel each time you want to make love, so you need to adapt to having sex at home. By six weeks, most babies fall into some sort of eating and sleeping routine. If that routine doesn't occur naturally, I suggest you try to impose one.

Parents who allow their children to stay up till all hours of the night are making a big mistake. The longer they permit their babies to stay up late, the harder this pattern is to alter. Eventually, these children begin school and must wake up at a scheduled time. Parents' laxity about enforcing a bedtime makes the transition much more difficult than it needs to be.

Let me get back to the new parents and the impact the baby has on their relationship. The two of you need time to be together as a couple. You need to develop your baby's sleeping and eating routine in order to avoid interruptions at all hours of the night. I'm not writing a parenting book, but if you want your romance to maintain any sparks, set aside time for sexual relations. For new parents, that means working to put your babies to bed at reasonable hours.

> **Q.** My husband almost never comes home from work before 8 p.m. That hour is when I like to put our two-year-old son to bed, but my husband wants to play with him a bit after he gets home. Of course, they horse around and that activity gets our son all excited. When I finally put him in his crib at 9, my son's too worked up to fall asleep. Most nights he ends up screaming until I retrieve him and I start the process of putting him back to bed again. This routine leaves us no time for romance. How do I change this situation?

A. I suggest that Dad change his routine. He can roughhouse with his son when he first comes home; then he should start a tradition of reading his son a bedtime story. Story time may help your son switch gears. Your son should be in his crib before the story starts; you can try to create a lighting situation that allows enough light for your husband to read while being dim enough for your son to sleep. If you establish this routine, your son can learn to fall asleep at an early hour and the two of you can share some time alone.

Locking the bedroom door

When people think of sexual aids, they generally think of vibrators, dildos, and the like. But for parents of small children, the number one sexual enhancement device is a little hook-and-eye lock for the bedroom door. (I don't own shares in a hook-and-eye company. I only mention these locks because they're the cheapest to buy and simplest to install. Any other locking mechanism that effectively keeps children from entering your room during an awkward time is fine.)

I receive many letters from parents asking me what to say to their children who barge in on them while they are making love. If these parents had locks on their bedroom doors (and used them), they wouldn't need to ask this question.

But the child's reaction isn't the real concern in this situation. In most cases, a child isn't affected a great deal when this interruption occurs. (See the sidebar "Noises of the night" for an exception.) However, you may start to worry about the possibility of a surprise visit, and this worrying may negatively affect your sex life. You shouldn't have to listen intently for sounds outside the door while making love. This distraction is definitely going to inhibit your sexual enjoyment. So each and every time you make love, you must lock your door.

Some parents refuse to accept this advice. These parents are afraid that their child may cry out to them and they won't hear the cry if their door is shut. I believe this fear may be unfounded. Unless you live in a very large house, you're going to hear a crying child even through a closed door. And, you may consider the option of using a baby monitor — turned to low — in order to relieve your anxiety.

An alternative to a lock is a chain. A chain permits you to leave your bedroom door ajar so that you can hear any cries and avoid any unwelcome visitors. Your friends and relatives may find a chain lock on your bedroom door odd, but if you're comfortable with this solution, ignore these folks and install one.

Noises of the night

Most children I know could sleep through a freight train rumbling through their rooms. Occasionally a child wakes up on his or her own, perhaps from a nightmare, and if the timing is right, the child may hear the two of you doing the wild thing.

The sounds two people make while engaging in sex are not what children might expect from an act called *making love*. Based on the noises alone, a child may think his father is hurting his mother. At the very least, these noises are going to be confusing. If the child says something about having heard you, you must explain that what was happening was pleasurable. Your child doesn't need to fully understand; he or she just needs to be comforted that mom and dad aren't doing any physical harm to each other.

If you are worried about what the children may think if they hear you, turn on the radio in your room. You don't have to put it on so loud that it covers the sounds you make (because that noise may actually wake them). But if the radio is on, it gives you an opportunity to say, "Oh, you must have heard the radio."

Showing Affection

How you react to sexual matters is largely influenced by the society in which you live. In some societies, members of a tribe all live in one large communal house, and having sex in private is just not an issue. Are children brought up in such an environment psychologically damaged? You may say just the opposite: Viewing sex between adults as a perfectly normal act is actually healthier than being raised in an environment where you are denied the opportunity to view any human physical interactions.

You probably were not raised in such an openly sexual environment. The inhibitions you inherit may be unavoidable, but their effects may be mitigated.

Part of you may want to hide all your sexual feelings from your children, but such a sterile environment isn't good for you or them. The more inhibited you behave as they grow up, the more likely that your children will feel inhibited as adults. Although some sense of modesty is important, too much may limit the joy and pleasure that comes from sharing love. You may prefer that your children don't come barging in on you while you are making love, but you should let them see that the two of you love one another. That means the two of you should kiss, hug, and hold hands in front of the children. You probably already exhibit these signs of affection toward your children; therefore, your kids know that these are signs of love. Why shouldn't your children see that you love your spouse as well?

Making it real

A peck on the cheek is not a real kiss. A quick squeeze is not a real hug. If your only signs of affection for your spouse are brief and unfeeling, your children don't see the true affection you have for each other. On the other hand, you don't necessarily want to grind your loins into one another as the kids stare open-mouthed.

Clearly the more open you are about showing your affection from the time your children are old enough to notice, the easier it is to maintain these activities. If your children rarely see you hug closely, they may react negatively to seeing it for the first time.

By the way, you shouldn't be showing affection to each other only for your children's sake. Giving signs of affection to each other all through the day is absolutely a part of foreplay. If you remain physically close at other times, when the opportunity for sex does occur, getting in the mood is easier. You don't need to break the ice because you don't allow the ice to form in the first place. So what exactly should you be doing?

- Hugging
- Kissing on the lips
- Holding hands while walking or watching TV
- Sitting on laps
- Dancing cheek to cheek
- Rubbing backs

Keeping each other at arms' length

Some people refuse to show any affection in front of their children. Some of these people were raised by parents who did the same, so public displays of affection make them feel uncomfortable. Although I don't expect these people to totally change their stripes, they should make an effort to take a few baby steps in the direction of being affectionate in front of their children. Not only will these parents set a better example for their children, but they will also help their relationship grow stronger.

Some men fear that if they get too close to their wives they'll get an erection, which the kids will notice. For the most part, I don't think that children stare at their parents' crotches. Kids usually regard parents as if they were a little like pieces of furniture. Your kids know that you're there, but they probably don't pay very much attention to what you're doing most of the time (especially if you're asking them to put out the garbage or empty the dishwasher).

Even if they do notice a bulge in dad's pants, they're probably not going to think, "Oops, Daddy has an erection." I believe that a father keeping his wife at arm's length is much worse than risking a bit of embarrassment about having to explain away the environment inside his trousers.

Baring It All

Most adults don't worry about being naked around little babies or even toddlers, but as their children get older nudity becomes more of an issue. I'm often asked whether parents should cover up, and I think the best answer comes not from me but from your children. Your average child is likely to start feeling uncomfortable about nudity at some point; the specific age when this occurs is not dictated by any guidelines. You don't want to embarrass your children, so the moment you notice your child feeling embarrassed, that's the moment when you should start covering up.

The biography of Katharine Hepburn indicates that her father made a ritual of having family members around him when he took a bath. He even permitted his children's friends, of either sex, to drop in; this activity went on right through their adulthood. If your children don't kick up too much of a fuss about seeing you naked and you are not uncomfortable, you may never need to worry about covering up. But if your children react negatively, I advise you to heed their complaints and act a bit more modest when they're around.

Finding Private Time When You Have Teens

The time comes when your children stay up as late as you do, or even later. And because teens know about sex, they won't misinterpret whatever noises they may hear. If you are fairly open through the years about loving each other in a physical way, you just need to forget about the fact that your teenagers can hear you and know what you are doing. (Your children probably don't want to think that you are sexually active; they may turn up the stereo or TV to drown you out.) But if you are doing your best to keep your children in the dark as to your sexual activities, your eavesdropping teens are definitely going to put a damper on your sex life.

The good thing about teens is that they don't usually stay on the home front. You may pretty much rest assured that on weekend nights they are going to be elsewhere; just make sure to use these moments of privacy to their fullest advantage.

Another habit of teens is to sleep as late as possible on weekend mornings. Again, you may put this time to use by making love while they're catching up on their beauty rest.

If your kids range in ages from pre-teens to teens, you may find yourself in a bit of a quandary; your children are too young to go out on a Saturday night and old enough to figure out what you are doing behind your closed door. Finding time for a bit of privacy is difficult. All I can say to these parents is that you'd better not overly develop your sense of modesty. If you do, you may be waiting a long time for some private, tender moments.

If you bring up your children so that you can trust them to stay alone when they reach their teenage years, you might consider taking some weekends off by yourselves. You may tell your kids that you decided to take up bird watching or museum haunting, activities that should keep them from wanting to join you. Make sure someone can check on your children to ensure their safety; then treasure the time alone.

Discovering Your Children Are Sexually Active

Eventually your children follow in your footsteps and become sexually active themselves. You may hope that this event doesn't happen until after they walk down the aisle with their loved ones, but waiting until marriage to have sex doesn't always happen. Some couples face more than one challenge when their children become sexually active; the fear of STDs or pregnancy may cause parents to experience a few sleepless nights. In addition, discovering that their children are sexually active may make one or both of the parents self-conscious. If thoughts of their children having sex creep into their minds while they're trying to make love, these thoughts may interfere with their ability to get aroused.

You can't do much about this situation except to try as hard as possible to concentrate on your partner and your own arousal. Face it; the reason you have children is to ensure that your genes continue to survive. The only way for your genes to continue after your death is if your children have children; in order for your children to reproduce, they must become sexually active. This stage in your child's development may seem difficult, I admit, but eventually grandchildren are the result. And once you have grandchildren, you appreciate how the cycle of life continues.

Chapter 15

Heating Up the Empty Nest

*L*et me start with the bad news. Two people spend 20 years or so concentrating their attention on their children (as well as on their jobs and housework). Their children leave their homestead, and the couple finds themselves alone. The adjustment the couple faces now that their children are grown and out of the house is going to be difficult. This couple may suffer from what is called *empty nest syndrome.* Basically, this term means that the couple let their relationship deteriorate to such an extent that, without the children acting as the glue to hold it together, their relationship may fall apart.

"Whoa there, Dr. Ruth," I hear some of you saying. "You mean if two people manage to remain married for all those years, just having the kids hit the exits may be enough to break them apart? You're exaggerating, aren't you?"

Sadly, I'm not. I see people in my private practice all the time whose marriages fall victim to empty nest syndrome. After the kids are gone, these couples can't find a good reason to stay together. Their relationship is like a car that has been slowly eaten away by rust; when it gets to the point that you can't put your feet down on the floorboard without scraping the roadway, the car goes to the junk heap.

So what's the good news? You may prevent and even repair empty nest syndrome if you're willing to work at your relationship. Repairs to a relationship need to be done well before the rust gets out of hand. If you address the symptoms of empty nest syndrome early enough in your relationship, you may avoid major trauma when your children leave home to start their own lives.

Identifying the Empty Nest

Empty nest syndrome has many faces. The syndrome often rears its ugly head and results in divorce. Other times it creates strain and difficulty in a relationship without completely tearing it apart.

Together but alone

Plenty of couples continue to live under the same roof as husband and wife long after their children go off to college or land jobs and move out on their own. These couples may never divorce, but that doesn't necessarily mean that their marriages work.

How do you recognize a marriage that suffers from the ravages of empty nest syndrome? Perhaps the husband and wife continually display anger at each other, resulting in constant bickering. Or maybe they don't say anything to each other at all. They may develop completely separate interests — he's out on the golf course all day and she's playing cards with her friends all night. Television may be their favorite companion, each watching separate shows in different rooms.

If negative emotions build up for a decade or two, they are quite ingrained. Each partner has little foibles that drive the other to distraction. When she sees his cigar ashes on the rug she wants to scream. When he waits for her to finish putting on her makeup, he wants to drive away to the party without her. It gets to the point where he drops some ash on purpose and she spends as much time as she can putting on her lipstick.

Some couples do a very good job of hiding their problems; their families, friends, and neighbors are clueless as to the true nature of their relationship. They may even appear to be an ideal couple. The fact remains that theirs are fractured marriages and in most cases, these Humpty Dumpty relationships cannot be put back together again.

In other cases, everyone knows that the husband and wife constantly fight, but those people closest to them do everything possible to keep them together. Certainly, the children don't want to see their parents get a divorce. And friends of the couple don't want to choose between them. So their circle of family and friends pressures them to remain a "couple," but all the pressure in the world can't restore the love that led them to walk down the aisle in the first place.

Sadly, some romances are beyond rekindling. Living together, maybe even having sex occasionally, doesn't make a romance. You can't call two such people strangers; after all, they know each other inside and out. But if absolutely no spark exists between them, you can't categorize this husband and wife as a couple, either.

I'm describing two people who either should have gone for therapy or contacted a divorce lawyer long ago. But "for the sake of the children" they fought their urge to split up and they remained a couple. They didn't break off communications completely because they could always talk about their children. They didn't go to the movies as a couple but did see films with their kids. They didn't take a romantic vacation but did travel with their children. They didn't want to see each other but they did attend PTA meetings, soccer games, and school plays together. Their kids kept them so busy that they didn't have time to think about separating. But after their children are gone, they really don't have an excuse to be together.

Is there any hope at all of restoring this and relationship? Quite frankly, probably not. My advice to couples with these severe problems is to see a therapist. When such couples come to see me, I honestly can't offer much help. Each partner's love tank for the other is bone dry. They may feel contempt, disdain, disgust, and even hatred for each other, but no love.

In search of common ground

The couples I just described have severe cases of empty nest syndrome; their relationships may be too far gone to repair. Not every case of empty nest syndrome is fatal to the marriage. Some couples suffer from milder symptoms. Rather than feeling negative toward each other, some twosomes may simply be bored with each other. If these bored couples are willing to work at their relationship, they can renew their romance. They can't expect this renewal to happen without effort.

Steve and Judy

Steve and Judy are both lawyers. He's a trial lawyer who gets wrapped up in cases and doesn't surface for weeks at a time. She has a private practice and is very active in community service. During the course of an average week, Steve and Judy rarely are home on the same nights. On weekends, with all the activities their kids have, they don't get to see much of each other — one is off to a soccer game while the other is at ballet class.

On the weekend after they took their youngest child off to college, Steve and Judy found themselves with a lot of time on their hands. The privacy seemed like what they'd always wanted, but they both felt awkward. Steve was accustomed to doing the food shopping most of the time. When Judy volunteered to go with him, he was delighted. But Steve had developed a technique of getting in and out of the supermarket at high speed. Judy preferred to compare prices and read all the labels, which left him frustrated.

As the weekend wore on and they did various things together — taking care of the garden, watching TV, going to the video store to select a movie — they both started to realize that they didn't have much in common. There was really nothing that they wanted to do together. Late Sunday afternoon, Steve was out back shooting hoops, something that he used to do with his son. When both Steve and his son played basketball, Judy had never felt jealous. But now the thought occurred to her that her husband wasn't playing basketball by himself just out of love for the sport; he didn't want to spend the hour before dinner with her.

People like Steve and Judy are quick to say that they love each other. The fact is that they have so little in common — outside of their children — that they don't know how to spend time together. Couples like this are at a crossroads, and many of them choose the wrong path.

Choosing a Path

If you have children, you inevitably face the day when the last of them departs. You can't prevent your kids from growing up and leaving; their departure is out of your control. What you can control is how you respond to your newly found time alone with your mate. You can choose to make the situation negative, or you can actively work to make it positive. In this section, I show you the potential fruits of your choices.

Avoiding the home front

Faced with an awkward situation at home, some couples opt to rededicate themselves to work. These couples take whatever free time they acquire and spend it at the office. They work late, go to the office on weekends, and bring work home. Do these couples really need to work as often as they do? Probably not. But saying "I have to work" gives them the opportunity to escape from their spouses.

Throwing yourself into work may be particularly dangerous to your relationship if your partner has a job where overtime simply isn't demanded. He or she is left at home with no kids to fill the time. Maybe your partner never resented your long hours before, but now your dedication to work appears to be directed at him or her. Your partner may feel that you work extra hours to avoid spending time renewing your relationship.

If work isn't the culprit, other activities may substitute. A round of golf can take up a whole afternoon. Gardening can take hours. Even chores can be stretched out so that they keep one person occupied while the other sits elsewhere alone.

Of course, some people truly love to play golf, garden, or work long hours. A golf widow may become very angry that her husband is on the links (I deal with that issue in Chapter 19), but she must be careful when judging his motivation. If his motivation for playing golf is from his love for the sport — not his desire to avoid being with her — she can't say that their problem is due to empty nest syndrome. Only when one partner intentionally uses an activity as an excuse to avoid the other partner does empty nest syndrome come into play.

Making the effort to connect

What should couples do when faced with empty nest syndrome? Actually, what they should do is not nearly as important as *how* they should do it — together. I'm not saying that a couple needs to be together 24 hours a day, 7 days a week. That goal is impossible. They just need to spend some quality time together so that they reestablish the contact they once enjoyed.

Couples facing an empty nest need to choose activities that enable them to pool their intellects, destroy boredom, and share interesting conversations. If they truly enjoy their conversations, when they see each other, they smile instead of feeling depressed. This doesn't mean that he gives up golf or she stops working in her garden. The goal is to consciously put aside time to partake in activities that they both enjoy and can do together.

Want some specific ideas for how to revive your intellectual connection?

- ✔ **Share a hobby.** If each of you has hobbies that the other does not find interesting, come up with a new one both of you can share. Make the search part of the fun. Discuss different activities that you could do together and spend some time trying them out. Play some chess. Go antiquing. Collect Native American jewelry. Search for buried treasure on the beach. Camp out in the woods. Start a business selling home-made pies. Solve the Sunday crossword puzzle. Surf the 'Net looking for the ideal place to retire. Join a local theater group. Shoot home movies that you script yourself.

- ✔ **Share a sport.** If golf is not the game for both of you, take up tennis or bowling. If you don't want to be competitive, go hiking or skiing. Pursue activities that are less tame by taking up mountain climbing or parasailing. Get a kayak and explore all the nearby lakes and streams. Rent a bicycle built for two and explore the back roads. Set up a volleyball net in the front yard and invite the neighbors. Buy a Ping-Pong table for the basement.

- ✔ **Volunteer.** Spend every Saturday serving lunch at a soup kitchen. Visit a senior home and read the residents books or take them out for strolls in the fresh air. Tutor children. Plan a fundraiser to fight cancer. Clean up your church or synagogue or mosque. Teach at a Sunday school program. "Adopt" an elderly person in your neighborhood and drop in to keep him or her company or to help with housekeeping.

✔ **Become more civic-minded.** Collect signatures to put a stoplight on your corner. Form a block association. Join the historical society. Stuff envelopes for a candidate you support. Run for office yourself.

✔ **Educate yourselves.** Take art classes at a local museum. Take continuing education courses at a nearby college. Buy a tape and teach yourself how to dance the tango. Pick an historical period, like the Civil War, and read about the subject together. Select a style of music that you both don't know much about, start a collection of *Best of* tapes or CDs, and try to develop an appreciation for it. Learn to play musical instruments.

✔ **Turn into travel buffs.** Take a trip. Make planning the itinerary part of the fun; learn as much as possible about your destination. On weekends, explore nearby towns and find out as much as you can about them. Learn their history and study their architecture.

✔ **Become more social.** Give parties, but not just for friends. Invite people you know slightly or not at all, such as couples you see at church but hardly speak to or neighbors who live at the other end of the block or down the hall or on another floor. Buy tickets to local charity events and make a point of talking to as many people as possible.

✔ **Fix up your home.** Even if you are all thumbs, you can learn to become handier. Make the lessons more fun (and less frustrating) by working on your home improvements together. Pick a room, maybe one of those left behind by one of your kids, and turn it into a study. Paint it, or put up wallpaper. Build shelves.

Changing your attitude

Now that more "together" time is available, you can knead that soft spot in your heart for your partner that became a little hardened from lack of use. It's one thing to say that you love someone but another to actually feel it. If you've been like two ships passing in the night for the last decade or so, the fact that you haven't exactly been mooning over your partner is only natural.

How do you get sparks flying again? Here are some suggestions:

✔ **Think about your partner.** When you first dated, I'm sure that thoughts of your partner cropped into your head all the time. As the years went by and you got a lot busier, you may have gone all day without once thinking about him or her. Now you need to reprogram your mind and your heart, so you must consciously think positive thoughts about your partner. Prominently place a picture of your spouse in your office, or even two or three pictures. Write down some of the highlights of your years together, keep the list in your pocket, and read it now and then. Sexually fantasize about your partner during a free moment.

✔ **Make dates.** Remember when you were in the dating stage? You'd talk on the phone, pick a time and a place to meet, and feel nervous for hours before the date began. Instead of just assuming that you'll see your wife or hubby on a Tuesday night, go back to making dates. Without kids to worry about, you don't need to go straight home after work. Select a restaurant and meet there for a romantic dinner.

✔ **Give gifts.** I don't just mean on birthdays and holidays. When you walk around on your lunch hour, think about buying your mate a little something. This gift could be as simple as a favorite candy bar or a magazine you think he or she would enjoy. The value of the gift has no relationship to the money you spend; the worth is measured by the warmth you add to each other's hearts. You feel good buying the gift and your partner feels good receiving it. That's what's important.

✔ **Avoid criticism.** No one is perfect. Sometimes you screw up no matter how hard you try. Spouses need to let each other make mistakes. Remember that you're trying to promote good feelings, not make your partner feel worse about something he or she has accidentally done wrong.

✔ **Give compliments.** After a number of years, you may take your partner for granted. Not only will your partner appreciate any compliments you throw his or her way, but also your own attitude improves each time you give one.

To tell the truth?

What if you really struggle to find ways to compliment your mate? Maybe the woman you married was gorgeous and thin with great legs and lovely skin, but now she's pudgy and wrinkly. Maybe the man you married was strong and handsome, but now he's flabby and balding. You know that you're supposed to give each other compliments, but should you just lie?

First, you should know that I believe in white lies. I see nothing wrong with trying to make people feel good. If she has gone to the beauty parlor, make sure you notice her hair and tell her that it looks good. If he buys a new suit, make a positive comment about it. If she's wearing a different perfume and you enjoy the aroma, tell her.

Compliments don't need to relate to physical appearance at all. If he cooks a good meal, let him know how much you admire his prowess as a chef. If she repairs a leaky faucet, praise her for being so handy around the house. You can boost each other honestly if you take the time to compliment the things that make each of us special.

Steaming Up the Nest

Couples who suffer from empty nest syndrome almost always have a boring or nonexistent sex life. Sex is an important ingredient in cementing a relationship. If your sex life cooled off over the years, you should take immediate action.

Private lives

Empty nest syndrome offers you one advantage: complete privacy. With the kids at home, you may have always remained covered up unless the bedroom or bathroom door was closed; now you can bounce around the house in your birthday suit. (Just make sure to leave a bathrobe by the door in case the FedEx man rings the bell.) Your body may not be as svelte as it used to be, but that doesn't mean that it's not sexy. In fact, clothes may push skin into awkward looking bunches; many people actually look better when they're naked.

I can suggest to couples that they make love in the kitchen, on the living room floor, or on the dining room table, but these locations aren't usually convenient with kids in the house. An empty house opens up the possibility of adding variety to your lovemaking in terms of locale. When the kids are all gone, your entire home is an empty canvas where you can paint your own erotic pieces of art.

You can start your brush strokes somewhere else, but your bed may remain the most comfortable place to end your sexual masterpiece. You may start fooling around on the couch while you watch TV; as soon as the show is over, head on over to the bedroom. Or you can have dinner in the nude with your chairs right next to each other as you feed each other, lick off that bit of mashed potato that "accidentally" dropped in his or her lap, and retreat to the couch before clearing the table.

Time is on your side

In addition to being able to vary the locale of your lovemaking, you're now more free to engage in sex at the moment of your choosing. Make love before dinner. Or during halftime of the game. Or right after breakfast. You decide.

You may also decide in advance the time you will make love. When your kids were around, you could never be sure exactly what hour they'd all go to bed and fall asleep. You might have said to each other in the morning, "Let's make love tonight," but if Johnny had a bad cold or Suzie had to stay up late study-ing for a test, your plans wilted. As empty-nesters, you can say, "This after-noon, let's shop for groceries; then let's make love."

"But Dr. Ruth," you say, "that's silly. Why make love after going to the super-market? That's such a weird time."

My answer is: Exactly! Sometimes sex is better at odd times. Imagine the dif-ference between going shopping and looking forward to making love right afterwards and going shopping when sex doesn't follow this task. Suddenly your shopping trip is more than an exercise in filling your cupboards; it's foreplay.

On grocery-shopping day, don't wear undergarments. A woman may choose to wear a sexy pushup bra and leave the top button of her blouse undone. Instead of slouching into separate corners of the car, sit close together. He can put his hand on your knee. Kiss for a long while before you exit the car. When you select vegetables in the produce department, stand close together with your hips touching. (No one else will know, but you'll probably exchange some heat in that touch.) Wink at each other over the shopping cart. If he says, "How about getting some whipped cream," you can both giggle. And standing in line to pay, you'll both know that you're getting closer to the moment when you can tear your clothes off. I expect that by the time you get your groceries home, you won't give a second thought to leaving them on the kitchen counter while you retreat to your bedroom.

You can't pull off these afternoons with your kids around. After they leave, a whole new sexual world opens to you. Dive into it. Make a point of doing things differently. Both of you need to stir things up and to go along when one partner suggests doing something new. If you don't like what you try, you never have to do it again. Don't limit your options ahead of time. Whenever you can, surprise each other.

What else can you do with all this new privacy?

- **Take your morning shower together.** Most of the time showering together doesn't lead to sex, but don't be afraid to be late for work once in a while.

- **Go for a moonlight drive.** Find a spot where you won't be interrupted and hit the back seat!

- **Rent erotic movies.** If you worry about what the neighbors think, drive to another neighborhood to rent them.

- **Greet the sunrise.** Don't fight the fatigue. When you both come home from work exhausted, have a light supper, set the alarm for dawn, and go to bed. In the morning, open the curtains, and as the light creeps into your window, compete with the sun for making the warmest glow.

- ✔ **Scent your world with flowers.** Buy a load of roses, cover your bed with petals, and settle down into the aroma.

- ✔ **Write an erotic story.** Spend a night writing together and acting out all the "good parts."

- ✔ **Rent some costumes.** Spend an evening playing Romeo and Juliet, Bonnie and Clyde, or Cleopatra and Marc Antony.

- ✔ **Create your own game show.** Watch your favorite quiz show and play along using the "at home" rules — the person who answers wrong has to take off an article of clothing.

Seizing the Moment

If you're a new empty nester, I assume that you're somewhere between your late 40s and early 60s. Statistically, you're likely to live till you're in your 80s; that's another 30 years or so — a long time. Thirty years may be longer than the time you spend raising your children. Your kids set the agenda for all those years, now you're in a place where the agenda is wide open. New possibilities arise, as do new questions:

- ✔ Do you stay in the same job?

- ✔ Do you retire early?

- ✔ Do you continue to live in the same house?

- ✔ Do you live in the same town?

- ✔ Do you want to be a snowbird?

Growing older isn't an easy proposition. You can ease the burden by growing older next to someone you love and who loves you. You share an enormous memory bank with this person. Becoming an empty nester may seem like a tremendous stumbling block, but it can also be an enormous opportunity. Be aware of the pitfalls, dedicate yourselves to overcoming them, and make the most of this particular stage in your lives.

Chapter 16

Working Too Hard for Romance?

"Rosie the Riveter" started a trend during World War II. Women who had previously devoted their days to caring for home and family started taking jobs outside the home in greater numbers. This trend exploded in the 1960s and 1970s. Today, 60 percent of all women ages 16 and over and 75 percent of women between the ages of 25 and 64 are in the workforce. Women make up 46 percent of the overall workforce in the U.S.

These numbers represent an incredible change that our society has undergone in the last 50 years. We still can't fathom all the repercussions of this change, although I am very familiar with one area that has been impacted dramatically: romance. Frequently, both partners work outside the home, return exhausted at the end of the day, and endeavor to maintain the household and raise the children. Romance gets shoved into the third row of the family's minivan, if not forced out altogether to cling to the roof rack.

What's the solution? Should one of you quit your job in order to save your romance? Obviously that answer isn't practical for many people. You don't want to create such financial distress that you add an extra layer of tension to your household. The solution lies in prioritizing romance in your daily schedule so that it appears high on your "to do" list. Even if you can't squeeze a lot of time out of your everyday lives to devote to romance, just a few minutes spent wisely can bolster your relationship. This chapter walks you through the process of prioritizing romance in your schedule and offers suggestions for ways to spend those precious few romantic moments.

It's not all bad news

The last couple of decades didn't bring only negative news *vis a vis* romance. Thanks to the work of Masters and Johnson, society has been enlightened in regards to sexual functioning — including a woman's need for foreplay and afterplay. As a result, many more women are sexually satisfied. Because of the Pill and other advances in contraception, the fear of unintended pregnancies is reduced. Sex may truly be enjoyed for pleasure instead of as solely an act in the procreative process. In addition to the sexual advancements, the new respect many women found while proving their equality on the job resulted in significant improvements to the relationship between men and women. Both partners benefit when they're operating on an equal footing, because romance is supposed to be an exchange of emotions, not a one-way street.

So while many more couples complain that they're too tired to have sex or can't find the time for romance, at least men and women approach the problem from very similar viewpoints. Not very long ago, men and women both believed that only men were supposed to enjoy sex. In Victorian England, mothers advised their daughters to put up with their husbands' demands and "lie back and think of England." For women, sex was about making babies, not about gratification. Today, most people are aware that both men and women are supposed to have orgasms. Society still needs some educating, but the word is definitely out.

Overall, I think that the benefits of the societal changes of recent decades outweigh the negatives. These positive changes affect both sexes. Men know that by giving their wives orgasms, they find the sexual experience more enjoyable as well. Women know that sex may be enjoyed purely for the pursuit of orgasms and not just as a means to become pregnant. You may experience moments of frustration when sex has to be put on the back burner due to the pressures of everyday life. But try to remember that your increasing sexual awareness means when you do have time for sex, it is a more satisfying experience than it would have been 100 years ago.

Recognizing the Need for Romance

Most of you recognize that you need sex. You cannot help but feel your sexual urges. A sexual urge is not quite like hunger, thirst, or the need to urinate (all of which eventually become overpowering). You may repress your urge for sex a lot more easily than these other bodily functions. Yet, no matter how consistently you ignore the tickling of your libido, some little creature continues to haunt the back of your mind whispering "sexxxx."

Very rarely do you experience the same urgency about romance. Few people hear little creatures in their minds whispering "romaaaance" on a daily basis. The need for romance lurks inside of you the same as the need for sex, but the romantic urge is much more subtle. That subtlety explains why romance may be easily overwhelmed by the day-to-day rush.

Romance also takes more time than sex. In the time you share a candlelit dinner, stroll along the lake, or dance a slow waltz in each other's arms, you could probably wash three loads of clothes, check your e-mail, and replace your threadbare underwear by ordering new ones online. While the short-term effects of putting chores before romance (such as a clean house and new underwear) may seem positive, the long-term effects may seriously and negatively impact your romance. A little more dirt in your household may add a lot more satisfying years to your relationship.

Making Your Mate a Priority

Your first step toward managing your time more efficiently requires realizing the importance of romance. You can't possibly prioritize romance if you don't appreciate its worth. Is romance more important than feeding your kids? Absolutely not. Is rekindling your romance worth opening a can of SpaghettiOs so that you're not too frazzled to become aroused that evening? Absolutely.

The day has only so many hours, and some of those hours must be reserved for sleep. Undoubtedly, in order to find time for romance, you take away time from doing something else. If you borrow that time from your household chores, it may mean that your house is slightly messier than you like, your kids don't always eat home-cooked meals, the yard work is postponed, or the dog misses his grooming appointment. On the other hand, the time you steal away from your scheduled tasks also means that you and your spouse may kiss, hug, cuddle, and enjoy sex — not a bad trade-off.

Letting the laundry go

Fred and Jan

Fred and Jan have three boys, and two of them are twins. Jan is a perfectionist, and despite the three-to-one odds she faces every day, she manages to maintain order in her household. Raising three small boys and keeping a neat house is wearing Jan out. Fred talks to her about letting up on her pursuit of a perfectly cleaned house, but she doesn't listen. The kids are asleep by 8 p.m. and Jan soon follows because she can't keep her eyes open. Fred finds himself alone every night, watching TV, and growing more and more frustrated.

Many people try to live up to standards set by their own parents. For some women, that means trying to keep the house as clean as Mom did or making sure everyone in the family has drawers full of clean laundry every day. The problem with trying to hit this standard is that your life is different than your mother's was. Especially if you work outside the home, your schedule simply cannot allow for perfection in the household. You must actively work on adjusting your expectations.

Maybe you're not a neat freak like Jan, but you may be faced with other pressing responsibilities. For example, maybe Monday night your son has a Little League game, Tuesday evening you attend a PTA meeting, and Wednesday you are faced with a choice of doing laundry (because no one has clean underwear to put on Thursday morning) or keeping a romantic date with your spouse that the two of you have planned for a week.

If you choose to do the laundry, I think you make the wrong choice. Changing your underwear every day is a luxury, not a necessity. I know what your mother always taught you; your mother doesn't have to know. Maybe she had more time available to wash the clothes, or maybe she neglected the romance in her life. I tell you right here and now that clean underwear is not as important as romance.

Is it frivolous to want to keep a romantic date with your husband instead of doing the wash? Maybe, but you need some frivolity in your life. You can't work every waking second. Forget about romance; that kind of life is simply not worth living. You should enjoy life, at least part of the time. If some task like laundry has to go by the wayside once in a while, it has to go.

"But Dr. Ruth," you say, "my husband is never going to understand. I've lived with him for a dozen years. Believe me when I say he'll fuss the next morning about not having any clean underwear."

I'm a realist. If your husband doesn't understand, grab a pair of his undershorts from the laundry pile, dip them in some hot soapy water in the sink, and hang them up to dry. This duty will take just a few minutes and solve the problem. Another simple and obvious solution is to make your husband responsible for his own laundry. Anyone can operate a washing machine; you can offer some pointers if he doesn't feel comfortable at first.

Ideally, the two of you will discuss the importance of romance, split the household chores to allow more time for rekindling, and work together to keep your home fires burning. (I talk more about the division of labor in the following section.)

Asking for help around the house

If the list of chores you face every day is overwhelming, the two of you need to talk about dividing the responsibilities. Don't let this discussion stray into abstract territory; keep it simple. Decide the chores each of you can tackle; make sure the weight of the household sits on both sets of shoulders. If you aren't satisfied that your partner's list of duties is equivalent to your workload, explain what daily tasks he or she should complete to balance the load.

Don't allow excuses to get in the way of this division of labor. If he has never prepared a meal before, point out some simple recipes from a cookbook and offer some pointers, or encourage him to pick up dinner from a supermarket deli. If she has never mowed the grass before, show her how to start and use the mower safely. Making excuses for each other is counterproductive. Find ways to accomplish what needs to be done. Dividing the duties may not be a perfect solution, but if your tasks are completed with a little time spared, then you have a little more time to put romance back in your lives.

Both men and women sometimes play at being all thumbs to get out of a task. If your partner tries to bow out of a chore by claiming ignorance, break the task down into smaller pieces, and assign simple steps that even a six-year-old can accomplish. And speaking of six-year-olds, don't be afraid to make your kids help out, too. Acting the part of a martyr by trying to complete all the household tasks by yourself is not conducive to good family relationships. Each of you has to stand up and earn some respect.

Scheduling romance

Most people find dancing cheek-to-cheek romantic. Without a wedding on your calendar, you probably don't see yourself waltzing in the near future. What if you say to your partner, "On Wednesday night at 10, would you like to dance with me in the living room?" Your mate may look at you strangely, but he or she may just say "yes." Pick some songs you'd like to dance to, load the CDs into your stereo, and spend half an hour tripping the light fantastic in your living room. Maybe dancing is something you can schedule every week. Or maybe you can both agree to spend that half hour doing some other romantic activity every week, if one of you doesn't care for dancing.

You need to be creative in order to fit romance into your life. If you can't block out hours of free time, squeeze some romantic minutes in here and there. Don't expect the moon. If you dream about an entire romantic evening — including flowers and a candlelit dinner followed by dancing under the stars — you may never get your wish. Be a little practical and add small tidbits of romance to your daily life. Each small bite may not satisfy you like one big meal, but even a big meal must be consumed one bite at a time. Find ways to connect the individual bites together in your mind.

Battling fatigue

I realize that your busy schedule is not the only factor that affects the amount of romance you enjoy in your life. If work and household chores sap all of your strength, no matter how much you crave romance, you may prefer to substitute sleep for a romantic interlude. Just as you can learn to schedule time for romance, you can learn to conserve your energy for a little rekindling.

Say you make a date with your partner for some cheek-to-cheek dancing at 10 p.m. on Wednesday. Five o'clock rolls around and a pile of work still sits on your desk. If you attempt to empty your in-box, you'll be so tired by 10 that the dancing music will lull you to sleep. I applaud diligence at work. My suggestion is to work diligently the other four days of the work week in order to free yourself for the day you schedule romance. Of course, you occasionally may be stuck spending some extra time at the office on your scheduled romance night, but don't let that happen every week. Blowing off your romance night in order to work sends a clear message to your spouse that romance is not high on your priority list.

Playing the Martyr

Some people enjoy playing martyr. These folks feel that unless they complain about their packed schedules, their lives aren't worth anything. Their existence is validated by being too busy, too overworked, and too short of time. (I'm not saying these people aren't busy, but they may be too busy for their own good, and yours.) They don't sit down and prioritize because they're not looking for lighter workloads. These busy bees enjoy telling everybody, especially their partners, how crazed their days are and that there is no time left for their relationships.

If your partner behaves this way, you may hesitate to ask for more time from him or her because you don't want to add any extra pressure. Although your thoughtfulness is commendable, it doesn't do much for the state of your romance. If the romance in your lives runs dry, your partnership is in danger. A love affair that isn't valued by your partner may not be worth keeping together. Something has to give, and the something shouldn't exclusively be the time you spend together. At some point you have to say "Basta!" (which means *enough* in Italian — a good language for being direct).

I know some people hold down two and even three jobs in order to make ends meet. Some people own mom-and-pop businesses that operate from 6 a.m. to 10 p.m. seven days a week. Some lawyers are forced to work 100-hour weeks. These people may not have a choice but to labor long hours and put work ahead of everything else. If your partner is in such a situation, you can't do anything except put up with his or her work situation or leave. The good news is that most people do have jobs that leave them some wiggle room, and these jobs allow them to prioritize romance in their weekly schedules.

How can you spot the true martyr? If your partner says that she must spend the evening working on the computer, ask some questions. Is the work for a presentation she is giving the following morning or next week? Can she put off the work for an hour or two to fit in a little romance? If she's an accountant and tax time is near, of course she faces a heavier work load. Discuss with your partner the urgency of his or her work; determine if the work in question is pressing. Together you may find that you can fit your work deadline and romance into your schedules. Be sure to let your partner know that your relationship has to be put on an equal footing with work.

If you don't speak up, your situation will only get worse. People who martyr themselves this way do not change on their own. You can't say to yourself that next week, next month, or next year things will improve. You need to communicate to your partner that you expect some immediate changes.

Notice that I don't add "or else" to that statement. I don't believe threats are conducive to positive changes; they only bring up negative feelings. Obviously, the "or else" is understood; by issuing a challenge, you only get the other person's defenses up.

You want your partner to see the light, to understand where you are coming from, and to agree that he or she needs to pay more attention to your relationship. Chances are that your partner wants to keep the relationship going but is simply too wrapped up in work. If your partner has lost interest in you and prefers work over your relationship — so be it. At least that truth has been brought to light and you can move on.

Making Time to Make Love

People with very busy lives find making time for sex almost as difficult as making time for romance. I say *almost* because the need for sexual release builds up after a while. Therefore, most couples eventually find time to have intercourse. But the gaps among lovemaking encounters definitely cause frustrations.

Sticking to a schedule

If your days and nights are harried, you probably need to schedule time for sex. That's not to say you can't enjoy spontaneous sex, but waiting for just the right moment may mean waiting a very long time. You may schedule Wednesday nights and Saturday mornings for sex, guaranteeing that the two of you will be canoodling at those times. Spontaneity is exciting, but anticipation may also cause your hearts to flutter. Your Wednesday night plan for sex should get your libido thinking about sex on Wednesday morning. With any luck, by the time you fall into bed together on Wednesday night, you'll be ravenous for each other — not a bad thing at all.

Running out of time

Some jobs just don't leave people much free time. What if your spouse holds one of these jobs? How do you fit in some romance and not feel constantly frustrated? I recommend arranging some romantic moments yourself. You may meet your partner for lunch, bring one red rose to place on his or her desk, and share a sandwich. Write him or her e-mails during the day — you may receive a quick "I love you" response. Pick out your husband's tie or your wife's blouse in the morning, and picture your spouse working throughout the day; your spouse may think of you when admiring his or her reflection in a mirror.

Another difficult situation for couples trying to keep romance in their relationships occurs when they work opposite shifts. No other jobs may be available, or one parent may always need to be home to take care of the kids. I obviously can't advise anyone in these situations to change. (If you can't afford daycare, working opposite shifts may be your only option.) I can recommend that you place a time limit on the opposite shift situation. Say to yourselves, "We'll do this for two years." Leaving a light at the end of the tunnel makes the situation easier to tolerate.

I do think that planning your sexcapades can work wonders for your sex life. I want to add that you may want to be careful not to fall into a rut. Certainly any spontaneous sex you add to the mix helps you to avoid being too rigid in your routine. You should also add some variety to your method of lovemaking. Variety means that even if you do it at the same times every week, at least the sex is not always the same or even in the same place. Also, consider changing your schedule every few months or so.

Taking it slowly

The French are noted for saying *vive la difference*. Men and women have achieved much greater equality over the past several decades, but this equality doesn't mean that their essential qualities have become the same. A woman still needs more time than a man to become aroused, and an important factor in generating that arousal is romance.

If you spare only five minutes to have sex, the odds are that she isn't going to achieve orgasm. A woman isn't at fault for requiring more time to reach orgasm any more than a lefty is at fault for writing with his left hand. (I could add that a shorty like me can't be faulted for needing a stepstool to reach the top shelf — okay, the middle shelf, too.)

I know that the scientific community searches for a miracle "cure" to enable women to function sexually like men. The medical advance would aid women in achieving orgasms as quickly as men. I understand the desire for this scientific breakthrough; I'm all for the occasional quickie. There are times when it would be nice for both partners to have orgasms in five minutes or less. Let me add that I'm also concerned about such a breakthrough. With a miracle pill for women, fewer and fewer couples may bother spending an hour or more at lovemaking, and that would be a shame.

Sex isn't just about orgasms; it's about a meeting of two people in so many intimate ways. Sex becomes a poor imitation of its potential if you rush in and out. For one thing, quick sex loses almost all of its romance. If you have five-minute encounters all the time, you no longer are making love; you're simply humping away for a few minutes like wild animals. If the two people having sex are not sharing their love as well as their bodies, then one of the main reasons for monogamy is removed. Two people need to devote themselves to hugging, kissing, caressing, stroking, and all of the other components of lovemaking in order to differentiate intercourse from masturbation.

As you see, I'm all for maintaining the romantic aspects of sex. I also know I'm not a miracle worker. Time is our most precious commodity because it's absolutely finite; I can't give you more of it. All I can do is help you to manage your time a little better and shift the balance a bit more in favor of love and romance.

Building Up a Romantic Reservoir

Romance, like light, is both a particle and a wave at the same time. Compared to sex, romance is harder to get your hands around. But romance is also more versatile than sex. Versatility is important when you can spare little time for your relationship.

Sex is fairly structured, because it is physical. You go from one stage of sexual arousal to the next in an orderly fashion in order to reach orgasm. Blood flows to your genitals when you are aroused and dissipates after you reach orgasm. You can't spend 15 minutes getting aroused, stop for a few hours to make dinner, put the kids to bed, jump into your partner's arms, and expect to be right back at the peak of arousal. Sex requires a physical build up and release — with no interruptions.

Romance is more of a psychological than a physical sensation. You can experience romance incrementally. The little love note your husband left in your purse has an effect every time you read it. The flowers on your shelf at the office whisper "I love you" every time you glance at them. The picture of your main squeeze on your desk makes you forget about your boss every time you see it. A series of tiny romantic moments may build on each other. Spend a few moments each day devoted to reminding your partner that he or she is important; these moments are never wasted.

An increasing sexual life span

Due to advancements in science, the average life span is growing; people commonly live well into their 80s and beyond. As long as you're healthy, you may have sex for that entire span. Potentially, when you retire, you spend time together to make up for those busy days when you were rushing by each other.

You can't take advantage of this added time together unless your relationship is still operating smoothly when you retire. You need to put in the time and effort now to ensure that you stay together and feel romantic toward each other later.

Speaking Up

Don't deprive yourself of some romance by keeping what you would like a secret. Speak up and tell your partner what you need. This request is particularly important if the days are rushing by like a springtime torrent. Remember that if you feel crazed, so does your partner.

The hunger for romance may be pushed aside; it may even be forgotten by your partner. Romance may be higher on your priority list than your partner's, so you both need to make an effort to raise it up a notch or two.

Q. When my husband and I dated, he was very romantic. Once he sent me flowers three times in one day. Since our wedding day, his romantic gestures have subsided. I never get flowers or many other signs of affection, unless they're connected with sex. Has he stopped loving me?

A. Men are taught that to win the love of a woman, she has to be romanced. Men see plenty of examples in the media. If you watch popular TV shows, how often do you see husbands being romantic? Not very often. Why not? Because a husband romancing his wife is less dramatic than a man romancing a woman who might tell him "no." I'm sure that your husband does still love you, and he thinks that just by sticking with you he is doing everything necessary to demonstrate his love. Let him know that you need other signs besides the fact that he crawls into bed next to you every night.

 If this scenario describes your husband, be prepared to talk openly about romance. Give him some examples of what you mean by romance. For example, maybe he's a fan of a certain sports team. His car may display a bumper sticker with the team's logo, he may wear a baseball hat with the team's name, and he probably watches all of his favorite team's games. Can he offer a logical explanation as to why he's such a fan? No, because his connection to the team is not logical; it's emotional. Use that example to help him see that your need for romance is just like his feelings for his team — your desire is not logical; it's emotional.

You both know that when his team wins, he feels excited. By contrast, when his team loses, he sinks into a funk for days. Let him know that he has the same power over you. If he does something romantic, you're high for days; if he ignores romance altogether, you may slip into a gloomy mood. He is able to make time to root for his team despite his busy schedule. Work with him to find time to root for his partner as well.

Romancing Each Other Long Distance

The airways and highways of America are filled with people who must travel for their jobs. I know this fact well, because I travel a lot and meet so many of these traveling workers. At the extreme are truck drivers and airline and shipping personnel; their jobs involve being away from home for long stretches of time. Most business travelers hit the road only every few weeks or every few months.

But whether a spouse travels constantly or just once in a while, distance always impacts a relationship. The person on the road may be so busy that he or she barely has time to think of the loved one left behind. The person staying at home may actually feel angry at the traveler because of all the extra duties he or she has to carry out alone. Or the opposite scenario is possible, where the person on the road is homesick and misses his or her spouse terribly while the one staying home enjoys not having to answer any demands. You can't predict your reaction if you or your partner must travel for work, but you can be on the lookout for problems that may crop up.

Keeping in touch

Good communication is obviously key to maintaining your romance while apart. Often the person on the road must bear the brunt of maintaining communication because he or she may not be accessible every minute of the day. Certainly cell phones may help the person staying at home feel more connected to the person traveling. But a phone call placed at the wrong moment may interrupt business rather than establish a romantic link. A pager may be a better tool for communication because it allows the traveler to call back at a time convenient for him or her, unless the coded message indicates that there is an emergency.

If you travel a lot, bring along a few reminders of home. These reminders may help alleviate loneliness by mentally connecting you to your spouse and family. Pictures are the best such reminders; they are flat and light and you can stick them into the edge of a hotel room mirror. Other reminders may be anything from love letters to paper scented with a favorite perfume to a pair of undergarments.

Resisting temptations

If you are away from home, lonely, and sexually frustrated from not spending much time with your partner, you may face the danger of giving in to the temptations of the road. You may meet someone who is also away from home, lonely, and sexually frustrated. You may seek comfort from each other and find it very easy to fall into each other's arms.

The partner left at home on a continuous basis may encounter similar temptations. In a way, these temptations are even more dangerous because they run a greater risk of developing into a long-term affair as opposed to a one-night stand.

Romance is a crucial weapon in the battle against such urges. You cannot completely isolate yourself from temptation when you're away from home. You don't choose whom you sit next to on a plane or select the gender of the people you meet with on business. Just because the desire strikes doesn't mean that you should give in to it. If you place that picture of your lover on your hotel mirror — or at least firmly in your mind — you may flirt a bit but you'll maintain the wherewithal to pull back before things go too far. Envelope yourself in an aura of romance, dream of the love in the picture, and shun taking flirtations to the next level.

And if your libido starts getting the better of you, do something positive to fix the situation. One possibility is to engage in some phone sex with your mate back home. If that's not possible, then don't hesitate to masturbate. At the very least, it's the only truly safe way to have sex away from your partner.

Relieving Your Stress with Romance

Just in case you need one more reason to foster romance in your relationship: I find that romance helps you to relieve the stress in your life. Cuddling up with your loved one reinforces the sense that you are not alone with your troubles. Romance proves to you that someone cares deeply about you and can literally give you the strength to go on.

Feeling protected

From time to time, you may feel that the world is out to get you. At these moments you need a safe harbor, a place where you feel shielded from the troubles of the world. A romantic environment is the ultimate safe harbor. This environment is the one place in the world where no one can bother you. You're under the protective shield of the person you love, and so for at least those few moments, you can relax.

It's ironic that people in the most need of the soothing effects of romance are the ones who feel that they don't have the time for romance. A short romantic interlude allows you to breathe deep and gather your strength to go on. Avoiding romance makes you feel disconnected from your partner and adds to your sense of unease. People who are the busiest need to take time out from their work and family lives to allow the healing powers of romance to work their magic.

Escaping the work world

A full work week doesn't allow time for you to fully indulge yourself in romance. Sometimes the best you can manage is a compromise between work and play. When you get some time off, be very careful not to waste these precious moments. Plan your vacation so that you include as much romance as possible. These idyllic moments give you a goal to aim for during the rest of the year.

If you have children, finding romance on a vacation is going to be a little more difficult, but it's not impossible. See Chapter 8 for some hints on how to make the most of your vacation days.

Chapter 17

Romancing Financial Difficulties

• •

• •

Although many types of stress may reduce the romance in your life, some of the most damaging relationship problems result from financial difficulties. This phenomenon is not universal. If you lived in a country where most people were poor, your love life probably wouldn't be greatly affected by your lack of money. (Of course, if your family were starving, that's another story.) You would probably accept your poverty as a way of life, and as long as you had enough to eat and a roof over your head, you'd need only a gorgeous sunset to create some romance.

Because you're reading this book, I can almost guarantee that you don't live in a poverty-stricken village. I'm willing to bet that all your neighbors have decent homes, two or more television sets, computers, nice cars, and many of the other trappings of modern society. Even if you're not aware that you're trying to "keep up with the Joneses," subconsciously you are. If your car is a little older than everybody else's on the block, that fact may bother you.

Besides feeling envious of your neighbors' wealth, you may feel dissatisfied with your income. If you earn more, you tend to spend more, so even couples with incomes that seem quite high may struggle to make ends meet. These struggles can most definitely have an impact on your romance.

Money is the root of many relationship problems, whether the issue is saving versus spending or what to do with a sudden windfall of excess cash. In this chapter, I show you how to work through some difficult financial situations and emerge with your pride, and your relationship, intact.

Calculating Your Own Worth

Should your self-esteem be tied to your financial status? Of course not. If you're happy with your job and you get rewards from working that can't be measured by the dollar amount in your paycheck, earning less than your neighbors shouldn't bother you at all. But just because something *shouldn't* bother you doesn't mean that you aren't disturbed by it anyway. You are affected by the society that you live in, and Western societies admire wealth.

Let me return to the car example. If you have a car that is eight years old and still runs well, you don't need to buy a new car. You may live in a rural area where you can't see your neighbors' cars each time you walk out the door and, therefore, the fact that you drive an older car doesn't bother you as long as it gets you where you're going. Or you may live in a suburban community where all your neighbors' cars are parked in their driveways and yours is the oldest one on the block, in which case you probably feel disappointed as you climb into it.

Human nature drives us to compare ourselves and our lives to those around us. You can fight off feelings of insecurity by justifying to yourself that you don't need a new car, but that fight eventually saps you of some energy. On the opposite end of the spectrum, if you have the newest car on the block, the pride you feel climbing into it probably gives you an energy boost. You feel on top of the world, and your spirit may even improve your love life.

I don't want to sound like an ad for buying new cars. I don't drive a fancy car myself. The point I'm trying to make is that you are affected by what society thinks, even if you don't want to admit it.

What can you do to avoid feelings of insecurity like this? Take stock of the things you have that money can't buy, such as love, health, and the non-monetary rewards of your job. If it helps you, make a list of all these and post it on your refrigerator, or the dashboard of your car! And if you see any deficiencies in these areas of your life, decide that you are going to do whatever it takes to make necessary improvements.

Just the way a car owner may wax a car to bring out the luster of its paint, you can polish your romance or your health so that you can extract every possible good feeling from it. And if you go out for a jog, be sure to look down your nose at anyone driving by — no matter what type of car they have.

Avoiding a Bankrupt Romance

All couples disagree about financial issues from time to time; that's natural. Money may play a big role in determining the quality of your life, and you and your partner may have very definite ideas about how it should be spent (or saved). You may consider money issues important, but money issues shouldn't rule your life or your relationship. In the following sections, I offer advice on how to respect your partner's stance on money issues and resolve financial disagreements without depleting your romance.

Overcoming money worries

If you constantly worry about money matters, those worries occupy the place that should be reserved for romantic thoughts. Our brains are only so big, and if they're filled with worries, romance has a hard time fitting in.

You may have plenty of money and still fret about your finances. Perhaps you play the stock market, and you obsess about every little up and down of the Dow. That kind of worry also blocks your romantic leanings.

What I suggest is that when you start worrying about money, replace those thoughts with more romantic notions. You can't always manage to substitute one thought for another, but it will never work if you don't give it a try. I know that financial matters can exert a strong influence on your thought processes, but don't tell me that sex can't do the same. So after you've checked your portfolio and made any necessary decisions, or written checks to cover all your outstanding bills, attempt to put these financial loads out of your mind by thinking about the last time you made love to your spouse.

As I'm sure you've noted, I often recommend seeing a professional when a problem gets out of hand. The same advice applies here. If you find yourself dwelling on some financial issue, be it a lack of money or what to do with your money, think about going to a financial advisor. I'm not so concerned with whether or not this person can bring you a windfall, but rather with whether an advisor can unburden you of having to make these types of decisions. The goal is to free your mind to think about the really important things in life, like your spouse.

Facing everyday money woes

Mistakes are part of the dues one pays for a full life.

— Sophia Loren

Some people live under constant financial pressure for years on end. This pressure can definitely take a toll on their love lives. While I don't have an MBA and can't tell you how to get your financial house in order, I may be able to help you alleviate some of the pressures that financial difficulties may cause your household.

Vera and Ken

Ken has a decent job on Wall Street, and Vera works part-time at a clothing shop. Their incomes should be sufficient to sustain their lifestyles, except that Vera can't keep herself from passing up a bargain. She loves clothes and receives an employee discount where she works. Frequently, her take-home pay is in the negative column because she spends more money on clothes than she earns. A jewelry store across the street from her work has cases of antique jewelry — which Vera adores — and a stop into that shop during her lunch hour pushes her credit-card bills sky high.

When Ken asks Vera to cut back her spending, she tells him to stop worrying because he receives a large bonus at the end of the year. Vera explains that she is just spending the bonus ahead of time. Spending money he hasn't earned yet makes Ken nervous. His view of Vera is changing as a result of her spending. She is no longer the sexy woman he married but a person who represents danger. Ken finds that he isn't turned on by her; he's turned off. She complains that he isn't acting romantic toward her anymore and demands to know whether he has a mistress. Ken laughs to himself at the question because the truth is, even if he wanted a mistress, Vera makes sure he can't afford one.

Sticking together

The most important step you must take is to face financial problems as a couple. You may frequently blame your partner for your financial woes, putting your romance into a state of permanent bankruptcy. Of course, sometimes one person is responsible for the financial problem. Perhaps, like Vera, this person spends excessively and he or she refuses to work harder or to seek a better-paying job. If that's the case, the problem is more than a financial one. A couple facing this situation may need marital therapy. But if your financial troubles are circumstantial (say there was a lay-off at work or the car blew its engine), you need to act in unison by working together to face your financial situation.

In one sense, working together on your finances may be a boon to your romance, because any time that you work as a team you enhance your relationship. Conversely, if you constantly bicker about money without reaching positive solutions, you damage your romance. Attitude is key; it determines whether you help your relationship along or deflate it.

Overcoming adversity definitely brings two people closer. If you eat beans and rice for dinner for the third night in a row, you can either get cranky or laugh about it. If you keep your sense of humor, you may find that you can enjoy that meal more than you enjoy one in a stuffy fancy restaurant. Love doesn't need diamonds, fur coats, or fancy cars to flourish. Cliché or not, the best things in life truly are free, including love, sex, gorgeous sunsets, and wildflowers. These freebies are available to all. You need to make the time to enjoy them. The more romance you include in your daily life, the easier your financial difficulties are to bear.

Gaining perspective

I don't want to make light of financial problems. When your car breaks down and you can't afford to have it fixed, of course you feel frustrated and angry. With your car out of commission, you may find you must walk through a downpour to the supermarket in order to purchase a container of milk. When you return from the grocery store, you may be sore as hell and not ready for romance.

You need to put such experiences into perspective. Everybody, rich and poor, encounters frustration. How you react to these incidents determines the impact they have on your romance. If your partner comes in from the rain, soaked and depressed about not having a working automobile, thank him or her profusely with a hug and a kiss. If you're the soaking wet one, accept that gesture with gratitude rather than letting your festering anger ruin the moment.

Remember to watch out for each other when you're under stress, including financial stress. You may notice that your partner is a little down. Make an effort to cheer him or her up. Plan an evening stroll so that the two of you are active and not just sitting around consumed with worry.

You often hear the phrase "keep your head above water" in regard to financial problems. By helping each other, you're much more likely to succeed at staying afloat. If you fight each other, drowning becomes a distinct possibility.

Talking about your differences

Not he who has little, but he who wants too much is poor.

— Seneca

Perhaps you are both big spenders. Your savings may be low, but you may be quite happy and feel romantic toward each other. At some point, you may regret your high living, but you're adults. You understand the consequences of not saving for the future.

Problems arise in relationships when the two partners don't share the same ideas about money. One area of conflict springs from the issue of who controls the purse strings. In the days when most families had only one wage earner, the person with the job usually made the financial decisions. Today, most families live on two sources of income, and one person doesn't control how the pie is divided.

Money is a serious subject. The two of you need to talk about your incomes and agree on how they should be spent. Your spending and saving expectations may differ. Your differences need to be resolved. When you discuss these money issues, don't exaggerate your partner's saving or spending habits; these misrepresentations only create more disagreements.

Dealing with a penny pincher

A certain breed of individuals likes to count every penny. To these bean counters, spending of any kind is unbearable. Folks like this aren't likely to change. Their views of money are deep-seated. Whatever causes people to behave in this manner, penny pinchers aren't likely to ever enjoy spending money.

If your mate can't stand to let any money slip through his or her fingers, you must make a choice. Either you accept your partner's behavior or you leave the relationship. On one hand, you could learn to live without fancy things and love this person for his or her other qualities — you may even live quite harmoniously. One the other hand, you may not be able to tolerate wearing last year's (or last decade's) fashions while plenty of cash is available in your joint checking account to load up your closet with the latest designer outfits. If you fight about this problem during your entire life together, both of you will struggle to savor any romance.

If the two of you can't find a middle ground that's satisfying, consult a financial advisor. Although you may not adhere to this person's every suggestion, the plan that he or she develops may offer some good financial guidelines to help settle disputes between you and your partner.

Tackling long-term financial decisions

Many areas for dispute surface when it comes to finances. Here are some questions you may wish to ask your partner in order to resolve financial disputes:

- Should you pay off your credit card balances?
- Should you begin saving now for your children's education?
- Should your savings be placed in a secure account?
- Should you invest in the stock market?
- Should you develop a retirement plan?

The items you purchase may also be subjects for discussion. Some people spend lots of money on clothing, furniture, or tools. Others don't. If you like antiques and your partner doesn't, you may debate whether an antique purchase is an investment or a frill.

Cars raise money issues, too. How long should you drive your current automobile before replacing it? Should you lease or buy? What model should you purchase? Should you buy a new or used vehicle?

I'm no expert on how to deal with money issues. You may need a whole book that addresses all your possible family finance questions. Luckily, my friends at IDG Books Worldwide have published other books on these subjects, such as *Personal Finance For Dummies.* To help the two of you cope with financial questions, I suggest that you read a book such as this.

Making the most of what you've got

Of course, no matter how strongly you may want to solve your financial difficulties, and no matter how great the advice you get, there may be no way to get around them. Does that mean that the state of your romance needs to remain crippled? The answer is, only if you let it.

Earlier in the chapter I mentioned eating beans and rice three times a week. If you're eating plain beans and rice, then that's going to be tough on your taste buds. But what if you doctor this combination by adding different spices each time? It will still be beans and rice, but if they're tasty beans and rice, then you may even look forward to dinner.

The same principle applies to your love life. Romance costs even less than beans and rice. What you must do is invest some of your imagination into making the most of romantic moments. For starters, don't bring up financial troubles over dinner, but keep the conversation upbeat. Set aside specific times to deal with financial issues, and don't let them leak into other moments you spend together.

Here are some tips for generating romance on a tight budget:

- ✔ If you can't afford to send real flowers, then draw some on a sheet of paper.

- ✔ Massages don't cost a cent, but they show you care and give the recipient a lot of pleasure.

- ✔ Say "I love you," "thanks," and "I respect you" often.

- ✔ The lower your bank account, the more hugs and kisses you should exchange. Hug each other tightly to show that you're in this together.

- ✔ Try sleeping in the spoon position (side by side, facing the same direction, with your bodies pressed together). By sharing body heat, you'll also warm up your spirits.

- ✔ Turn off the TV, turn on the radio, and share a slow dance or a fast boogie.

- ✔ Most importantly, if you see that your partner's spirits are down, show some solidarity and do something to pick them up.

Struggling through Unemployment

Probably the worst financial worries result from losing your job. Unemployment may introduce financial worries and a raft of disturbing emotions, depending on your personality. Even the threat that your job may be pulled out from under you can have a serious effect on you and your relationship.

Losing a job strikes a savage blow to your ego. If your ego is strong, you may bounce back soon enough. If your ego is already on shaky ground, you may end up feeling entirely worthless. Your ego may hit rock bottom, and you definitely can't create romance when you are feeling so low. A job loss may even lead to clinical depression (see the "Clinical depression" sidebar), which makes it hard to get out of bed, let alone invite someone under the covers to share that bed with you.

While some people experience depression as the result of a job loss, other folks may react by becoming very angry, especially if they feel they were treated unfairly. You may be part of a whole team that got axed and therefore aren't taking the layoff personally — you probably don't feel that your job was downsized because of anything you did. Being singled out and sent to the unemployment line may hurt you on a more personal level. Your personality may be endowed with a short fuse, and adrenaline may course through your bloodstream in vast quantities when you learn of your layoff. Thoughts of revenge, not romance, then fill your mind.

Clinical depression

You may often use the word *depressed* to describe your emotional state. This state is fairly common; many folks get a case of the blues now and then. But some people suffer from *clinical depression,* which is a serious problem. Clinically depressed people require professional help; this help may be in the form of medication to help alleviate their depression. Many factors trigger clinical depression, including losing a job.

How do you recognize if you are clinically depressed (or if your partner is)? Following are some signs to look for:

Eating problems (either lack of appetite or overeating)

Sleeping problems (either sleeping too much or not enough)

Low energy

Low self-esteem

Inability to concentrate or make decisions

A feeling of hopelessness

If you, or someone you love, is demonstrating two or more of these signs (particularly if you recently experienced a known trigger of depression such as the loss of a job), you must seek professional help. See Chapter 20 for information about locating a therapist and what to expect from your visits.

If you are fired because of something you did, or failed to do, ruminations and regrets about whatever caused your severance from a regular paycheck are going to play like movies in your head. Over and over again, you'll rehash the scene that brought on this disaster. These reruns make romantic feelings toward your spouse as rare as new episodes of "I Love Lucy."

As you may imagine, the best cure for unemployment is to find a new job, especially one that pays more than the job you lost. I was fired once, and I was very upset at the time. But the firing turned out to be a good thing. In fact, I may not have become Dr. Ruth if I hadn't lost that job. But I know that not everyone bounces back in this way. The older you are, the harder it is to find a job at the same level as your old one. It's possible to find fame and fortune when you're in your 50s, but it's not the norm. If you find yourself unemployed in your middle age, look for examples of people who made great leaps when they were the same age. Use their stories as inspiration so that you can believe it's never too late to succeed. On that list could be my friend Judge Judy (we share country homes on the same lake), artist Grandma Moses, or author Frank McCourt.

If you don't find a job right away and you need to settle for one that offers a lot less prestige and income, how will your new circumstances affect your romance? Many people choose to wallow in their misery, walking around with their grumpiest pusses on and refusing to be comforted. The result? Romance withers. Maybe their libidos can kick through the doldrums every once in a while, but generally they find that their sex drive gets buried under the ashes along with romance.

Coping with bitterness

In some ways, losing a job resembles mourning the loss of a loved one. Certainly the loss hurts when it first happens, but eventually the pain is supposed to wear away and you begin to function normally again. However, losing a job can lead to a continuing series of negative emotions. After some time has passed, you may get over your resentment towards the individuals who fired you, only to find yourself angry at people interviewing you for new jobs if they fail to appreciate your talents. Every letter of rejection brings all the bile right back to the surface. A job hunt that lasts for an extended period may mean that you anticipate rejection and get angry at people who haven't even seen your resume.

This cycle of bitterness can last a long, long time. Not only does it damage you, but it also affects your loved ones. Your temper may leave no room in your heart for romance. You probably won't miss romance during this time, but your partner will. Not only do his or her romantic needs go unfulfilled, but living with an angry person can be very disconcerting. Your partner never knows when your anger is going to erupt because particular situations don't cause your outbursts — your underlying bitterness does.

Unemployment poses another danger as well; it can sometimes lead to substance abuse of either alcohol or drugs. When someone sits around all day with nothing to do other than to fume about out-of-reach demons, he or she may seek comfort from a bottle or a pill. If you or your partner tread this destructive path, seek help as soon as possible.

If your relationship has a strong foundation, it should be able to withstand several months of disruption. Hopefully, the two of you share a deep enough reservoir of love that you can both weather this particular storm. I hate to relay that not every story has a happy ending. Maybe your next job is not weeks or months away. Maybe your next position is years away or never materializes at all. Or maybe the next job is several steps *down* the ladder of success.

Q. My husband worked as a manager at the same plant for 20 years. The factory owners decided to close the plant and lay off over 1,000 workers, including my husband. With such a flood of people looking for work, my husband couldn't find a job for over six months. He was very upset. We weren't in any danger of losing our house because I work as an office manager at a law office and bring home a decent salary. Eventually, my husband took a job working as a salesclerk at a local discount store. I didn't want him to take the position because I felt he should hold out for another managerial job. My husband said he couldn't stand staying at home any longer. Though he now goes to work every day, he's no happier than he was before. In fact, he's downright miserable. When he gets home, he sits down with dinner in front of the TV and doesn't say a word. He's polite but doesn't act like he loves me at all. We haven't had sex since the day he was laid off from the plant. We may as well be two strangers living under the same roof instead of husband and wife. I can't see our situation improving. Is there any hope? Am I doomed to either live with someone whose emotions are shot or get a divorce?

A. Your husband's self-esteem was obviously very dependant on his job. Not only has he lost the status he derived from his work, but he has also become financially dependent on you. This financial dependency may make him feel even less in control and perhaps less of a man. This reaction is not uncommon and can be a very big problem. Your husband has to understand that his behavior is hurting the two of you and that he is risking the one anchor he still has in life, your relationship. The best way for him to break out of his depressed state would be to speak with a professional counselor. You may need to be very firm with him about taking this step. If he absolutely refuses, you should go to the counselor yourself. Discuss your situation with the counselor and review your options.

If your employment future looks this bleak, you may not be able to let go of your bitterness. A married couple may swear at the altar to stay together through all sorts of difficulties, but a major personality change due to a prolonged lapse in employment can do terminal damage.

Helping your partner heal

Anyone who is fired feels some pain and negative effects from the loss of his or her job. The depth of the pain and the length of the negative reaction depend on the individual. If one of you loses a job, both you and your partner can take action to alleviate the discomfort.

Taking comfort in the truth

People with financial difficulties often experience denial. Rather than go over their finances to see what their assets are and try to design a budget that they can meet, they ignore the situation. Of course, they can't really ignore it. Deep inside they worry about how they will manage.

Most of the time, people with financial troubles feel a lot better when they do their homework. With a little effort, they can find ways to make their limited finances stretch further and last longer.

If your partner is in denial about your financial straits, you must help him or her face the truth. Add up all your financial assets, figure out how much money is coming in, and look for expenses that you can cut. If your partner won't join you in this task, at least share the results with him or her. Those results may be somewhat comforting.

Smiling as you tighten your belt

Both of you should make every effort to cut back on spending voluntarily. If you say "I can give up this or that" with a smile on your face, your partner may feel better. He or she will know that you're sacrificing, and a little acting on your part may make the process of cutting back more palatable.

If you are employed and your partner is not, you must be certain not to treat your partner like a slave. If he or she refuses to help out around the house, you share a bigger problem and may require professional counseling. Hopefully, your partner takes on some extra chores during the time of unemployment; try not to make these tasks seem demeaning. Don't order your partner around — make suggestions instead. Write your grocery list together. And if your partner brings home a brand you don't like or fruit that's slightly spoiled, don't get upset about it.

"Mistakes" made by an unemployed person may be cries for help. If your partner feels self-pity, he or she may seek attention from you, of any sort. Demonstrate patience, love, and understanding, and the result will be curative. Blow up, and you can damage your partner's self-esteem further.

Searching for a new job, together

Helping an unemployed partner prepare a resume is another important task. Your partner may not find the writing easy when deciding what to leave in and what to leave out. Having another person's critical (but not too critical) eye can be very helpful. A resume to be proud of can give your partner's ego a boost.

One of the key ways to find a new job is through networking. Networking involves telling other people — family, friends, people you know in the business world — that you need a job. But what if the unemployed person lacks the nerve to tell family and friends that he or she is unemployed? In this situation, a significant other can step in and get the word out. Networking may not lead to a new job right away, but you never know unless you try.

Sharing a romantic unemployment

How can you make the entire unemployment experience more romantic? If you adopt the right attitude, you both may find romance — even in this seemingly desperate situation. If one partner is unemployed, he or she can handle a lot more of the household chores, which will free up time that both partners can use. The bad news is that you may only be able to afford a macaroni and cheese supper. The good news is that you don't need to clean the dinner dishes right away because the unemployed person can scrub them tomorrow during the day. Use the time that would be spent doing dishes to go for a walk, hold hands, and put your arms around each other. The intimate contact should make both of you feel better. This contact may not lead to sex, because unemployment can wreak havoc with a person's libido, but a few more strolls to watch the sunset just may get him or her back in the mood for love.

If you are unemployed, what else can you do to increase the romance in your relationship during this stressful period?

- Run a hot tub for your mate when he or she comes home from work.

- Mix a batch of frozen margaritas; you can both wash away some of the cares of the day.

- Be a good listener. You may feel jealous that your partner has a job and you don't, but by listening to his or her tales of workplace woe, you strengthen your relationship.

- Help your kids finish their homework before your partner comes home. That should free up some family time.

Above all else, be patient with each other and remind yourselves daily that unemployment doesn't last forever. When that new job finally arrives, share a romantic celebration that shows your partner how much you appreciate what he or she has been through during this stressful period.

When she earns more than he

This issue is not financial, but psychological. Many men admit to being upset by their spouses earning more than them. Even among those men who say they don't care, I bet most of them would be bothered if actually faced with the situation.

Why should a woman's higher income affect her partner? The man has traditionally been the breadwinner in most families. Even today, most men earn more than their wives. Part of the reason is gender discrimination, and part comes from the fact that women take time off to have children and get shunted to the so-called "mommy track."

Given this history, you can understand why a man may feel uncomfortable if his partner earns more than he does. But to be blunt, a man must accept the fact that his partner makes more money and move on. Certainly, her income improves the family's finances when she earns the most money she can; everyone's bottom line benefits from her wages.

A note to women: If you earn more money than your husband, be extra careful with his ego. You can't merely say, "Get over it," just as your husband can't tell you not to cry when you see a romantic movie. A hundred years from now, men may no longer care whether or not their wives make more than they do, but today men have legitimate grounds for feeling uncomfortable at being number two in the household. Following are some tips for surviving this potentially uncomfortable situation:

Let him get the check. When you dine at a restaurant and he insists on putting the bill on his credit card, don't make a fuss, even if you pay the monthly bill.

Don't make him ask for cash. If his spending cash comes out of your pocket, instead of giving him money to spend, leave the cash in a place where he has easy access to it.

Keep your salary differences quiet. When you're at a party, don't brag about how much money you make or, worse, put down his job in any way.

Avoid using your higher salary as a weapon. During a fight between you and your partner, try as hard as you can to not bring up the fact that you make more money than he does.

Rolling in the Dough

For most people, the term "financial difficulties" applies to not having enough money. Some people actually encounter the opposite extreme: a mother lode dropped upon their doorstep. A very few people win the lottery or a sweepstakes. A more significant number come into large inheritances or strike a gusher in a business venture.

Can there be too much of a good thing? You bet there can. Maybe this good fortune happens when he's in his 50s, and he decides he wants a younger wife. Maybe both partners start running with a faster crowd and get hooked on drugs. Or maybe they move into much ritzier digs, far from all their old friends, and discover that it's quite lonely at the top.

If you find yourself sitting on a pile of money, I'm not going to try to convince you to donate all of your cash to my favorite charities so you can avoid developing relationship problems. I do urge you to be careful about the way you spend your windfall. Don't go overboard with your wealth. Take your time spending it so that you can enjoy your new purchases. Maybe you want to fix up your old house or buy a vacation home. Or maybe you want to pick up and move altogether. Keep in mind that while good fortune may be smiling down upon you now, you never know what's around the bend. As a couple, keep all four feet on the ground.

Being able to afford a trip to the desert island everyone dreams of can certainly add romance to your relationship. But you may get so caught up in your new lifestyle that you forget about being a couple. You need to be careful not to allow material things to get in the way of your romance. A nouveau riche couple may find themselves spending even less time together than they did before — he takes up golf in an even bigger way and she commits herself to extensive redecorating of their house. It's great to come into a windfall, but be careful not to let the green ones get between you and your sweetheart.

Chapter 18

Rescuing Romance from Life's Hardships

The heart cannot be broken. The heart can be wounded so it seems the whole universe is a place of incredible suffering. But the capability of the heart to endure suffering is unlimited.

— Henry Miller

I sincerely hope that you never have to test Henry Miller's testament to the strength of your heart, but tragedy knows no bounds. As teenagers we often act as if we are indestructible, but as we grow older, we see all too many signs of how frail our bodies actually are. And although health concerns are the most common hardship we have to endure, plenty of other hardships trouble us as well.

How can romance survive life's crises? First, look back on the definition of the word that we are using in this book: Romance is the context in which the emotion of love exists. Can love exist within a context full of tragedy? Of course it can. If the person you love falls ill, do you stop loving him or her? Of course not. In fact, as you watch your partner suffer and bravely battle whatever demon has grabbed a hold of him or her, you may end up feeling even stronger love. Your heart may feel like breaking at seeing someone you love suffer, but that doesn't negate the power of your love. And the person with the illness may love you more too, because we often place more value on something when we're about to lose it than we did when it was readily available.

Certainly the writers of romantic novels, plays, and movies know this to be true. Rarely do you find a storyline in which romance is in full bloom while the sun shines brightly and all is well. More often than not, the hero and heroine are fighting the forces of nature or evil, and because they are thrown together in the midst of a crisis, they fall in love with each other. Their love strengthens with every danger they face.

Of course, in a fictional world, the heroes don't have to deal with feeding the kids, doing the laundry, and handling last-minute assignments from the boss while scaling whatever hurdles are put in front of them. So although hardship *per se* may actually help to create a romantic setting, crises can wreak havoc on romance when added to the stresses of real life.

This chapter offers guidance for keeping romance in the picture when you and your partner face a serious illness, the death of a close friend or family member, or even a natural disaster. You may still doubt that romance can survive in such trying circumstances, but as I show you, attitude is everything.

Understanding Fear

You should start by understanding why crises have such a profound impact on our relationships. Crises generally evoke an emotion that deadens romance: fear. Say the word *cancer* to yourself, and your heart probably skips a beat. Say that word while thinking about your partner, and you may feel like you'll never catch your breath again. If you experience the fear that emerges from a great hardship, then you may find that all thoughts of romance become locked in the deepest vault of your heart. You may not even want to look at your loved one because a glance can set off an emotional upheaval.

If you're not in the midst of a crisis situation, you can be objective and realize that allowing fear to overcome you is a mistake. Fear drives a wedge between you and your partner so that at the moment you need each other the most, you find yourselves drifting further and further away. If fear has already entered your consciousness, then driving it back out is difficult.

Using anger as a disguise

Anna and Sam

Anna and Sam were both 80. Anna had undergone a triple by-pass two years earlier, and then her husband, Sam, had his turn. Although Anna hadn't suffered any complications from her surgery, Sam developed breathing problems in the hospital that continued even after he came home. He was always short of breath and couldn't put more than a couple of words together at a time. Each time he tried to say something to her, Anna would cut him off.

She'd start to yell at him, telling him to be quiet because she didn't have the time to stand around waiting to hear what he had to say.

Although Anna seemed to be angry at Sam, the real motivation for her outbursts was that she was deathly afraid. She didn't understand why Sam was having such breathing problems. The doctor said it happened to some people, but because she had come through the same surgery with flying colors, seeing her husband barely able to speak and unable to take even a few steps before he had to lean heavily on his walker frightened Anna. She lived in constant fear that his heart would give out from the strain of undertaking everyday activities like getting out of bed. She couldn't take watching him have a heart attack, nor could she stand the thought of having to face the world alone.

Rather than voice her fears to Sam, which would have required admitting them to herself, Anna took the opposite tack. She'd bark at him constantly because watching his struggles brought her own fears to the surface.

Fear often fools its victim by taking on other faces, as it did with Anna. Sometimes, a sick person's partner appears to be angry all the time. The healthy partner snaps at the ill one and offers absolutely no sympathy. The healthy partner may appear to have a heart of steel when the reverse is true. Another common result of fear is that the healthy person spends as little time with the ill partner as possible, because just seeing the devastation of illness makes him or her sick with fear. That person may claim to need to spend extra hours working and hire a nurse to take care of his or her partner. He or she may try to push the ill partner into going for extra rehabilitation because of a desperate need to drive away haunting nightmares.

All these reactions stem from fear. If you are in that situation, you may be terrified that you are on the verge of losing your lover and afraid that if you give in to your real emotions, you won't be able to handle them. So instead of the compassion you'd like to offer, your fear twists your tongue, and the loving words you intend to say turn into angry jibes. If your partner already feels somewhat guilty for making your life more difficult, then hearing these hostile attacks only makes him or her feel worse.

Facing mortality

Seeing someone who is very sick also makes us afraid of our own mortality. In our day-to-day lives, we often don't pay much attention to our health. But when you watch a loved one fighting a serious disease, you naturally think, "That could be me." Lurking in the background are the thoughts of what will happen if this condition is fatal: "What will happen to me, the one left behind? How will I handle being alone? Will I ever have another partner?" These thoughts are accompanied by added guilt, because you feel that you're supposed to be concerned only with your partner. Because you are relatively healthy, you aren't entitled to any sympathy, or at least not yet.

Allowing yourself to think the worst

Can you totally repress your fears? Not really. You can mask them, but they continue under the surface. You have to learn to cope with fear. You can't go around crying or shaking like a leaf all day. But you also have to let yourself experience some fear as an escape valve. If you keep fear bottled up inside, it grows in strength and comes out in some of the ways I discuss in the preceding section. My advice is to permit yourself a short period, once or twice a day, when you let yourself think about the worst:

- ✔ What happens if he dies?
- ✔ What if she never regains the use of her legs?
- ✔ What if I'm faced with the decision of whether or not to terminate life support?

After you spend five or ten minutes staring your inner fears in the face, you can put them back in your emotional storage chest so that they don't become overwhelming.

You can ask these soul-baring questions of yourself out loud, but I wouldn't invite anyone else into this conversation except a professional counselor. If you reveal your inner fears to friends and family, they may bring the issues up at times when you don't want to deal with them. They may think that they are being helpful by talking about them, when at that particular time you may need all your strength and can't deal with them. If you have a sibling or friend whom you really trust and who knows when to listen and when to keep quiet, then you could confide in that person. But because you want to limit the time you spend giving in to these fears, you may be better off facing them by yourself within a time period that you can control.

Coping with Chronic Illness and Disability

Some maladies strike you hard and then allow you to recuperate. Others do their damage and then linger on, maybe forever. For example, if you've been in an accident and become a paraplegic, unless medicine takes some major leaps in the near future, you're probably not going to regain the use of your legs.

Some people faced with such a calamity give up, while others do their utmost to make the best of their situation. The latter are often called "heroic" or "brave," though in a way their paths actually are easier — admitting defeat to a physical ailment ultimately makes living with the condition worse. Certainly a person who is fighting the ailment is going to offer more to his or her romance than one who has lost all hope. In cases where the ill or disabled person feels hopeless and ready to give up, professional counseling must come into play (see Chapter 20).

Fighting for life (and romance)

A chronically ill or disabled person who fights to maintain a good quality of life gets many rewards for his or her efforts. He or she gains increased self-respect with every hurdle cleared. That person also, I hope, gains improved health and strength over time.

But having someone fight so hard to maintain and improve his or her life has a down side. In order to clear everyday hurdles, a person with a chronic condition must spend lots more energy than a healthy person does. Just walking across the street may be a major battle. If healthy people have a hard time finding the time and energy for romance, imagine what chronically ill or disabled people go through to fulfill their romantic needs and the needs of their partners.

Respecting the right to romance

Because romance is a private matter, we often don't consider that people with physical impairments must struggle to sustain their love lives. If someone asked you what you would miss most about being blind, you could come up with a laundry list of items, but you may not mention a lack of romance. In fact, many of us look at people with physical afflictions as being asexual, which is far from the truth.

People with disabilities or chronic illnesses often find adapting to every other aspect of their lives easier than struggling to keep romance alive. If matters are really bad, their partners may even leave. And single people who are ill or disabled, whether they are newly alone or were single when disaster struck, generally have more difficulty finding partners than healthy singles.

Because society tends to look at romance as a luxury, we don't offer much help to people with chronic health problems who need to nurture or find romance. If chronically ill people are forced to live in a hospital situation, we actually put up barriers to romance by making privacy virtually nonexistent.

Instead of being disturbed by thoughts of ill or disabled people loving their partners and having sex, we should ask ourselves, "What if that were me? Would I want to spend the rest of my days in solitary confinement?" The answer is almost certainly "no."

We must all change our attitude when it comes to illness, disability, and romance. I have long called for making private rooms available to people who must live in long-term care facilities. These could be used by couples or even single people who need some privacy to masturbate.

Battling bitterness

If you suffer a chronic illness or disability, becoming bitter is easy, and bitterness can destroy a romance. You may vacillate between feeling sorry for yourself, contemptuous toward your healthy partner, and angry at the world. All these emotions are understandable, but you must make every effort not to let them linger. If any one of them sticks around indefinitely, your relationship will take a strong, possibly fatal, hit.

If your partner takes care of you, you have an extra hurdle to overcome. Undoubtedly, you feel a measure of guilt about the sacrifices your partner makes. A common way of dealing with this guilt is to convince yourself that you deserve your partner's full attention — that you should expect nothing less. This is a dangerous attitude to take, because it eliminates the need for gratitude. You should remind yourself daily that although you cannot feel guilty for your physical condition, you can and should feel grateful to have a partner who is so dedicated to you that he or she is willing to change everything in order to care for you.

I fully expect that you will experience days when your situation feels overwhelming and you struggle to find reasons to be happy. Here's a suggestion for getting through those rough moments: a "feel better" collection. I have a special drawer that I keep full of letters and mementos that make me feel better. I suggest that you start your own collection of mementos that remind you of how much you are loved. If your partner goes out of his or her way to do something special for you, write a note about it and put it in a drawer or box. I'll bet that very soon you'll have quite a collection of such notes. When you're having a bad day, pull these notes out and read them. They will give your spirits a lift, and instead of being crabby toward your significant other, you'll be able to put on a big smile.

Caring for an ill or disabled partner

Assuming that someone who suffers a chronic illness or disability has a partner and that the relationship survives the stress of the crisis, we must recognize that both people suffer because of this dramatic change. For example, maybe the couple used to play tennis together. The healthy partner can still play, but he or she may feel guilty about finding someone new to play tennis with. His or her partner can't enjoy the sport anymore, so the healthy person may somehow feel wrong for enjoying it.

A more severe situation occurs when the healthy person must take constant care of the sick one. The healthy partner can become virtually homebound. That person may set aside career, friends, and hobbies indefinitely in order to provide the necessary care.

If the ill or disabled person has limited mobility, life for a couple can change in thousands of ways that may seem minor but become very significant when combined. For example, the couple goes to a wedding, and she has no one to dance with. They're at a party, and he has to get food for her before he can eat. The doorbell rings while she's upstairs and he's downstairs, and she has to run to answer it. The healthy partner must be extremely brave and committed to the relationship to stay through the situation.

Resenting the sacrifice

Some people make such sacrifices with heavy hearts. They force themselves to take care of their sick spouses because they feel they must, but they resent every second of it. Obviously, romance cannot survive in such a relationship.

Even someone madly in love who has to take care of all the extra duties involved in assisting a disabled person is going to have days when his or her energy is completely spent. On those days, the caregiver may snap at anyone seemingly without reason. As long as the bad mood isn't constant, the couple can still derive much pleasure together.

However, the person who is a caregiver totally out of duty, without a trace of love or warmth, will always be miserable. Romance shouldn't be allowed to evaporate because of a health crisis; it needs to be intensified. Helping romance grow in the face of a crisis is difficult, but the rewards are commensurate with the effort.

Asking for help

If caring for your partner takes up every second of your day, then it will be impossible to find time for romance. Don't try to be a hero or heroine and do it all yourself. If you can get help, do so. (Because every illness is different, I suggest that you ask your doctor about where to get help.) If no social service agencies can offer any aid in caring for your partner, and your budget doesn't allow you to hire an aide, then ask family and friends. Many people may want to help you but don't know how. Or maybe they even offered assistance when the problem first occurred, and you turned them down. In general, people feel good donating a few hours of their time to a good cause, and you'll feel much better if you get a break from constant caregiving duties.

If you can free up some time by asking for help, you probably need to spend some of it taking care of yourself. You may want to get away from the house for a while. Whether you go out for a nice lunch alone or spend time visiting with friends you rarely see anymore, make sure that you spend some of your free time pampering yourself so you feel stronger when you return home.

In addition to pampering yourself, spend some of your free time pampering your romance. Plan a picnic so that when you and your partner are alone again, you can venture into the sunshine and enjoy some summer fun. Go shopping for a CD of romantic music that you both can enjoy. Rent some romantic movies. Whatever you do, devote at least part of your time away from your partner a thinking about how to make your time together more romantic.

Approaching the subject of sex

Before deciding whether sex is possible for you and your ill or disabled partner, you must get an all clear from the doctor. Not every doctor will raise the subject of sex without prodding. If the doctor finds the subject embarrassing, he or she may conveniently forget to mention it. But even if you are embarrassed as well, you have to know the answer to this question. If you have any doubts about whether intercourse is safe or even possible, the two of you may avoid sex and possibly miss out on lots of pleasure. So make sure that you bring it up, and don't settle for a simple yes or no answer if you have more involved questions. You're entitled to get these answers, so take the lead if that's the only way that you can get the information.

Sometimes, the ill or disabled person cannot fully enjoy sex. He or she may have lost the ability to have an orgasm or lost interest in sex. But just because that person can't enjoy all the benefits of sex doesn't mean that he or she should avoid taking part in any sexual activity.

> **Q:** My husband suffered a spinal injury and lost the use of his legs. He is no longer able to have an erection. Because he cannot enjoy sex, he has given it up entirely. If I ask him to hold me in bed, he'll do it grudgingly but only for a few minutes. When the sexual tension gets too bad, I sometimes masturbate, but I really hate doing it. I wish I could get him to touch me and bring me to orgasm, but he refuses. Is there any way that I can get him to help me with my needs? I do so much for him, so I don't feel that I'm asking too much.

> **A:** Your request is a legitimate one, but he undoubtedly feels bitter about having lost his ability to have erections and orgasms and can't find enough concern for your needs to overcome these feelings. Saying to him, "In exchange for all I do, you could at least help me sexually," would be difficult. I know that you don't want his attentions to come as a result of blackmail. You need an intermediary to talk to him. If you could get him to see a marriage counselor, perhaps that person could help him understand how you feel and change his attitude toward your sexual needs.

Bringing your partner to orgasm doesn't require the same level of physical activity as playing tennis or dancing. If you can move only one hand, you can pleasure a partner. And although your partner may find someone else with whom to play tennis or go dancing, you probably don't want him or her to find a new sex partner.

A healthy partner continues to have sexual needs and feel aroused, so even if sexual activity does not give you sexual satisfaction, you should make every effort to take part. I hope that you derive some pleasure from being touched and stroked in return.

Some healthy people lose their desire to have sex with their disabled partners. Perhaps you still have strong feelings for your partner and help to care for him or her, but you aren't able to become aroused because of the changes in your partner's body. In such instances, a sex therapist, who has the training and experience in this area, may be very helpful. I would strongly urge that the healthy partner not give up on having sex but instead seek help in order to restore what was lost.

Although an illness or disability may change the nature of how you engage in sex, by making certain positions impossible or forcing you to be slightly less vigorous, you shouldn't allow that to spoil sex for you. (See *Sex For Dummies* for some ideas about positions to try.) Make up for your physical limitations by spending more time slowly giving each other whatever types of pleasure are available.

Healing through romance

When one of you is facing a devastating illness or disability, make every effort to tap into the power of romance. It not only keeps your relationship strong so that the two of you can face the situation together, but it may help the partner suffering physical ailments to heal more quickly.

What can you do to foster romance when a partner is suffering greatly? You can spend time holding hands. Stroke your partner's head. Cuddle. Bring up past experiences that were pleasurable. Even if your partner is so sick that you can't tell whether he or she is able to grasp what you are saying, talk about your pleasant memories. A partner who is extremely ill undoubtedly feels fearful. If you can take his or her thoughts to a pleasant place, even for a few moments, you can provide a wonderful respite from suffering.

This outpouring of romance should continue even after the healing process is well under way. Hospitals may get patients out of bed much quicker than they used to, but the healing process can't be rushed. Conversations that you have about the good times can be therapeutic; they help put your partner in a better frame of mind and may speed up the healing process.

Deciding to sever your ties

When you got married you swore an oath to stay together through both sickness and health, and you may have meant it at the time. But when faced with the reality, not everyone can cope.

No breakup is ever easy, but one that takes place under such circumstances is going to be extremely rough on both parties. Looking at this situation from the outside, it may be easy to lay the bulk of the blame on the healthy half of the couple, but that's not a fair assumption to make.

I certainly recommend that couples severing their ties in the face of a health crisis use the services of a marriage counselor to ease the way. In fact, I think this is more important than when both people are healthy. The healthy person may have an overwhelming need to resume a normal life, but if his or her ties to the ill person can be partially maintained, the ill person may benefit. I'm not saying this will always work out, but marital therapy may help to lessen the bitterness over the breakup.

Dealing with Death

None of us is fully prepared to deal with death. In some societies, people accept death as an integral part of everyday life, but most Western societies focus on the living. When we encounter this natural but very mysterious aspect of our humanity, we often have great difficulties dealing with it. If a family member, particularly one of your parents, passes away, you or your partner may encounter serious psychological repercussions. The person who has suffered the loss will naturally be in mourning for a while. But how long that mourning period lasts is where problems can arise.

Mourning too long

A mourning period has no set period of time. You can't say that you should be getting over your loss after one week or one month. That time period is unique to each individual and depends on your psychological makeup and the relationship that you had with the person who died. If you were close, you will never forget this person, and your relationship really will not end. But after a certain time, you have to accept this person's passing and be able to function normally, and that is when mourning will be over. Even if that doesn't happen right away, some progress should become apparent as the weeks pass, especially where your relationship with your significant other is concerned.

You may find that you have difficulties making this adjustment. Maybe you become overwhelmed by guilt. Or perhaps you were psychologically dependent on the deceased, and you just can't separate yourself.

By allowing romance back into your relationship, you would make real progress toward resuming your normal life together. But perhaps that is not your goal. Perhaps, because of some guilt that you bear, you feel that if you allow yourself to move on, you will forget about the deceased person. You mistakenly feel that by letting the mourning period drag on, you somehow atone for your guilt.

Your partner may also feel handcuffed by this situation. He or she may feel uncomfortable trying to rekindle your romance because of the priority that mourning is given. Your partner may feel that instigating romance is disrespectful, and so he or she treads on eggshells around you, which only prolongs the problem.

Helping your partner overcome grief

The partner who is not in mourning has a responsibility to the relationship to help end the grieving period. He or she should at least try to lift the mourning partner's spirits, and if that's not possible, then he or she should strongly suggest that the grieving partner seek the help of a counselor.

If you try to lift your partner's spirits, don't just announce, "Honey, the mourning period is over, and I'm going to get you out of your doldrums." That's not going to work because it's artificial. Instead, you have to take action that will have the same effect without being so blatant.

First, try to brighten your partner's environment:

- ✔ Put fresh flowers around the house.
- ✔ Keep the curtains open during the day, and turn on lots of lights at night.
- ✔ Put some up-tempo music on the stereo.
- ✔ Prepare some meals that are very tasty, maybe even spicy.
- ✔ Invite lively friends over, and clue them in to what you are doing.

Also try to get your partner out of the house:

- ✔ Go out to dinner. Even if you only go to McDonald's, at least the atmosphere will be upbeat.
- ✔ See a funny movie.
- ✔ Anytime the sun is shining, go outside. Sunshine is a great antidepressant.

In your conversations, try to be future-oriented:

- ✔ Make plans for a trip.
- ✔ Talk about upcoming events, even if the conversation is as simple as what to make for dinner.
- ✔ Try not to do all the talking; get your partner involved.

As I said, mourning has no set time period, but if you've been trying your best to break through the sadness and you're not making any progress after several months have passed, then you should consult a counselor. It could be a religious leader, a social worker, or a psychologist. The counselor will be able to help you evaluate the situation, and can work with your partner if necessary. If your partner is severely depressed, he or she may need to see a psychiatrist, who can prescribe medication.

Suffering a mutual loss

Tragedy knows no bounds, so a death may strike both of you with equal force, such as the death of a child or mutual close friend. Your relationship then becomes an important lifeboat. If you can help bring each other out of mourning at about the same time, then I'll bet that your relationship will be even stronger. If one of you is lagging behind, then the other should attempt the strategies I discuss in the preceding section. And again, if you can't do it alone, then get professional help.

Sticking Together after Losing Everything

Illness and death aren't the only hardships you can suffer. Every year, tens of thousands of people are adversely affected by disasters such as floods, mudslides, hurricanes, tornadoes, and earthquakes. And many calamities, such as auto accidents and fires, are created by human activities.

Adversity of any type can definitely bring a couple closer, but it can also split them apart if they're not careful. I think that most people depend on their partners for support, but sometimes the level of stress caused by a disaster can make one person turn against everything and everyone. People can become overwhelmed and withdraw into themselves. Rather than try to salvage what they have left, such as relationships with persons they love, their desire to run away from a world that has hurt them is so great that they even try to distance themselves from their partners.

In a sense these people are also mourning, though in this case they mourn the loss of inanimate objects, like the contents of a house. If these possessions took a lifetime to accumulate, their loss will be quite discouraging. Having to start over, especially after a certain age, can make a person want to give up.

Helping your partner find hope

Can you actually experience romance while living in a Red Cross shelter or a relative's spare bedroom? I think those situations are a "package deal." After a disaster, hope is more important than romance, so your job is to give your partner hope. If he or she sees you rolling up your sleeves and trying to put your life back together, then he or she may be dragged into action, too. Eventually, as you start to make some progress at restoring your household, you both should feel more hopeful about the future.

Notice that I said *should*. In some cases, the burden is just too much. Then the partner who is coping with the situation should contact the proper agencies to get help. If you've just lost everything, then you probably can't afford a private counselor, but federal, state, and local branches of government do provide assistance for people in need, and that includes counseling for those who can't deal with the crisis.

Finding romance in hardship

I'll assume that you've made some progress and are on your way to creating a new life for yourselves. Isn't that situation similar to when the two of you first got together? Is there a more romantic time in a couple's life than when they are just starting out and the whole world waits for them? Potentially, this new beginning for the two of you could be quite romantic.

If you live through a natural disaster or fire, the two of you will most likely be spending more time together. Obviously, you'll both be working hard to gain back some of what you lost. But I hope you can do much of that work together. Remind each other to savor every small victory. Although I don't wish this type of situation on anyone, I do think that each new purchase the two of you make after losing all you own will have a great deal of meaning. Don't miss an opportunity to thank each other for working so hard and being so strong.

Rebounding After a Crime

Thankfully, crime statistics have been decreasing recently, but tens of thousands of people still are victimized by crime each year. Some crimes, such as having your car stolen from a parking space, have little impact on your romance, despite their financial wallop. But when the victim and criminal come face to face, no matter what the actual crime is, the victim will suffer some psychological consequences.

When other people's problems impact you

The sky doesn't always have to fall on your head in order for your life to be turned upside down. Suppose that your father-in-law dies and your mother-in-law decides that she's going to move in with you. Or your brother loses his job and is thrown out of his house, and he and his family are camping out in the living room. This type of change throws your family dynamic into a tizzy.

Any loss of privacy detracts from your state of romance — that's a given. An old adage says that no good deed goes unpunished, and if you allow someone else to share your living space, then that good deed will have its cost. If you and your partner allow this incursion to get under your skin, then the new arrangement becomes even more challenging.

My advice to people living under such conditions is to develop a thick skin. I'll give you an example. When you use the toilet, you always close the door, right? Well, in the military, you wouldn't have the luxury of a door or even a stall around the toilet because battlefields don't have such amenities. And you know what? Soldiers in basic training learn to adapt. How does the military apply to your life? Perhaps normally you might not hug and kiss in front of other people, and you might be hesitant to make noise while having sex if you know others can hear. With long term houseguests in the picture, you have to let your modesty drop off your shoulders like an unhooked bra. Your relationship is too important to have it become a shadow of its former self because of your good deed.

If a woman is afraid that her home is no longer safe from thieves, then she's going to be uncomfortable closing the bedroom door and becoming aroused. If she has been raped, the scars of that episode can cause arousal problems for the rest of her life. And a man who has been carjacked once may never again feel comfortable going out for a drive.

The human spirit is amazingly resilient. For example, think of Senator John McCain, who was a POW in Vietnam and went on to run for president. He certainly had problems in his life after that experience, but he was able to overcome the torturous conditions he endured.

Resilience requires willpower. You must say to yourself, "I am not going to let some miserable criminal ruin my life." You may be scared, but if you force yourself to face your fears, you can overcome them.

Fear can take a terrible toll on romance, as I discuss earlier in the chapter. That one strong emotion can block out many others, particularly those as fragile as the feelings that arise from romance. So if you want the rest of your life to be elevated by romantic feelings, you have to employ all your willpower to overcome your fears. It won't be easy, but your yearning for romance can also be a great motivator. Tell yourself, "Yes, I'm afraid, but I want to be able to love my partner fully and completely, and I'm not going to let fear stop me." Eventually, fear will fade back into the dark recesses of your psyche where it came from, and you can have a fulfilling life. And if you can't do this on your own, then go for counseling. In many states, such counseling may even be automatically provided for victims of a crime.

Knowing When to Leave Romance Alone

Have you ever had one of those weeks? You know the kind — the babysitter had to go back to Ireland, the car's transmission died, the roof sprang a leak, and both kids came down with the flu. Any one of these problems would be annoying and stressful but manageable. When you put them all together, you're ready to pull your hair out.

In this chapter, I insist that you can find romance in sickness, death, and disaster. But guess what? I'm not touching a bad week with a ten-foot pole. After it passes, you can look back at a bad week and laugh, but while you're going through it, romance is the last thing on your mind. In fact, you don't want to associate the word *romance* with a week like that because you could taint your idea of what romance means.

No relationship can be romantic every single day. Life is too complicated for that. Try not to force romance into every day, but don't allow romance to drift so far off shore that you can't pull it back. If you have a week without a whiff of romance in it, don't sweat it. Trust that the next one will be better and more romantic.

Part V
Troubleshooting Your Love Life

The 5th Wave   By Rich Tennant

"I don't know, Mona—sometimes I get the feeling you're afraid to get close."

In this part . . .

Most couples can kick start their romance on their own, if they're willing to devote the time and attention it deserves. But sometimes, the issues prohibiting romance are too serious or complex to handle on your own. In those instances, you need to seek outside help for your relationship. This chapter helps you identify when that type of assistance is needed.

In Chapter 20, I help you decide when to call on the services of a marital counselor and show you ways to locate a professional you feel comfortable working with. Chapter 21 offers an overview of common physical problems that impact sexual relationships and helps you identify when it's necessary to seek medical help for the sake of your romance.

Chapter 19

Navigating Common Traps and Pitfalls: TV to the Internet

In This Chapter

▶ Learning to control your TV habits

▶ Using the Web wisely

▶ Keeping sports, shopping, and other hobbies in check

▶ Creating a routine that allows for romance

*I*n the "good old days" (whose good qualities may actually have existed or may be a figment of our collective imagination), we definitely had far fewer distractions in our lives. Life was simpler before television, VCRs, DVDs, cable, satellite dishes, remote controls, stereos, personal cassette/CD players, MP3 players, hard wired and cell phones, beepers, Nintendo, GameBoys, PlayStations, PCs, Palm Pilots, Instant Messenger-ing, and the World Wide Web.

But I can't personally testify that the average living room in the "good old days" experienced lots more romance just because no tangled web of extension cords and cables was clinging to the baseboards. Maybe before people could make the interior of their homes brighter than Dodge City at high noon, couples merely yawned out of boredom after the sun set and went to bed a whole lot earlier. I'll bet that when candles were the only way of keeping the darkness at bay, nobody thought of their dim, flickering light as being very romantic.

But whatever life was like before the Invasion of the Electronic Gadgets, we are all well aware that these beeping gizmos suck time out of our lives now. Today, many people look up from their PC screens to see the sun rising in the East, having spent the last 10 hours surfing the Internet. I'm sure that pulling an all-nighter didn't happen very often when the height of a night's excitement was playing cat's cradle with a piece of yarn.

Have all these gizmos endangered romance? Maybe not any more so than the two wage-earner family, instant mashed potatoes, and artificial flowers, but they certainly have had a negative effect. Sadly, when we have to decide between spending time on a romantic expedition and spending time with an electronic device, the bells and whistles of the electronic world often win out.

As I mention in Chapter 5, the modern era has brought both good and bad influences with regards to romance. Being able to send a personal e-mail to a loved one is great. Ordering flowers online can be a real time-saver. And for those couples who want to try out some sex toys, being able to have them delivered directly from your PC to your front door removes all the embarrassment, assuming your postal delivery person doesn't x-ray the contents of every box he delivers. But if couples aren't careful, these same tools can reduce the romantic elements of their relationships to a few bytes.

In this chapter, I examine the dangers posed by these electronic marvels as well as other potential intrusions on your love life. I also offer suggestions for what you can do to rekindle the romance despite all these distractions.

Tuning Out the TV

When radio was at its zenith, families would gather around to listen to the stars of the day speak to them right in their living rooms, so early radio served as a unifier. And in the early days of television, when the set was huge and the screen was small, families continued to assemble together to watch their favorite broadcasts from the limited choices available.

Later, costs decreased, so now many homes have two or more sets. Channels proliferated, so that many programs are available for every possible family niche, including the dog. With the advent of the remote control, men and women drifted off into differing viewing habits. The bottom line is this: Television ceased to be a unifier and became a divisive force. While he is in the den, thumb glued to the remote watching ten sporting events at the same time, she is in the bedroom watching a movie that a few months ago could be seen only in theaters. A romantic picture this isn't.

In my opinion, Americans watch too much television. This habit is not only bad for their romances, but it eats up time they should spend on other things as well. Yes, some wonderful programs exist (including some documentaries that I have produced). But many people don't sit down to watch a specific program that they've selected ahead of time. Instead, they hunt around for something and often settle for a program that is not worth their time.

Focusing your viewing habits

I know that I can't get Americans to stop watching television, even if I promised everyone great sex. We're hooked; there's no getting around it. But

I do have some suggestions to make TV slightly less obtrusive and your home environment slightly more romantic:

- **Never put the television on as background noise.** Many homes have a TV constantly on in every room. I don't know how the people living under this bombardment can even think, but I do know that they can't hold a conversation. This habit does terrible harm to your relationship. Personally, I don't think you should have the TV on as background even if you're all alone, but when your spouse or children come home, shut that TV off so that you can communicate with each other instead of allowing that box to do all the talking.

- **Do not watch television during dinner, unless you are eating alone.** Dinnertime is the perfect opportunity for a couple, or an entire family, to share conversation and reconnect after having been away from each other all day. This process is very important for rekindling romance. With CNN and other news channels, you can get the news at any time, so don't force yourselves into silence at the dinner table because of the TV.

- **Think about what you want to watch ahead of time.** If you're struck with the urge to vegetate for a bit by staring at the tube, then select a program from the paper and tune in to that one show. If you want to hunt around during the commercials, feel free to do so, but turn the set off at the end of the show you originally selected. That will limit the time you spend in front of the TV.

- **Plan your viewing times together.** If he wants to watch something from 8 to 9 p.m. and she wants to watch something else from 9 to 10 p.m., then the whole evening will be devoted to television. If you have two TV sets, I suggest taping the 8 p.m. show, so you can each watch your shows at the same time and spend the hour between 8 and 9 doing something together. It doesn't even have to be particularly romantic — you could be doing a load of laundry together — but as long as you're paying attention to each other, the time spent will be good for your relationship.

- **Don't count TV time as romantic time.** If the two of you do watch a program together (yes, it does happen once in a while), don't count that as quality time, unless it is something like a documentary on The History Channel that leads to a discussion. Intellectual stimulation is romantic; paired vegging out isn't.

- **Keep late night viewing to a minimum.** I told Johnny Carson that he was partially responsible for reducing the sex lives of Americans. Jay Leno, Dave Letterman, and a host of late night news anchors now share that same responsibility. Although watching late night television is okay, it shouldn't become a religion so that you have to watch the news or a talk show every single night. Making love to your partner, or even talking with him or her, should take priority over any TV program. If you can't break this habit in a piecemeal fashion, then you're better off stopping altogether.

Giving romance a sporting chance

It may seem like discrimination against men, but I have to put watching sports on TV into a category of its own. And yes, I know that many women watch sports with the same fervor, but you can't really compare the numbers.

In the not-too-distant past, an occasional sporting event was shown on TV; now they're nonstop. You could literally give up watching sports that are played with a round ball and still find yourself glued to the set for hours on end. The networks know that men like sports, and the beer and car industries want to be able to reach this audience with their commercials, so together they've put on a never-ending show. The problem is that increased viewing of sports programs, particularly on the weekends, reduces the amount of time couples can spend together.

Jim and Judie

Judie knew when they were dating that Jim liked sports, but he always made time for her, so it didn't seem to be a big deal. They got married in June, and although Jim would watch the occasional baseball game, again Judie found that it didn't interfere with their activities. But then September rolled around and football season started. Jim was suddenly unavailable every Sunday afternoon. Judie had always loved the fall weather, but no matter how crisp and blue the sky was, she couldn't get Jim away from the TV set on Sunday afternoons.

Football started to become a sore point with them. Judie would ask Jim during the week if he would go to a barbecue at some friend's house, but he would have to check the football schedule first. On Sunday, Judie would sulk and bang things during the game, which would get Jim annoyed, and they'd often fight. And then if Judie wanted to see a friend for drinks during the week, Jim would object, citing her complaints about his football watching. These fights continued until Super Bowl Sunday had passed and Judie got her husband back on weekends. The next year, as summer drew to an end, Judie dreaded the arrival of another football season.

Trimming back your viewing time

I know that most men are not going to give up watching sports entirely, and everyone is entitled to some relaxation of his or her own choosing, but men can do several things to keep this habit from destroying all romance in their relationships:

✔ **Let your significant other know ahead of time when the must-see games are going to air.** That way, she can plan her weekend without getting blind-sided, setting you up for a 15-yard penalty.

✔ **Be willing to tape the occasional game and watch it at a more convenient time than during her sister's wedding.** It's certainly possible to keep from finding out the score, and the advantage of watching a taped game is that you can fast forward through all the commercials, half-time reports, and end of game time-outs so that a three-hour game can be watched in about 15 minutes. (Okay, I exaggerate, but you can definitely save at least an hour.)

✔ **Try not to mix seasons.** Don't start watching football until after the World Series, don't start watching basketball or hockey until after the Super Bowl, and don't start watching baseball until after the basketball or hockey play-offs. This should help to knock off a good 25 percent of your sports viewing, while allowing you to catch the most important games of each season.

✔ **Consider watching only the second half of all sporting events.** Many games aren't decided until the end anyway.

✔ **Never watch golf or bowling on TV unless you're recuperating from triple by-pass surgery and need the calming effect.**

You're right, all of these tips are aimed at cutting down the amount of time you spend watching sports. Is this fair? I'm going to let you answer that question. I want you to guesstimate how much time you spend every week watching sports. You watch more sports during some seasons than others, but try to come up with an honest average. Then try to guesstimate how much time you devote every week to spending some quality time with your significant other. If, by some miracle, those two numbers are in balance, then you probably don't need to cut back your sports viewing. But if the numbers tip heavily on the side of sports, then you may want to admit that some correction is in order.

Using the extra time romantically

Ladies: If he's giving up watching all or part of a game, or if he's taping a game for viewing later and tells you about it, be ready to reciprocate. Put aside whatever you were going to do, and do something — take a walk, play tennis, plant a bush in the garden — together.

Gents: It's possible that your mate doesn't have time for romantic activity. While you watch ball games, maybe she usually does laundry or helps the kids with their homework. She may not be able to drop what she was doing to do something entertaining or romantic with you. Does that give you the right to go back to watching your full quota of sports? Absolutely not. Instead, offer to help her out. Believe it or not, doing the laundry or helping your son with his science project gets you points for being a romantic if it frees up some time for your blushing bride. If she gets some room to take a deep breath, she may actually be able to allow some romantic feelings to seep into her consciousness, and who knows what results that will get you.

One more thing: Don't go up to your mate and say, "All right, I turned off the game, so what do you want to do together?" If you want to be romantic, first assess the situation. Is she up to her knees in work of some sort? If that's the case, offer to help. If she's sitting reading the paper, ask her to go for a swim, visit some garage sales, go to the local farm and pick apples, or anything else you feel like doing.

By the way, substituting *engaging* in a sport (including, but not exclusive to, sex) for *watching* sports isn't a bad idea. If the two of you are playing tennis against another couple, you can still root for the home team while burning off some calories and acting as teammates.

Surfing the Internet without Drowning Your Romance

Surfing the Internet can be more useful than watching TV. If your kids need socks and you go on the Internet to order them, then you're not wasting time or taking yourself away from your partner; shopping online probably takes less time than going to a store and buying the socks. The problem with the Internet is that after you get sucked in, getting back out is sometimes hard. You go looking for socks, but then you decide to check the weather, look at your stock portfolio, find some new recipes on the cooking sites, and so on. The next thing you know, you've lost an entire evening.

Mankind has a natural inclination to explore. With a billion or so Web sites available, wanting to see what's out there is natural. But spending too much time on your explorations could have quite a negative impact on your relationship.

Because the Web is somewhat interactive — you get to decide where you want to go next — it's a place the two of you can explore together. You may not have the same style of exploration, but you can adapt to each other. So maybe surfing the Web could bring you closer together if you do it as a team, sort of like Lewis and Clark.

Cheating via the Web

Pitfalls lie in wait on the Web that are even more dangerous than television or sports. The Web offers distractions, such as chat rooms and sex sites, that don't necessarily have redeeming values and can cause divisions in your relationship.

I am frequently asked whether cybersex is cheating. In order to answer, I'd like to digress for a moment and touch on the subject of masturbation, because that is the activity most frequently resulting from cybersex.

Consider a hypothetical couple, Arnold and Betty. They usually have sex together twice a week. In order not to discriminate, I'll give you two scenarios:

✔ In scenario one, Arnold often works late, so he comes home very tired. Having sex with Betty twice a week is all he desires. But Betty would like to have sex more often, so on some of those nights when Arnold stays late at the office, she masturbates while reading some erotic literature on a Web site.

✔ In scenario two, Betty is perfectly satisfied with having sex only twice a week. She really doesn't want to have sex more often, but that leaves Arnold feeling overly aroused on some nights, so he relieves those feelings by masturbating while looking at the images that he has on an erotic CD-ROM.

In both scenarios, the partner who is not masturbating doesn't feel cheated because he or she doesn't want to have sex more often.

Now look at two other scenarios:

✔ Betty likes to spend some time in chat rooms. She meets a guy she likes, and they spend lots of time chatting. One thing leads to another, and they start having cybersex, meaning they are both masturbating themselves while telling each other what they are doing to arouse the other. This relationship fulfills most of Betty's needs for sex, and so she starts turning down Arnold for sex more often so that they're making love only once a week. Arnold feels cheated.

✔ In scenario two, Arnold starts getting up at night to look at porn sites. So many sites and such a variety of sites are available that he finds himself unable to stop. Each time he does this, he masturbates, so when Betty cuddles up to him looking for some lovemaking, he often turns her down, as he feels quite sated.

Now I'll go back to the question of whether cybersex is cheating. In the first two instances, the other party wasn't being cheated out of having sex, and so I don't see any problem with this. But in the latter two scenarios, the person masturbating was very much involved with his or her favorite form of cybersex, so much so that it did take away from the partner. So in those cases, I consider cybersex to be cheating.

Still, no hard and fast rules about this exist. Basically, this call is based on common sense. Many people hope that I'll say their cybersex lives are not cheating because they are not actually involved with another live person. But they know perfectly well that their behavior does take away from their relationship with their partner and must be considered cheating.

I'm not saying that cheating via cybersex is the same thing as actually engaging in sex with another person. You can't catch a disease to transmit to your partner or cause an unintended pregnancy via cybersex. And cybersex can never be as intense as real sex. But cybersex can still damage your relationship, and even if this damage starts out as a small crack, it could grow to the point where some months or years later you find yourselves completely split from each other.

How common is it for people to get hooked on cybersex? I've read some articles where huge numbers are tossed around, but I always take such studies with a grain of salt. However, I do get letters from people who complain about a loved one who can't kick the cybersex habit. If it is happening in your relationship, then it doesn't matter how many other people on your block are having this problem; the only thing that matters is that your relationship is suffering.

Using the Web to pleasure both of you

I don't like forbidding people from doing things. I know I don't have any real authority to back up such a decree, and if you're really hooked on cybersex, you're probably not going to listen to me anyway. Also, I prefer to give people positive advice rather than negative rules. So this section contains some suggestions of what you can do if you have problems with cybersex. If these don't work, and if you can't break yourself of this habit, then you should give serious consideration to seeing a sex therapist.

✔ **Have a cybersex relationship with your partner.** Most people develop different personas during their Web chats. Pretending that you are someone different, maybe someone more daring than the real you, is one appealing aspect of these chat sessions. Why not try this with your partner? One drawback would be if you have only one computer at home, or one phone line, because then you can't chat in real time; you have to send messages one at a time. On the other hand, you can make love together in real time, so that's a major plus.

If you do decide to try this, and you're going to make up a cyber persona, you may want to try switching sexes for a while to see how that feels.

Another variation, which would allow you to have real time chats, would be to act as a couple. Maybe you could find another couple to have cybersex with or have a cyber threesome with one other person. Or the two of you could pretend you're one person, each taking turns at the computer.

✔ **Look at erotica on the Web together.** Many sites show nude pictures, both male and female, although nude female pictures predominate. Even if the woman doesn't find the pictures very sexually arousing, the curiosity factor may make such nosing around more appealing than simply looking at anonymous models spreading their legs. If the two of you have sex after a viewing session, that should make looking at such pictures as a couple much more satisfying.

✔ **Take your own erotic photos.** For a variation on the erotica theme, the woman could dress up in various outfits and wigs and the man could take digital photos of her in various states of undress. You could save them in your computer so the man can fulfill his voyeuristic tendencies by "surfing" for pictures of his own mate. (Just make sure the kids can't get at them.)

✔ **Write a sexual diary.** Each of you could write a fictitious diary of sexual escapades for shared reading pleasure, and put those in your computer. These diaries might then serve as a road map for actual sexual activity, if both of you feel comfortable enacting particular entries.

Nonelectronic Distractions

Although technological advances have made TV and the Internet among the greatest distractions couples have to fight against, some good old-fashioned distractions that have been around for years still exist. In this section, I cover the main culprits, from golf to the kids to the telephone.

Feeling addicted to golf and other sports

Golf can take time away from romance just as easily as a TV or computer can. In warmer climes, golf can be a year-round romance destroyer if the golfer insists on playing every week. You can't take off three or four hours every weekend without that having a negative effect on your relationship. If you're watching sports on TV, at least you're in the house and can answer a question, like "What did you do with the kids?"

Any sport can become addictive, from running and aerobics to weight lifting. In moderation, these activities are good for you. But we all know people who take them to extremes. For example, they're still running five miles every day even though they have to wear all sorts of bandages around various joints and they limp going up and down stairs. These people have pushed their bodies too far, but they can't quit.

I'm not a specialist in helping people get rid of addictions, but if you or your mate is heavily involved in a sport, then you know that it can take its toll on your relationship. If someone is running every day for an hour or more, not to mention warming up, cooling down, and showering, then much of that person's free time is given over to the sport. Because free time is something we're all short of, devoting adequate time to relationships will be difficult.

Don't be lulled into a sense of complacency just because these sports promote good health. If one partner sits at home feeling lonely while the other is off running a race every weekend, or if one partner feels frazzled because he or she has to get the kids off to school every morning while the other partner runs, then the relationship suffers.

Relationships are a little like golf. Unless you practice at getting better, you're going to hit all your balls too far to the left or right or into a sand trap. You have to be willing to put as much time, if not lots more time, into working at your relationship as you put into improving your sports performance. What it all boils down to is how much you value your relationship, and if playing golf or lifting weights means more to you than spending time with your mate, then you have a problem.

The solution is not to merely give up the sport in order to spend additional time with your mate; that sacrifice will probably make you miserable. For all I know, you took up golf or running in the first place as a means of getting away from your mate. The answer to this problem is to try to improve your relationship so that you enjoy being with your mate. For that to happen, you both have to work on this together. You have to find common ground — things that you like to do together — and then do them.

Think back to when you were first dating. Maybe you liked going to the movies. Maybe you enjoyed hanging out with a group of friends. Probably you liked having sex. Do you do these things very often now? If not, make them priorities.

If the two of you don't enjoy being together, then it makes perfectly good sense that you'd prefer to play golf or go to the gym rather than be with your partner. Cutting back on those activities is pointless unless you fix the underlying problem. If you've really grown far apart, then you may need the professional help of a marriage counselor.

Shopping till you drop (your spouse)

Some people shop for necessities, and some people shop as a pastime. We can't escape having to shop for groceries or clothes that have been outgrown, but for some people, the urge to shop is as much an addiction as the urge to surf the 'Net for erotic images.

The business world has learned how to capitalize on this addiction by making shopping as convenient as possible. They have built huge edifices filled with stores and surrounded by parking lots to make it easy to spend money. Some people can't resist the pull of the shopping mall. Combine this itch with the ability to charge your purchases, and this can be a dangerous enterprise, as many people have discovered after being buried in mountains of high-interest debt.

But this is not a financial book, so although I may caution you about shopping beyond your spending limits, my real purpose is to point out how shopping can tear at the seams of your relationship. Shopping not only steals time from your romance, but by causing fights over money, it also can ruin any chances of rekindling your romance for quite some time after you return package-laden from your latest shopping expedition.

Certainly, some people shop as a way of satisfying other needs that are not being met. For example, if a man spends inordinate amounts of time working and his wife doesn't work (or only works part-time), she will have many empty hours on her hands. She may turn to shopping with the false idea that the satisfaction she gets from her purchases will sate her thirst for companionship. As with all addictions, the fix is only temporary. You can have a closet filled with clothes and wake up to find that you need to go shopping for more. The fact that spending your partner's hard earned money causes him some anguish may add to the sense of satisfaction, but in the end it's a losing proposition.

If you have too much time on your hands, the way to avoid using that extra time to shop is to do something else with it. Your real need may be to spend some quality time with your mate, but if that is not possible in the immediate future, find other, more useful ways of spending those hours:

✔ **Take a course.** Study a subject that appeals to you (like Greek mythology or American history), take a course that teaches you some useful skill (like how to invest the money you save by not shopping or how to repair your car), or learn a skill that satisfies some inner creative urge (like painting or sculpture).

✔ **Donate your time to charity.** This could be a long-term commitment to one organization, which (in addition to helping some needy people) would put you into contact with other like-minded people. Or you could take on some volunteer activity in a private capacity, like visiting a housebound person or tutoring a child confined to a hospital for long-term care.

If shopping has become a substitute for a loving relationship, then these are only short-term cures. You must find ways of reestablishing your relationship with your partner so that you don't find yourself in this position. On the other hand, perhaps you have no likely alternative because your spouse will not cut short his work days. In this case, you may want to put even more of yourself into activities like the ones I suggested so that you can fill your life with purpose rather than just filling your closets.

Going overboard with your kids' activities

I deal with this subject in some depth in Chapter 15, but it's worth bringing up here as well. Obviously, you have to take care of your children, and that can take lots of time. But you can actually overdo it, which is not good for your relationship with your children or with your mate. If you're running around driving your kids from soccer games to piano lessons to play dates, feeling totally frazzled by it all, how much time is left for you to spend with your spouse? Not enough, I'm sure, and that's going to eat away at your relationship, which isn't good for anyone.

In addition, your kids need some one-on-one time with you. If you're always on the go, even if it's on their behalf, the relationship you have with them is also being eroded.

If you feel that your life is too complicated, you should probably cut back on some of these activities. What you trim is up to you, but make a commitment to cutting back. And then be careful not to make the mistake of substituting some other activity to replace your duties as soccer mom or dad. Use the time you free up to stay at home and talk to your mate or play a board game with your children. Eventually, you'll get used to having a little inactivity in your life and will feel much better for it.

Becoming tied up by the telephone

I spend lots of time on the phone, and it is a wonderful gadget, but it's definitely a modern appliance that can take over your life and do serious damage to your relationship. If your phone rings all night long, or if you're the one making other phones ring, you can end up spending much more time talking to people outside your home than to your mate.

Maybe your spouse isn't complaining. While you're on the phone, he's perfectly content to watch television. So you two "lovers" spend your nights almost as completely apart as if you lived in separate apartments.

You can handle the phone in several ways:

- **Use an answering machine to screen your calls.**
- **Get out of the house, and leave your cell phone off.** When you're taking a walk together, concentrate only on each other.

> ✔ **Declare a phone-free time.** Let your friends and relatives know that they shouldn't call you after, say, 9 or 10 p.m. unless they have an emergency.
>
> ✔ **Set an old-fashioned egg timer near the phone, and turn it over when you pick up the phone.** After the three minutes are up, announce that you have something to do and cut off the conversation. Obviously, that won't work every time, but it may help cut down on the overall time you spend talking.

Of course, on nights when your mate is off bowling, you can chat as much as you want.

Working at home

You may need a home office for several reasons. Perhaps you or your mate has given up going to the office in favor of telecommuting. Or maybe one of you has a business on the side. Or you need to work more than 40 hours a week but also want to have some time to be with your family, so you go home, spend some time together, and then go back to work.

These are all good reasons to have a home office, and they may even help to bring you closer together. But a home office can also tempt you to spend more time away from your partner. Maybe you have dinner with the kids and read them a bedtime story, but then you work till long after your mate has gone to bed, so you don't even share a goodnight smooch. And the lure of your home office on weekends can leave no time for doing anything fun or romantic with your spouse.

> **Q:** My husband is a salesman who is out on the road most of the day. He used to go back to his office in the afternoon to do all his paperwork, but then he set up a desk with a computer in our bedroom so that he could make a few more sales calls during the day and do his paperwork at night. I hate the way our bedroom looks now. He has papers all over the place, and I'm forbidden to touch them. And he gets so wrapped up in his work that he never seems to have time for me anymore. I can't even go to bed and cry about it because I'd disturb him. I know we need to save money so we can buy a house, but that might take another couple of years and I don't know if I can stand this situation that long.
>
> **A:** First, think about your décor. I'm against turning bedrooms into offices. It's just not the right atmosphere for romance. Invest some of the money you're saving and get a computer desk that folds up when not in use so that it looks like a cabinet. Put it in the living room. If it doesn't fit, put it in the bedroom but insist that he put all his papers away so that it can be closed up when not in use.

Next, you have to set up a schedule of "dates." Make plans to go out together two nights a week, and on those nights he has to stop working earlier and go back to his office to do his paperwork. Even though he'll have the room for a home office outside of the bedroom after you have a house, it's important that you establish the habit of making time for each other now.

If a home office is interfering with your romance, then you have to find ways of getting yourself away from the office. Maybe you need to go out to dinner more often. Or simply post hours when you'll be home working and when you won't. Or perhaps you and your mate should have a talk about your finances. Do you need the extra income that comes from working such long hours, or is the time more valuable to you? In your calculations, remember that time is your only asset that has a finite limit, and you won't find out what that limit is until the very end.

Getting too gung-ho with civic activism

I believe that everybody should give back to his or her community. I'm the president of the YMHA/YWHA (the "H" stands for Hebrew) of the community where I live, and I'm very grateful to all those who volunteer their time on behalf of my Y. But although it's great to say "yes," you also have to know how to say "no." So many organizations need help that if one finds out you've donated some time, others will surely ask. And if you're interested in your community, you'll want to help them all. But you can't allow yourself to be spread too thin. It won't be good for the organizations that you already help, and it definitely won't be good for your romantic life.

Of course, you can do some activities together. Although helping to run a soup kitchen may not seem romantic at first blush, I think such an activity is very romantic. By doing a good deed as a couple, you cement your relationship with time spent together, good feelings shared, and a topic that interests both of you and can generate discussion.

But the converse is also true. If only one of you is always out of the house attending this meeting or that, when do you get to spend time together? And if the other person has no interest in what you are doing, you can't even talk about your activities or make plans concerning your latest venture. Again, you are faced with the task of prioritizing. Yes, you should spend some time being active in your community, but don't take your mate for granted. Even if he or she isn't demanding more of your time, set aside some time so that you don't end up being punished for your good deeds with a frayed romance.

The problem with good deeds is that they can make you feel self-righteous. If you're out bowling and your mate complains, you may understand his or her point. But if you're out helping in your neighborhood, you may think that you deserve a medal, not anguish from your mate. The only thing I can do here is to quote that old saying "charity begins at home." If you can't find some time to give to your partner, then you definitely don't deserve that medal.

Tapping into the Benefits of Routine

If one word can describe the life of a modern family, it's *hectic.* It seems as if we are not in control of our own lives. You want to scream "Stop!" but you don't have the time, and it wouldn't do any good. If you're stuck in that kind of lifestyle, you've no choice but to try to fit things in. Although your mother or grandmother always did her wash on Wednesdays, your washer is likely to be going at any time of the day or night. Who can set aside a day to do laundry? What an unrealistic concept!

Or is it? I don't necessarily mean that you should only do laundry on one day a week. Laundry doesn't take as much time as it used to, and it's more practical to spread it out during the course of the week. But how many times have you heard the cry, "I need a clean shirt" or "Where are my jeans?" Because nothing is done on a schedule, your family expects their needs to be met on demand. If you're willing to do laundry at 2 a.m., then why wouldn't someone ask you to? If you'll put dinner on the table whenever somebody asks, then of course your family will expect six servings.

As a consequence of spreading yourself so thin, romance — which needs some time to build up and work its spell — gets pushed aside time and time again. So what's the answer to this dilemma? Establish a routine and stick to it. Dinner is at a certain time, and everyone is supposed to be present. If someone can't be, then he or she can make a sandwich and clean up his or her dishes. If laundry time is Tuesdays and Thursdays at 8 p.m., then calls for a clean shirt on Sunday have to wait.

By sticking to a schedule, you can also schedule time for doing something romantic. You can actually get tickets to a play. Or make dinner plans with another couple at a hot restaurant. Or take dance lessons every Monday evening. Something may have to be sacrificed in order for you to do some of these things, but after you have a schedule, you can select what to move around or drop.

If you're always in crisis mode, romantic moments get pushed aside over and over again. But if you create a game plan and manage to stick to it most weeks, then you will find the time for doing some of the things you want to do. Certainly, a crisis will come up now and then, but if you can manage to squeeze in a little romance most weeks, then you'll discover that finding the discipline to make up a schedule and stick to it may be the most rewarding activity of the week.

Chapter 20

When the Two of You Can't Make It Alone: Going for Therapy

● ●

In This Chapter

▶ Determining when your relationship needs outside help

▶ Fighting common fears of therapy

▶ Locating a therapist you can relate to

▶ Finding ways to afford professional help

● ●

*F*rom time to time in this book, I advise you to seek professional help. You may find it strange to consider visiting a professional counselor in order to rekindle your romance. In most cases, I would agree — you and your partner can take the necessary steps on your own. But some relationships unravel to such a degree (or perhaps aren't so tightly raveled to begin with) that the fireplace is bare of even a twig to start the rekindling process. If that's the case with your relationship, the prudent thing may be obtain some professional guidance.

How do you make that judgment? Sometimes this decision is very easy. The two of you always fight, and you cry yourself to sleep every night. Or you feel so depressed about your marriage that you can't get out of bed in the morning. In these cases, you may not be able to heal these rifts on your own and you need professional assistance.

Maybe you're not quite at that crisis stage, making it more difficult to judge whether or not your relationship is beyond your ability to repair on your own. In this chapter, I offer some guidelines to help you decide if your relationship needs professional help. I also show you how to locate a suitable therapist and overcome some very common resistance to the idea of seeking outside help for your very personal matter.

Deciding That You Need Professional Help

What do I mean by *professional help?* Many people mistakenly believe that professional help means going to a psychiatrist who spends months delving into your past in order to try to figure out what is wrong with you, followed by years of analysis in order to cure your problem. If that describes your definition of *professional help,* I understand why you may shy away from this process. If you're short of time, adding a weekly visit to a psychiatrist for the next few years may make your stress level unbearable.

While some people require the expertise of a psychiatrist, most people with marital or sexual problems don't. You're not trying to alter your personalities; you're trying to rekindle your romance. A professional counselor has a variety of therapy methods to choose from. You may make progress in repairing your relationship after only a handful of visits. Very often the main roadblock to romance stems from a lack of communication. If the therapist can reestablish the connection between you and your partner, you may be able to repair much of the damage on your own.

For example: You love your spouse and you realize that your romance needs some heating up. You try to get that spark lighted but nothing is happening and you can't figure out why. You may even ask your partner directly what is wrong and not receive a clear answer. Other than a lack of romance, your relationship may appear to be fine.

You could muddle through for the next five or ten years without facing the problem. As I stress in Chapter 15, the time to repair a relationship is not when there's nothing left to repair. You need to rebuild bridges as soon as possible. If your efforts at reconstruction aren't getting anywhere, the time has come to seek professional help.

Overcoming Resistance to Therapy

Laurie and David

Laurie and David have been married for ten years and have two children, ages six and eight. Both partners hold down full-time jobs. Between their children and their jobs, their lives are often filled with stress. Laurie assumes that the reason she and her husband fight so much is because they are both so stressed out.

Laurie's mother, Alice, noticed that her daughter and son-in-law didn't seem to be getting along. Alice had previously paid a visit to a marital therapist to resolve some difficulties she'd had with her husband, and she made an appointment for Laurie to see the same therapist. At first, Laurie refused. She didn't think she needed therapy and she didn't have the time. Alice insisted and volunteered to take care of the kids during Laurie's appointment. Laurie gave in.

During that first session, Laurie admitted to the therapist (as well as to herself) that the fights were the result of more than just stress. Laurie realized that David resented her for making slightly more money than he did, even though he had a graduate degree and she didn't. As a result, he pushed almost all of the care of the kids onto her shoulders, in the hopes that she'd be unable to handle the pressure and quit her job. Laurie had no intention of quitting her job. Her resentment toward David was increasing daily; they hadn't made love in months.

Many hurdles prevent couples from making the decision to go for marital therapy. In Laurie and David's case, denial of the critical state of their situation became one primary cause for their relationship breakdown. Once a couple recognizes that they have a problem, the next common hurdle is not knowing where to go for help. Many people are stymied by the process of finding a therapist; Laurie was fortunate that her mother could recommend one. After jumping the hurdle of finding a therapist, couples may still not make an appointment because a stigma is attached to seeking therapy of any kind. People tell their friends and neighbors in great detail about a visit to the doctor for some medical condition, but these same people do everything possible not to let on that they receive therapy.

Guarding your secrets

Some couples don't seek professional help because they are afraid of opening up to a stranger. Certainly, no one should take the process of going for therapy lightly because it can be very difficult. For some time, you've been brushing your relationship problems aside — hesitant to speak with anyone, including your partner, about them. It's only natural that you find it a bit awkward to talk about these issues with someone you barely know. Remember, a therapist is trained to alleviate your fears, and after you end your therapy, you never have to see this counselor again. Therapy is a very private experience.

If you're afraid of seeking therapy, my advice is to put your first session in proper context and don't build it up into some big scary moment; you're not on your way to an oncologist who is going to tell you that you have cancer. Yes, you reveal secrets, but those secrets remain private. The therapist doesn't reveal anything to your partner that you don't want revealed.

As a therapist, I must ask you to give your therapist a fair chance. Although a therapist is similar in some respects to a physician, your treatment does not require a shot that makes you feel better in an hour or two. You and your therapist (and hopefully your spouse as well) need to develop a relationship in order to ensure effective treatment. This relationship takes work and time. Make sure that you give your therapist an opportunity to make some progress before you assume that the treatment isn't working.

Dreading a breakup

Another reason that some couples fear seeking professional help is they imagine the situation is much worse than it actually is. These couples fear that if they go to a therapist, the therapist will announce that the relationship is so far gone that the only solution is to break up.

I can't say that people never break up after going for therapy. However, that result is rare. Unless a couple is very close to the breakup point before seeking help, they should expect to improve their relationship with professional help.

Conversely, I know of some couples that actually require the help of a therapist in order to break off the relationship. Both partners know that they don't love each other any more but they stall putting an end to their marriage. Perhaps these couples stay together because they have children Or they stay together simply because of inertia. They both may be very busy at work, for example, and may believe that they don't have the time or the energy for a breakup. Many people are also afraid of being alone. Some folks just don't like change, even if they know it's for the better.

When you honestly scrutinize any relationship, you reveal some cracks. Because no one is perfect, no relationship is perfect either. You may have some cracks in the ceiling of your living room — that doesn't mean you sell the house and move. You just go through the annoying process of scraping and painting your ceiling You may repair the ceiling yourself or you may consider the job too complicated and call a professional. Like a professional house painter, a professional marriage counselor or sex therapist can help you solve problems that are complicated. Your professional house painter is unlikely to suggest that you sell your house instead of repairing your ceiling, and your therapist is unlikely to advise you to leave your mate instead of repairing your marriage. You may assume that after a few visits to your therapist, your relationship is going to be in better shape than it has been in years.

What if you discover that your relationship has deteriorated far more than you thought? When you bury your head in the sand for a long time, you may be in for this discovery. Say your partner hasn't been honest with you and he or she has been acting distant. You may assume that your partner's behavior is due to work and stress, but maybe his or her behavior is the result of an extramarital affair. This fact is revealed in therapy and may be the catalyst that leads to the end of the marriage. Ask yourself: How much of a marriage do I have if my partner is cheating on me and lying to cover it up? In these circumstances, therapy doesn't cause a breakup — it really only speeds up the process. I think that resolving such a serious problem in a timely manner is actually a good thing; stalling only wastes your time.

Let me give you another example. Say you're 35. You notice that your husband isn't as attentive as he once was, but you try to ignore this fact for five years. What's the result? First, you spend five years being very unsatisfied with your relationship. Then, at the end of the five years, you discover that he has been having an affair. You're now 40 and facing single life again. Stalling produces no positive results, only negative ones.

Plenty of people, men in particular, don't visit their doctors for their yearly physicals because they're afraid of what their doctors may find. These same men admit that visiting their doctors regularly is better than skipping appointments. They know that if their doctors detect problems early, these problems are more likely to be treatable. Going to a therapist is no different. Try to put your fears aside — the sooner you seek treatment from a therapist, the more likely that your relationship may be saved.

Finding a Therapist

Locating a therapist may be more difficult than finding a medical doctor. Because most people don't talk about going to therapy, asking your friends and neighbors for recommendations may be awkward. You may not want to admit that you need help and they may not want to admit that they've gone for help. So word-of-mouth, which is how many people find their medical doctors, is not always a fruitful option. On the other hand, if you do know someone who has undergone therapy, by all means, ask that person for a recommendation. If you don't mind letting other people know that you need help, you can spread the word and see what advice comes your way.

Asking for recommendations

I often give lectures. During these lectures, audience members sometimes ask questions. An audience member may be too shy to ask a question that reveals his or her personal circumstances. My advice is to say that the question is in regards to his or her friend's situation. Everyone in the room may suspect that the person asking really has the question, but they won't know for sure. (I also take questions on note cards in case this "friend" trick isn't enough of a cover for some people.) The same ruse may be used when asking for a therapist referral: You can say that you have a friend looking for a marriage counselor. I wish people didn't feel ashamed about these issues. But I can't just wave a magic wand and make the shame go away, so I recommend using a little subterfuge to locate a therapist.

Normally, when you need a medical specialist, you ask your general practitioner for advice. You may begin your search for a therapist the same way. Some GPs are connected to a larger group of doctors — maybe through a hospital affiliation or an HMO — and they are able to recommend a therapist. (*Note:* If your insurance policy covers mental health care, you may need to contact your primary care physician in order to ensure coverage; you may be limited to psychologists and psychiatrists who are part of your particular insurance plan.) Even doctors who are not part of a group may know of good local therapists to recommend.

If your friends or family doctor don't prove to be fruitful resources in your search for a therapist, contact the nearest teaching hospital. These large hospitals almost always offer referral services. Just call the general information number and explain to the operator that you are looking for a referral for a therapist. You should be connected to someone who can refer you to a therapist specializing in marriage counseling. You can also call a local college or university and speak with a professor from the department of psychology. Some of these professors may have private practices.

You can ask for a recommendation from a religious leader from your church or synagogue. Ministers and rabbis often make these references and know of counselors who are good.

If you want to take a more anonymous route, you can call the American Psychological Association, which has a referral number (1-800-964-2000). Of course, you can peruse the trusty Yellow Pages (available online as well); this source has plenty of listings of counselors.

The Internet offers many ways of finding health care professionals. Some databases charge the therapists to be listed, and some don't. The lists in these databases vary due to this circumstance. These online sources don't give any kinds of ratings, but at least they're a place to start. Among the resources are:

- ✔ Mental Health Net's Clinician's Yellow Pages, www.mentalhealth.net
- ✔ Find-A-Therapist, www.findingstone.com/find-a-therapist
- ✔ Psychotherapy Finances Mental Health Provider Directory, Therapist Directory, www.psychology.com/therapy.htm
- ✔ American Association for Marriage and Family Therapy, www.aamft.com
- ✔ Mental Health Infosource Professional Directory, www.mhsource.com/referral/docsearch.html

✔ The Internet Care Directory, `www.caredirectory.com/main.html`

✔ The Anxiety Disorder Association of America, `www.adaa.org/consumerresources/findaprofessionaltherapists`

For someone seeking a sex therapist, the American Board of Sexology (`www.sexologist.org/index.htm`) has a good listing. And if you don't have access to the Internet, you can write to AASECT (American Association of Sex Educators, Counselors, and Therapists), the organization that accredits sex therapists, at P.O. Box 238, Mount Vernon, IA 52314.

Narrowing the field

You may receive a personal recommendation and have a good idea of whether a therapist may be right for you. If you can't find a therapist through a personal recommendation, you may only have a list of names. This list is only a partial solution to your quest. Rather than going *eeny meeny miny mo,* I suggest that you call several of these professionals. Explain your problem, ask questions concerning their methods of treatment, and inquire about their fees. Call each therapist on your list before deciding to make an appointment. After your first visit, if you're not satisfied, try another therapist. That you feel comfortable with your counselor is important. You are free to choose; why not pick the one who seems to mesh best with your personality?

When you select the therapist you like best, discuss with this professional what you expect to get out of therapy. Your goals should be realistic. Don't expect that either you or your mate is going to undergo a complete personality change. You'll usually find that even some small improvements in the way you interact can make quite a difference. Your counselor should help you determine a course of therapy that meets your goals within a time frame that you both agree on. Outlining a program also helps ensure that your expectations are met.

Knowing What to Expect During the First Visit

When you visit your physician for your annual physical, the clinic staff usually takes some measurements (like your weight, blood pressure, and temperature) before your doctor examines you further. Similarly, a mental health care professional takes down some basic information before beginning your therapy.

Your therapist may start your first visit with sort of a status examination; he or she may ask you a lot of questions and expect honest answers. The answers you give are private, so be as honest as possible. By holding back, you make finding out exactly what's going on more difficult for the therapist.

Because this chapter is about therapy for couples, the therapist needs to speak to both of you. In the very beginning, you may be interviewed together. The two of you will also be questioned separately. In all probability, the two of you may answer the same questions differently; each of you has a different perception of what has been happening. You may not know the whole story and one of you may not reveal the whole truth when you are together. The mental health provider may compare your stories to get a clearer picture of what is going on. Eventually, you may visit your therapist together and speak more freely about your relationship. Some people just need time to open up. In time, the provider will feel comfortable enough with your situation to begin to offer suggestions.

Seeking Solo Help

Although you feel you need professional help to settle your differences, your partner may refuse to attend counseling sessions. Maybe he or she fears that the therapist will take your side. Maybe your partner is afraid of being forced to reveal information — information that he or she has hidden from you. Your partner may never choose to join you for a therapy session. Does that mean that you can't benefit from therapy? Absolutely not.

If you decide that both of you need help to repair your damaged relationship, that may also mean that you, personally, suffer from some mental anguish. You may not fix the state of your relationship but you may benefit from a professional's guidance.

The very fact that you see a counselor lets your partner know that you perceive serious problems with yourself and your relationship. Sometimes a partner who shrugs off your complaints as frivolous changes his or her mind when you reveal that you see a therapist. With any luck, your visits may be enough of an incentive to get your partner to pay a visit to the therapist even if the only motivation is to tell the therapist his or her side of the story. After your partner is in the "hot seat," a resolution of your relationship problems may then be possible.

Even if your partner never visits your therapist, your health care provider should be able to help you grow stronger and feel better about yourself — that may lead to a resolution also.

Anticipating Your Homework Assignments

Talking about your problems offers some relief for many relationship problems. In order to come up with workable solutions to your problems, you both need to improve your communication skills. The next step is to make some compromises in your relationship. Your therapist should offer guidelines that you can follow in order to accomplish these goals. I can't speak for others in my field, but let me give you an example of the type of homework that I give.

Barbara and Phil

Barbara and Phil admitted to not having sexual relations in three months. They were in their mid-30s and healthy. One night they tried to make love and Phil could not get an erection. He admitted to me that he had masturbated an hour before this happened. (He had not admitted this fact to Barbara.) Phil thought that Barbara had started her period and didn't want to have sex. She was very surprised at his inability to have an erection; the night before, he took only a few seconds to become erect. Barbara said some things she regretted. (She did not admit this fact to Phil.) They tried making love again the following night; Phil again could not get an erection. This sexual failure worried him. And Barbara's mind started to wander into all sorts of areas: "Is he having an affair?" and "Doesn't he find me attractive any more?" After a third occurance of this problem, Phil started to avoid Barbara altogether. She was overcome with worry to the point that she started smelling his clothes to find the scent of perfume.

Their problem is a very simple one, of course. When a man worries whether or not he can have an erection, his anxiety can make it impossible for him to have one no matter how hard he tries. His erectile failures become a self-fulfilling prophecy. All he needs is to have successful intercourse with his wife one time, and his problem may never reoccur.

First, I had Phil explain to Barbara what happened that first night so that her fears about an extramarital affair ceased. But I couldn't say anything to Phil that could guarantee his ability to get an erection, and his failing again could prove to be a serious setback. My assignment to this couple was to stop having intercourse. That night, they could touch each other and try to arouse each other, but after the touching and arousing they were to stop. Because Phil didn't have any fears about not being able to have an erection, he was able to become aroused. I banned them from having intercourse a few more times. When I removed the ban, Phil had no trouble and their problem was solved.

Deciding on the type of therapist

If your relationship problem is based on a sexual issue, you should meet with a sex therapist. Sometimes the specific nature of a problem is not so clear. All mental health providers specialize in a particular area to some degree. I do marital and couples therapy as well as sex therapy; sometimes, I help a client with other types of problems as well. If someone comes to me with a problem that is out of my professional realm, I recommend that person to a colleague. Don't worry too much about locating a therapist who specializes in resolving your particular problem. If you find a provider who appeals to you, go for a visit. Either that person can help you or that professional can refer you to someone who can. At least, take the first step — which is the most important one.

If you know what to look for, as I do, curing a problem like Barbara and Phil's looks easy. But this case wasn't a messy one. Some couples start to fight over a problem like this to the extent that their relationship becomes badly damaged. Barbara never really believed that Phil was having an affair, but she could have; then getting this couple back together would have been much more difficult.

The cause of their problem was apparent to me, but not to them. Phil and Barbara went through three months of needless torture because they didn't communicate with each other. By seeking professional counseling, they reached a positive resolution. That's why visiting a therapist is so important; you can't always handle a problem situation by yourselves.

Seeking a Second Opinion

What do you do if therapy doesn't work for you? A counselor may not be successful for two main reasons. The first is that the counselor is not the right person for the job; the second is that your relationship is not salvageable.

I learned first-hand the importance of seeking second opinions. I had some health scares in my life that turned out to be nothing at all. The way I avoided going under the knife was by seeking second and third opinions. The second and third doctors could have recommended the same surgery, but their opinions revealed that I didn't need it. In my case, the second and third opinions saved me from an unnecessary surgery.

If you go for marital therapy and find that it's not working, give serious consideration to seeing another counselor. Follow this advice especially if you feel in your heart that you can repair your relationship. Conversely, sometimes a couple goes to a therapist as a last ditch attempt to save their marriage; deep inside they know that their relationship is over. If that's the case with you, accept the reading of the first professional you consult. You and your spouse must honestly communicate about the progress you are making toward repairing your relationship.

Misusing Therapy

Not everybody is a good candidate for therapy. Some people try to use therapists to get what they want. These people agree to go for therapy but they have no intention of applying what comes out of it. They have preconceived ideas about their relationships and they stick to these ideas no matter what. After they leave the therapist's office, they may twist what was said in order to get their own ways.

Other people try to sabotage therapy. These people hold back, maybe saying nothing at all in response to the therapist's questions. Or they tell lies or even try to flirt with the therapist.

As you may imagine, a therapist can't do much in these situations. A counselor can try to get the offending party to change his or her behavior but can't offer a guarantee. If one partner insists on sabotaging the therapy, the other half of the couple must decide whether to continue the relationship or not. When a partner doesn't respect the guidelines set down by your therapist, perhaps the relationship is passed the point of no return. If that's the case, you must decide — with the help of your therapist — whether or not to stick by this person.

Digging Up Deeper Problems

Another outcome of going for therapy occurs when the therapist discovers some deeper problems at work in one or both partners. For example, if one of the two was sexually abused as a child, that abuse could signify the source of this couple's sexual problem. The abused person may not recall the abuse until undergoing therapy. That person may need to undergo therapy individually in order to deal with the underlying problem before the relationship can be repaired.

If a deeper problem is revealed through your marital therapy, I urge you to seek a second opinion. While a therapist may be able to bring out such deeper issues, that doesn't mean the therapist has the training to treat the specific problem that is revealed. I frequently say "I know what I know, and I know what I don't know." Although I realize my professional limitations, some therapists may not like letting a client slip out of their grasp. I'm not intimating that therapists hold on strictly for financial reasons, though that may occasionally be the case. Many professionals don't like to admit defeat. A therapist who has no experience treating a particular syndrome may want to give it a shot anyway. The only problem is that you become the guinea pig. If your history is complicated, the possibility of the therapist misdiagnosing your problem exists.

Finally, many people in the mental health field specialize. A therapist, psychologist, or psychoanalyst who has successfully treated many people with your same particular problem is the provider you want. If you doubt whether or not your therapist can handle some deeper issue that may come up, don't stick with this therapist out of loyalty. Look around to get the best treatment available.

Making Therapy Affordable

I know that health insurance plans vary in their coverage's of marital therapy. I also know that not every budget can withstand the cost of therapy. Don't assume that you can't get the help you need because your wallet is on the flat side.

Social workers often work for the state or for private agencies backed by private donations. These professional counselors either don't charge you or charge only a nominal sum. Visiting a social worker can be a little more complicated than visiting a private therapist. You may wait a longer time to get an appointment and the office may not be as nice. However, keep in mind that many social workers are well trained and can offer you help.

Social workers may not cost as much as private therapists, but they still should be qualified. You need to check out your social worker's credentials. You could be assigned a social worker who has many degrees and years of training or someone who has less education and experience. The social worker you're appointed to may not have the experience to help you; don't be afraid to ask to see a supervisor about getting a new social worker assigned.

By the way, a social worker who feels that your case needs to be viewed by someone with more experience should tell you that.

Another way of getting help that is not costly is to visit a member of a church's clergy — whether or not you belong to his or her congregation. People in religious orders help save many marriages and may offer you the help you need. A person of the clergy may also have access to emergency funds; if you need more specialized care, you may be able to secure some financial assistance with their aid.

Finally, some private therapists work on a *sliding fee scale.* This scale means that they may charge their full fee to people who can afford to pay it (or who have insurance that will pay it) and are willing to charge a cheaper rate to people with less money. You may find a therapist you like but whose rates you cannot afford; don't be afraid to ask whether a sliding fee scale is available.

Chapter 21

Medical Matters: When You May Need to See a Doctor

● ●

In This Chapter

▶ Keeping unwanted pregnancies and STDs at bay

▶ Identifying common female problems

▶ Combatting male health problems

▶ Avoiding halitosis and headaches that can deaden your romance

● ●

Sometimes, you can rekindle your relationship by yourself. Sometimes, you can revive it with the help of a therapist. And sometimes, you need a medical doctor, if not to actually rekindle your romance, at least to fix a problem that is preventing you from lighting that fire yourself.

Though I'm known the world over as Dr. Ruth, let me state right now that my doctorate degree is not in medicine. I did train to be a sex therapist under Helen Singer Kaplan at New York Hospital/Cornell University Medical Center, and I was surrounded by doctors, but that doesn't mean that I absorbed any medical knowledge through osmosis.

Because I received no medical training, I am very hesitant about giving any medical advice. For example, people often ask me about AIDS. They want to know the possible symptoms. Now, let's say I give someone a list of symptoms but I leave one off because of my lack of medical training. And let's suppose that this person has the one symptom I neglected to mention. Because of me, this person may think that he or she doesn't have AIDS. As a result, he or she may not practice safe sex 100 percent of the time. What if it turns out this person does have AIDS and has passed it on to someone else?

In order to prevent such disasters, I don't give you very much detailed medical information. On the other hand, I have many physician friends. If I do offer any medical facts in this chapter, you can rest assured that these facts have been substantiated by someone in the medical profession so that you won't get erroneous information.

I also ask you to use a little common sense. Every medical condition can possibly play havoc with your romance. You may have an ulcer, for example. Your partner may really like to eat at fancy restaurants where only rich foods that can upset your delicate stomach are served. This situation could cause a rift in your relationship. Or you may have trouble walking, and your partner loves long moonlight strolls — that could be a problem. You get the idea. If a medical problem not covered in this chapter could hamper your romance, then see a doctor about it. Don't play the martyr by living with the discomfort; doing so is unnecessary and potentially disruptive to your relationship.

In this chapter, I cover medical issues that primarily impact your sex life. I think this information is necessary because many people are ashamed to talk about their medical problems with their partners or doctors. As a result of their silence, they suffer needlessly. I'm going to give you a basic overview of some common problems in order to encourage you to seek help and to facilitate the office visit with your doctor.

Preventing Unintended Pregnancy

Let me start with something very basic: birth control. I've made educating people about birth control my personal crusade in order to prevent unintended pregnancies. If I can prevent only one such mishap as a result of this book, I'll be satisfied.

The method of birth control you use could impact your romance. If you do not have faith in the method you are using, or if your partner is not sure of its effectiveness, a subconscious fear of pregnancy could dampen the pleasure of having intercourse or make one of you avoid intercourse altogether.

It perturbs me that at the dawn of a new millennium, medical science is still searching for a method of birth control that doesn't have any drawbacks. The Pill is effective but has side effects and does not prevent transmission of diseases. A barrier method, like the condom, can prevent disease but is not 100 percent effective at preventing pregnancy. Sterilization is too final because you never know if you may want another child. (For a discussion of various types of birth control and their limitations, see *Sex For Dummies*.)

No perfect method of birth control exists; the two of you must talk about this issue and come to a mutual agreement. Go over the pros and cons of various birth control methods before engaging in sex. Once you agree on a method of birth control, you can be sure that your selection won't negatively impact your romance.

The condom is really the only viable method of birth control that does not require a visit to the doctor. A visit to an MD is going to be necessary in pursuing your birth control choice most of the time. Before both of you make your final birth control decision, set an appointment with your doctor and ask questions about various methods. Don't allow your doctor to convince you to use a method you're not comfortable with. However, your physician can give you the latest information about possible risks and side effects, especially as these apply to your personal medical history.

Stopping the Spread of STDs

The fear of causing an unintended pregnancy may remove the pleasure from sex. In addition, the fear of contracting a *sexually transmitted disease* (STD), such as herpes, chlamydia, or even AIDS, may also deplete your enjoyment of sex. If sexual partners are together for a long time, these fears shouldn't exist but sometimes do anyway. One partner may worry that the other is cheating — that's one potential cause of anxiety. Or maybe one of you has a long list of past lovers and refuses to be tested, so the concern about STDs is always present in your relationship.

You can rid yourselves of any such fears by both of you being tested. Your partner may refuse to go along with this, but your partner's refusal should not keep you from being tested yourself. The two of you may have been together for years and have been faithful to each other. In that case, if your partner were a carrier, you probably would have already caught an STD by now. If you get tested, the negative result may be a good indication that your partner is negative as well.

If you have strong concerns that your partner has an STD, be firm when you ask him or her to be tested. Perhaps when you first engaged in sexual relations you didn't have the conviction to put your foot down about this issue. But now you've been together for a long time and you have every right to voice your complaint. Your fear of STDs may harm the sexual side of your relationship. Your partner should go for testing not only out of love for you, but also to help put your romance in tip-top shape.

You may fear that your partner is having an affair and that you'll catch an STD as a result. You face a more serious problem than I can address in this book. You cannot rekindle a romance that is torn apart by infidelity without the help of a therapist. For the sake of your relationship, and the sake of your health, seek professional help as soon as you suspect this problem. (See Chapter 20 for guidance when looking for a therapist.)

Facing Female Problems

Most of you are aware that women experience physical and possibly emotional changes each month due to menstruation. Other common female problems are not so well known and can have big impacts on your love life. This section provides an overview of some of these problems and some general information about how they are treated.

Vaginismus

In the beginning of this chapter, I note that the fear of causing an unintended pregnancy or catching an STD may ruin the pleasure of sex. For some women, fears like these can actually make intercourse impossible or very painful. *Vaginismus* is a condition in which a woman involuntarily tightens her vaginal muscles, preventing her partner from being able to place his penis into her vagina. The cause for vaginismus is psychological and may include one of the aforementioned fears. Sometimes, getting to the root of the fear and removing the cause allows a couple to overcome vaginismus.

Some women cannot overcome the mental block that causes this problem. One form of treatment that may help is to use a series of *speculums* (instruments that gynecologists use to examine the vagina) or dilators. Each speculum or dilator used is slightly larger than the previous. Your doctor may slowly open the vagina wide enough for intercourse to be possible. If sex therapy cannot alleviate the symptoms of vaginismus, you should definitely consult your gynecologist.

Vaginal odor and dryness

Two other vaginal problems can affect sex and therefore, the state of your romance. The first problem has to do with vaginal odors. I often get letters from men who want to perform oral sex on their partners but are turned off by a strong, fishy odor. This scent is caused by an imbalance in the bacteria that are always present in the vagina. (The cause is generally not a sexually transmitted disease, though some STDs do cause infections that also give rise to an odor.) The smell, and an accompanying whitish discharge, can worsen after she engages in intercourse.

The imbalance of bacteria can be so minor that many women either don't notice they have an infection or don't bother to go to the doctor to get it treated. However, if the problem is turning off your partner, you should definitely get the appropriate antibiotic. If you notice any discharge coming from your vagina, and if your partner is not giving you the oral sex that you crave, definitely go to your gynecologist.

Another problem that some women encounter is vaginal dryness. I don't mean the dryness that occurs after menopause, which is very common and natural, but dryness that occurs in premenopausal women. Normally, the bartholin's glands produce a natural lubricant when a woman becomes aroused. This lubricant facilitates intercourse. If your partner tries to penetrate you before you are fully aroused, intercourse may be painful — your vaginal walls have not been given the chance to produce lubricant. You may experience dryness due to some other cause. If you experience dryness often, consult your gynecologist. Whatever the cause, don't suffer needlessly — use an artificial lubricant. Some brands, like Replens and Senselle, coat the vagina for several days so that you don't need to apply these lubricants just prior to having sex.

Urination during sex

Urination during sex is not uncommon for women — it sometimes occurs at the moment of orgasm and sometimes prior to that moment. The cause may be an irritable bladder or a weakness at the neck of the bladder. The first line of treatment is to make sure you urinate just prior to engaging in sex. Because most women with this problem lose only a few drops of urine during sex, you can also just place a towel underneath you and not worry about it. If you are embarrassed, you can ask your doctor for a medication like the kind used to prevent bed-wetting. This medication would reduce the possibility of urination occurring. If you frequently lose control at other times, in addition to when you have sex, you may be a candidate for an operation to strengthen the neck of your bladder. Again, my advice is to visit your doctor.

Fertility problems

Some couples make babies by accident while other couples try and try without success. If you fall into the latter category, fertility issues may negatively impact your romance. First, not being able to conceive is depressing and second, if you feel blue, sex loses a lot of its luster. Also, you may be seeking the advice of a fertility specialist. This professional may instruct you exactly when to have sex and when to avoid it — such a set of instructions isn't conducive to romance.

Perhaps you feel trapped by fertility problems, but you're not. Taking control of the process of making a baby does not mean that your lovemaking has to be routine or even dull. Even if it's not the best sex you ever have, sex to make a baby can be pretty good.

Here's an example: Your partner's sperm needs to be implanted into your egg outside of your womb. Your man has to go to the lab and masturbate in order to give the lab fresh sperm to work with. A lab technician may tell your partner to arrive by 8 a.m. and stick him in a room with some erotic magazines or, if he's lucky, some erotic videos and a VCR. Such a setting is certainly not romantic. Does the process have to be this way?

Why can't the two of you take part in the sperm producing process? Both parties can have an orgasm, although you must be careful to gather the sperm in a jar. Let's say the lab is nearby your home. Why not extract the sperm together at home and bring it to the lab? Even if the lab is too far away for you to transport the sperm in a timely manner, why not look for a nearby motel room that you could dress up with some candles and flowers? Why must you always give sperm on the lab's schedule instead of yours? The two of you may only be able to get together at 5 p.m.; tell the lab that's the time when the deed will be done.

Fertilizing the egg outside the womb may seem like an extreme way to make a baby. At the beginning of a couple's quest to have a child, they usually follow a schedule of when to have intercourse based on their doctor's instructions. Because doctors want the man's sperm to be of the optimum quality and quantity, his or her instructions state when to have sex and when to refrain from having orgasms. Therefore, the process can be a little more complicated than making sure that you have sex that one day a month when the woman is fertile. Nevertheless, the time period in question is not long, and you have the rest of the month to do what you please.

Make sure that you use the rest of the month to make sex as romantic as possible. Take lots of bubble baths together. Make love when you get home from work, have dinner, and then make love again. Take a nap lying on top of each other in a hammock, wake up, and have sex. You get the idea.

And what about the times when you have sex under your doctor's orders? Is he or she watching you? Do you have to be embarrassed about it? Of course not. Do you know what makes this sex unromantic? Your own mind. You may resent being forced to have sex at scheduled times, but you can choose to make yourself miserable about these conditions or make the process as pleasant as possible. Think about it. What are you being forced to do? Make love. Is making love really so bad under any circumstances?

If the process of overcoming fertility problems gets you down, change your attitude. When you start to feel negative, change your thoughts. Think about the last time you made love when you weren't filling a prescription, as it were. Remember how good sex felt and let those memories program your thoughts. Tell yourself that you are enjoying this particular sexual episode, and then enjoy it. If you insist on donning a long face, sex isn't going to be romantic or enjoyable.

Here are some other things you can do to help each other:

- **Put your best foot forward when you announce that the time is nigh.** Smile when you say it, pardner, and look like you want it too.

- **Use a new position.** You can even name it *The Baby-Making Position.*

- **Try different forms of foreplay.** Anything that you can do to make this act of sex interesting takes away from the fact that you are having sex on a schedule.

- **Try scheduling sex at other times as well.** That way, when you're doing "it" officially, the scheduled sex won't seem quite so strange.

- **Don't be too clandestine about your sexual activities.** Most couples facing fertility issues don't want to be bothered by a lot of questions, especially from eager-to-be-grandparents — that's understandable. But you may wall yourselves in; then, not only are you making love on a schedule, but also the act can seem as if you're doing it in a prison. Try to make light of what you're doing, to some extent, and maybe the process won't feel like such a burden.

- **Think sexy.** A positive attitude may actually help make that baby and it certainly creates an atmosphere that is a lot more pleasant. So, as your fertile time approaches, try to get yourself as aroused as possible. Wear your sexiest underwear. Show some cleavage. Be flirtatious and see if you can turn on some other men during the day as well as your partner at night. When the time comes to make a baby, you'll feel like the decision to be bumping and grinding is yours.

Peri-menopause

At the other end of the fertility spectrum is menopause, when a women can no longer be considered fertile. I cover this topic in Chapter 12, but here I'd like to mention the precursor to menopause — peri-menopause. Peri-menopause usually begins when a woman is in her late 30s or early 40s. Peri-menopause causes a slight diminishment in her hormone levels, and this, in turn, causes other symptoms. I won't list all the possible symptoms here, but among them may be some unexpected tiredness or mood changes that may affect the state of your romance.

If you are too young for menopause, you may be going through peri-menopause and not recognize it. You may blame your tiredness or mood changes on emotional, rather than physical, causes (and your partner may do the same). If you experience mood swings or fatigue, check with your doctor to see if you could be peri-menopausal. Knowledge of the symptoms does not prevent you from experiencing them, but knowledge may certainly help you understand them.

Mastering Male Problems

A man's ego is very tied to his "equipment" so that when men suffer from some physical problem, there is almost always a strong impact on a couple's romance. Getting medical help is really the only solution, so learn to identify these problems and then make sure that you do something about them as soon as possible.

Erectile dysfunction

I have to congratulate Bob Dole for having the courage, and I do mean courage, to tell the world that he had problems getting an erection as a result of his treatment for prostate cancer. Because he helped to announce a cure for this problem as well (the drug Viagra), he performed a double-good deed.

Erectile dysfunction (ED) is now out of the shadows. Whether it results from prostate cancer, diabetes, or some other physical cause, men who lose their ability to have an erection can now get help. Drugs like Viagra help many men overcome difficulties having erections; commercials for these drugs bring the problem to light on prime-time TV. New drugs are on the horizon, like Uprima. Hopefully, these new drugs will benefit others for whom Viagra didn't work.

A word of warning: Viagra is not a panacea. A pill alone cannot revitalize your love life if it has been neglected. Look at Chapter 12 for ways to supplement the new wonder drugs by spicing up the activity in your bedroom.

Tight foreskin

Some men have no problem obtaining an erection, but their penises are not circumcised and the foreskin does not pull back all the way as it supposed to. This tightness causes them pain. This condition is called *phimosis*. While phimosis normally becomes apparent during childhood, this problem can occur later in life as a result of infections. If his erections are painful, he may not be in a romantic mood very often.

If you have this condition, you should definitely consult with a urologist. You may have to undergo circumcision. Adult circumcisions may be more painful than infant circumcisions, but this procedure should cure the problem.

Suffering in silence

Despite the mass marketing of Viagra, some men still suffer from ED and other sexual problems in silence. Although women are used to going to the gynecologist to have their genitals examined, most men never visit a urologist. Even those men who have problems that would benefit from a urologist's attention avoid visiting the doctor. Many men pretend that they don't have a problem or just put off making an appointment until they reach a crisis stage. I'm not sure what causes so many men to act this way and the reason really doesn't matter. The partners of men who refuse to go to the doctor need to help these fellas in whatever ways possible.

If your man puts off a trip to the doctor, encourage him to make the appointment. Go with him if he wants. If he's anxious, assure him that you love and support him. You don't want him to end up suffering a condition that affects your romance.

Peyronie's disease

Many men's penises are slightly curved when erect. A more pronounced curve, which makes intercourse painful or impossible, is known as *Peyronie's disease*. This condition is caused by a thickening of the fibrous tissue on one side of the penis, which causes the curvature in the opposite direction. Although assorted theories for the cause of Peyronie's disease have been developed, no cause has been proven.

This condition may disappear on its own after a few months. Taking large doses of vitamin E is thought to be a possible curative agent. If the condition persists and is harming your sex life, surgery may be called for. Contact your doctor if your penis develops this condition. Your physician should be able to determine if you're suffering from Peyronie's disease and offer you the course of treatment that is best for you.

The bumps of love

Actually there are no such things as bumps of love; I just like the way that phrase sounds. Sometimes bumps do appear on a man's penis. If they are small lumps that look like little pimples and are all about the same size, 1–2 mm, they are probably *pearly penile papules*. Men usually develop these lumps in their teen-aged years but may not notice them until a woman points them out. Because they're normal glands, there's nothing you need to do about them. If you have bumps on your penis that are not so uniform in size, you should contact your doctor.

Testicular cancer

Most women are tuned into the fact that they need to examine their breasts regularly for lumps. Men should become accustomed to examining their testicles. I do my best to get the word out. One man actually thanked me because he examined himself after hearing me and discovered a lump that required treatment.

Tom Green's comedy may not appeal to everybody, but I commend him for publicizing his testicular cancer. He certainly made a lot of young men aware of this danger. Testicular cancer is much more likely to strike men under 35 than men older than 35.

You may not feel that having your testicles examined once a month by your partner is romantic. I like to think that any time your partner does something for you, the act should be considered somewhat romantic. Because this exam could save your man's life, ladies, don't shy away from this duty. Your examination may lead to other things, and well, you're not his doctor, so there's nothing wrong with getting personal.

Avoiding Other Romance Inhibitors

It's not just the area between your waist and knees that can physically inhibit you from maximizing your romance. Here are some other problems to look out for.

Keeping your breath sweet

Halitosis, or bad breath, is certainly not a life threatening disease, and you may not even think about going to your doctor about it. In fact, you may not know that you are afflicted with bad breath at all. But I get a surprising number of questions from people who like to kiss and get little response from their partners. In some cases, the cause is quite simple: bad breath. Nobody likes to kiss someone whose breath stinks, and because kissing is often the first step to other joys of sharing each other's bodies, it can act like the gatekeeper. If a couple can't get past this hurdle because of bad breath, the rest of their love life may suffer.

Obviously, if you ate garlic-laden shrimp scampi for dinner, you're going to have bad breath. But bad breath that comes from a specific meal is not a real concern, unless one partner always eats garlic or other foods that cause halitosis. However, if your partner has chronic bad breath, and especially if that keeps the two of you from kissing very often or very passionately, then this condition should be corrected. Breath mints and mouthwash are good places to start, but some cases of bad breath are more deep-seated and require a visit to the doctor or, even better, the dentist.

Bad breath does not come from your stomach. Dentists believe that gum disease is the primary culprit, though there is some theorizing that bacteria that collect on the back of the tongue may be the cause. You can try brushing your tongue when you brush your teeth, and you can even buy special tongue scrapers, though this sounds like a gimmick to me. Do make sure that you brush your teeth thoroughly and have regular check-ups at the dentist. (I sound like your mom now, don't I? But she wasn't concerned about rekindling your romance, I bet.)

Another possible cause of bad breath is a chronic sinus infection. If you have a nasal drip and bad breath that you can't get rid of, definitely consult with a doctor.

Preventing sexually induced headaches

We all know that there are real headaches and fake headaches. The fake variety are used as an excuse to avoid having sex, and while they are definitely a detriment to romance, they do not require medical attention. (They might fall under the list of issues handled by a sex therapist instead.) But some people get real headaches as a result of sex, and men are three times as likely to be the victims as women.

There are two basic types of sexually induced headaches. One is felt in the back of the neck and is probably due to muscle contractions. The victim of these headaches should try to relax his neck muscles and use positions that do not put a strain on the neck.

The other type of headache results in a severe pain just at the moment of orgasm. For this type of headache, consult your doctor to be sure that there is no serious cause and to determine if a prescription can help to alleviate them.

Working around your weight

I'm not speaking of the aesthetics of fat here, but rather that if one or both partners are very overweight, it can make engaging in certain sexual positions difficult if not impossible. If you are so overweight that it prevents you from engaging in sex, you should consult with a physician, because not only will this dampen your romance, but it may well lead to other ailments as well.

Men should also be aware that their penises extend below the level of their skin. A man who has a lot of extra weight in his lower abdomen is covering part of his penis that otherwise would be exposed. So losing weight makes sex easier in two ways; you'll have less belly and more penis protruding.

Part VI

The Part of Tens

The 5th Wave   By Rich Tennant

"THEY'RE A VERY PROGRESSIVE COMPANY-IT COMES WITH MATCHING COLORED CONDOMS."

In this part . . .

Need some quick tips for adding some spark to your relationship? Look no further — The Part of Tens is here. This part suggests romantic vacation ideas, unique dates to plan with your partner, variations to try in the bedroom, and Web sites to explore if you're looking for even more ideas for romancing your mate. If you take just some of the suggestions you find here, your romance should heat up in no time.

Chapter 22

Ten Romantic Getaways Sure to Create a Spark

• •

In This Chapter

▶ Taking a vacation without leaving home

▶ Finding romance in the city, the country, and abroad

▶ Cruising for romance by land and by sea

• •

*P*icture your romance as a damsel in distress tied to the railroad tracks. Somewhere off in the distance is a train running at full speed and blowing its whistle. Eventually, that damsel is going to go *poof* unless someone comes along and unties her.

Every now and then, your romance needs to be untied from the everyday stresses of life or it will get flattened to a point where it can never be inflated again. You need to free yourself from the binds of your job, your kids, your family, the phone, beepers, traffic jams, meetings, piles of bills, piles of laundry . . . you get the idea.

Don't necessarily pick your favorite type of vacation area for a romantic getaway. Choose one that offers the best environment for perking up your romance. Here are ten suggestions for vacation escapes, ranging from the very modest to the more elaborate.

Making Your Home a Hideaway

Where is the cheapest place you can go on vacation? Your own home. How exactly can your home be a getaway? One way to distinguish an at-home vacation from your normal life is to schedule it. When you go away for a vacation, you make plans, even if you're a free spirit who prefers not to make reservations. For an at-home vacation to be successful, you need to follow the same steps. Schedule your at-home vacation with no "real life" interruptions, and change your attitude as soon as your holiday begins.

Romance requires concentration. Every distraction that you remove from your environment makes it easier for your romance to flame up. You may have a hard time taking an at-home vacation because you can't ignore the housework that beckons. Creating a vacation atmosphere at home takes some practice.

For example, you may rely on the answering machine to record messages to avoid taking telephone calls. Then, you discover that the noises the machine makes (the clicks and buzzes that sound even if you turn the speaker off) are a distraction. You start to worry that the telephone calls you miss may be important. The solution? Unplug all of your telephones. Tell your friends, family, and coworkers that you're on vacation; then, they won't even bother calling. If someone close to you is ill or experiencing some other type of problem, you can check in with that person periodically. (You'd probably check on this person if you were vacationing out-of-town as well.)

Some people, particularly of the male persuasion, may think of an at-home romantic vacation as an all-day sex romp. While sex should certainly be allotted its time slots, there are many other ways of connecting that should also be included:

- ✔ If there's a new restaurant you've been meaning to try, make a reservation. Make it a late reservation, then make love before you go. When you get back, you can fall asleep in each other's arms.

- ✔ Go to the library, pick out a book you both like, and then sit on the back porch and read it out loud to each other.

- ✔ Rent a documentary about some foreign city you've always wanted to visit, like Paris, and then afterwards go for dinner at a local restaurant that serves the cuisine you'd find in that city.

Taking in the Sights of the Big City

Although some big cities have more attractions than others, they all have one thing in common: They make great places to hide. If you live in a big city, you can get away from it all quite easily by going to another neighborhood. For example: Perhaps you live in the 'burbs. A weekend stay at a downtown hotel can be a great getaway. You may discover activities and attractions that you never thought of visiting before.

A big city offers lots of distractions, and these distractions may help your romance soar. (Rather than distractions, maybe I should call them stimulations.)

✔ **Indulge in dining.** Find varieties of wonderful foods; when you activate your palette, your other senses are enlivened as well.

✔ **Explore the arts.** Visit museums and galleries to absorb different types of art. (This sparks your mind, and I believe your mind is your number one sex organ.)

✔ **People watch.** You encounter all sorts of different people. Some of these folks will tickle your funny bones, peak your interests, and fascinate you.

✔ **Take a walking tour.** You may be amazed at the varieties of architecture. Discover breathtaking views from your city's tallest buildings.

✔ **Window shop.** Even window-shopping may inspire you; the professionals who dress shop windows in big cities are a very creative lot.

Finding Seclusion in the Woods

If the two of you need to talk and become reacquainted after having spent months barely seeing each other, a vacation away from everything can be wonderfully romantic. You can rent a cabin, bring along some good wine and scented candles, and really get to know one another again — both emotionally and physically. Here are some ideas:

✔ **Build a fire.** If your cabin doesn't have a fireplace, build a bonfire outside (if it's legal) and roast some marshmallows, which you can feed to each other.

✔ **Make some music.** If you know how to make music, bring along a guitar or harmonica and serenade each other. For those not so musically inclined, bring along a tape or CD of old favorites that you can sing along to.

✔ **Go for a long hike.** Bring along a blanket so that when you get tired, you can lie down someplace private and add some spice to the hike.

Bug off: The problems with roughing it on vacation

Lots of people say that camping in a tent and roughing it are romantic ventures, and I agree. There are romantic aspects to it. But you know what? A bare-bones camping trip, with no luxuries, can also destroy romance. If it rains, if the bugs are out en masse, or if it's too hot or too cold, you may wind up feeling miserable instead of ecstatic. When you camp with little more shelter than your pup tent, you're at the mercy of the elements. If finding time to get away is hard to do and you can afford to do more than set up your tent in a campground, you might look for a better option. My suggestion is a woodsy setting with a roof over your head.

Strolling through the City of Lights

I know that I could tuck Paris into my discussion of big cities, but this metropolis deserves its own special section. I rarely make universal statements, but I'll stick my neck out here and say that for most people, Paris is the most romantic city in the world.

People often ask me where I get my energy, and I really can't explain it. The same is true with Paris. You can ask Parisians why their city is so romantic, and they may not have an explanation. One unique aspect of Paris that may factor into its romantic aura is its strict zoning laws; very few tall buildings are constructed here. The special light radiating from Paris skies is always around you. Another factor is the Parisian sense of style; wherever you look, you're surrounded by beauty. Dining on some of the best food in the world doesn't hurt, nor does admiring the great art in the city's many museums.

Paris is the ultimate strolling city. The center of the city, where everything you might want to see is located, is small enough that you can go everywhere by foot. As you soak in the ambience, you begin to glow with the same radiance that lights up the city. The next thing you know, that glow has infused your romance.

Paris is a great place to go sightseeing, and you should visit it once in order to take in all the sights and snap photos. After that first visit, you should go back merely to bask in the special light that only Paris possesses. I'd be very surprised if your romance didn't come back with a very dark tan.

Finding Inspiration in the Holy Land

I admit that Jerusalem is not as romantic as Paris, but it is my favorite city in the world. Jerusalem has a unique feeling that awakens your soul and also makes you better appreciate your partner.

The planners of the new Jerusalem have insisted that all of the buildings be constructed out of the same white stone. The stone makes for a very impressive, peaceful atmosphere.

What Jerusalem possesses, as does the entire country of Israel, is the heritage of the Holy Land. The holiest places of three great world religions are found here. These holy places have not always lead to political peace, but an inner peace may settle upon you when you visit. The sense of awe that ordinary mortals have being amidst these sites should bring the two of you closer together in ways no other place can. If your souls are connecting in a very special manner, you are drawn to each other in a way that can only strengthen your romance.

Setting Out on a Romantic Adventure

How many movies have you seen where a man and a woman are thrown together in some adventure? Although they start off hating each other, soon enough they fall into each other's arms. I'm not suggesting that you need to put yourselves in peril in order to pump up your romance, but sharing a trip that has just a touch of adventure can definitely bring you closer together.

What type of place am I suggesting? One suggestion is any country where you don't know the language and the vast majority of the natives don't know yours. Just choosing what to eat from a menu written in lettering you don't recognize can be an adventure. Picture yourselves exploring a *souk,* the maze of little streets found in the old sections of many towns in Arab countries. Or going on a safari. Or camping in the woods 50 miles or more from civilization.

The more you get the feeling that it's the two of you against the world, the closer you feel to each other. You revert to pioneer times when the man's job was to protect his spouse, and she felt protected by his big strong arms. It may not be politically correct to assume these roles at home, but being PC won't matter during this romantic excursion.

A romantic adventure offers the best souvenirs: the memories of the times you share. If you feel a little more alive on this particular trip, the memories you retain of those moments when you "cheated death" will be vivid. You can stir those memories by perusing the photos you bring back, and they will have a positive effect on your romance for the rest of your life.

Relaxing on a Tropical Isle

Why are tropical islands romantic? Islands bring out your sensuous qualities. You don't wear very much clothing, the sun and tropical breezes feel great on your bare skin, and the sun setting on the horizon equals romance. Sure, a few activities fill some free time, but mostly you just lie on a beach with nothing much to do but relax.

That last word, *relax,* is key. After a day or two, you really do forget all your cares; the armor you wear to ward off stress falls away, and the romantic aura captures you. Does it matter which tropical isle you visit? I don't think so. Many people have their favorite island destinations — I think that's great. But the differences can be fairly minimal as far as your romance is concerned.

When traveling with your children, consider visiting an island with a Club Med or similar resort that has a staff of experts who watch your children so that you can get some real R&R.

Cruising the High Seas

Cruises are designed to pamper you, and if pampering makes you feel relaxed, a cruise is most certainly a good place for you to restore your frazzled romance.

The good thing about a ship is that you're never very far away from your cabin. My advice to you is to visit your cabin as often as possible. You don't necessarily need to have sex each time, but privacy is hard to come by on a ship. In your cabin you have the opportunity to cuddle and neck and kiss. If these activities lead to sex, great. If they don't, you can go back on deck knowing plenty of other opportunities for lovemaking exist as your ship glides through the ocean.

Cruising the Highways

For landlubbers, a cruise along the nation's highways can also make for a romantic voyage. There's something about being locked away in a steel structure, whizzing by the open landscapes, that is very freeing. Inside your car, you have your own contained environment. You can say anything you want to each other and no one can hear you. You can sing along to your favorite oldies. You can feel free to stop and take a look if something outside the window catches your eye.

Until very recently, such a trip with children was the antithesis of romantic because of constant whining and curious little ears. Today, many vans are equipped with a TV, VCR, and headphones so that the little ones are not only occupied, they can't hear a word you say.

Although your trip may be fun if you take what comes and plan your days as you go along, make sure you know of some good hotels along your possible paths. You may use a cell phone to make reservations as you get close to hotels you have noted. Nothing spoils a romantic car trip more than being forced to spend the night in some sleazy motel where you don't feel comfortable.

Returning to Your Honeymoon Hotel

If you're married, I hope that the two of you had a great honeymoon. And if you went someplace special, you can definitely have a romantic vacation by returning to your honeymoon hotel. (I strongly recommend that you jettison the kids for this trip.)

This excursion may be even more romantic than the first time you made it. You may have been virgins the first time around and you may have been tentative about your lovemaking. But by now, you should know enough about each other's bodies to be able to drive your partner wild. With a treasure trove of memories to share, nostalgia will play a strong supporting role in the reenactment of this love story. Don't worry — you won't have any awkward moments of silence.

I want to add that it's important that you don't spend all your time reliving your past — especially if you're approaching empty nesthood. Use some of the time to make plans for the future. I'm not talking about financial plans, but strategies for how to keep your romance vibrant. Analyze why you needed this vacation in the first place, and take some new vows. These vows — which you write together in the spirit of your passionate second honeymoon — should be designed to protect and rekindle your romance.

Chapter 23

Ten Great Ways to Date Your Mate

*Y*ou live together for a number of years. You share the same bed for sleep and sex. You eat dinner together most nights and breakfast most mornings. Why, then, do you need to date each other?

The simple reason: Taking the person you share your life with for granted is an easy habit to get into. The fact that you have sex on a semi-regular basis, share a checkbook, and discuss whether or not to paint the living room does not mean that you have license to ignore the romantic quotient of your relationship. No couple should expect to be romantic all of the time; you do have a life that needs your attention. But the best way to make sure that you do have some romance in your relationship is to continue to date, just the way you did before you began to shack up.

If the sex the two of you enjoy resulted in some young ones sharing your living space, resurrecting the dating process is even more important. Kids easily suck up all your free time. If you want to ensure that you spend some time alone together, plan for it — don't leave it to potluck.

The definition of a date isn't set in stone. Yes, a date can involve sharing dinner in a restaurant, going to the movies, or dancing cheek-to-cheek, but a date can also involve other ways of spending quality time together. Part of the dating process centers on the activities you do together. Another part centers on the attitude that you bring to a date. You may dine in the most romantic restaurant in the world, but if one of you can't stop thinking about the big sales meeting scheduled for the following morning, the date is going to be a washout. On the other hand, even sharing a cold can of soup when a storm knocks out your electricity can be very romantic when the two of you ignore your circumstances and give each other your full concentration.

The Morning Date

On weekday mornings, you and your mate probably have a hard time dragging yourselves out of bed. But weekend mornings may be different. You probably aren't awakened by an alarm, and you don't feel rushed to jump into the shower. For these reasons, weekend mornings are a great time for a date.

Like any other date, a morning date takes planning. In fact, morning dates may require more planning than others. When you first get up, your creative juices may feel drained. How do you overcome your grogginess? Take the time to prepare. For example, if you want to have a romantic breakfast in bed, prepare a breakfast tray the night before. Set an electric pot to brew coffee so that it's ready when you wake up. You don't have to think about what to do when you plan ahead; just follow your own instructions.

A morning date needn't take place only in bed. The two of you could take a stroll to watch the sunrise, ride your bikes to a field to pick wildflowers, or put on your snowshoes to make the first tracks in the freshly fallen snow. Keep in mind that men experience the highest levels of testosterone, their sex hormone, in the morning. This high level of testosterone is one reason why so many men regularly wake up with erections. So, if your morning date starts out in bed, don't be surprised if it heats up quickly.

Lunch Dates

Lunch dates are a great way to keep your romance going during the week. If your offices are close enough to each other, meet somewhere for lunch. You don't have to meet in a restaurant. Maybe there's a park at the halfway point where you could brown bag it. I advise that you take advantage of your lunch breaks once in a while.

What's important about a lunch date is that you get to see each other during the day, which is not part of your normal routine. As I say many times in this book, boredom is very dangerous to a relationship. So for variety's sake, try to take a long lunch hour once in a while. You can catch up on your work by staying later at the office if you need to; the sacrifice will be well worth your while.

The menu for a lunch date is not critical to its success. Your time is limited; you may find the most convenient meal is to grab a couple of hot dogs from a street vendor. If the weather's nice, just sharing some unaccustomed sunlight on a workday can seem like a mini-vacation.

Both of you probably have work on your minds, so keep your conversations light. You may have more fun just looking at the other people sharing the sidewalks with you than trying to have a meaningful conversation.

Keep in mind that the best-made plans often go awry. Just because you decide in the morning to have lunch doesn't mean that both of you can completely control your workday schedule. If your partner has to get back to the office after 45 minutes or an hour, don't make him or her feel guilty for needing to cut things short. Let him or her off the hook and try to stretch out the next lunch date to an hour and a half. If you lay a guilt trip on your partner, he or she may think twice before agreeing to have lunch during the week with you again.

For the same reason, I caution against surprise lunchtime visits. Your partner may be extremely busy, and he or she may have to give you the cold shoulder. That chill can definitely harm a romance-rekindling project. If you have lunchtime plans that suddenly need to be cancelled because duty calls, don't make a face. By being flexible with each other about the timing, these lunchtime outings can be lots of fun.

Phone Dates

What if the two of you can't meet for lunch because the distance is too great? Does that mean you can't have a lunchtime date? Absolutely not. If you can't meet in person, use the phone. You can both find a phone out of the office to ensure some privacy and call each other. You may each have a cell phone — you can call from anywhere you like. If not, see if a conference room or nearby phone booth can offer the privacy you need.

Many couples spend a lot of time on the phone when they date and develop an intimate phone relationship. Then they move in together and that aspect of their relationship dies. Certainly, being face-to-face with someone is better than speaking with someone on the phone. However, some aspects of a phone relationship can't be replaced. When you talk on the phone, your voice goes directly into your partner's ear. You can keep your voice low and whispery to cultivate intimacy. Your intonations are very different than when you speak to your partner in person, even when your partner is sitting only a few feet away. You're more likely to say something silly or very personal on the phone than when your mate is in the same room.

Although talking to your spouse on the phone for a half hour before each of you leaves the office may seem absurd, sometimes the absurd is just what you need in a relationship. Make phone dates with each other and see what transpires. If you find something uniquely satisfying in this type of date, make sure that you continue to connect in this way with some regularity.

Traditional Dinner Dates

You eat dinner together almost every night anyway. Cooking can be time-consuming, and if your pantry is not well stocked, the resulting meal may not be that tasty. Many restaurants do their best to create a romantic atmosphere — why not let them work their magic both in the kitchen and the dining room once in a while?

Some couples who both work outside the home go out to dinner a lot; the act of sharing a meal in a restaurant becomes downright mundane. For those couples, I suggest keeping certain restaurants as "date" restaurants. Select from the remaining restaurants on your list when you're merely going out to kill your appetites.

What differentiates a date from just a meal? How much time you spend is one factor. If you linger over each course and don't mind that the waiter is taking his time bringing you the bill, that means you're deep in conversation and busy rekindling your romance. Another indicator may be what you order. For example, sharing a bottle of wine puts you in a different mood than drinking mineral water.

Keep in mind that not everybody finds a restaurant the ideal place for a date. The problem may be with diversions at the restaurant. Many places have a theme (sports, rock 'n' roll, and so on) that can be distracting. Or, the restaurant may be the trendy place to meet, and the crowds can interrupt your romantic dinner. At these types of establishments, your partner may get so involved in what is going on around him or her that full attention is not given to your conversation. If your twosome includes someone who is easily distracted, you're better off ordering takeout for your romantic dinner dates so that you can get him or her to give you undivided attention.

Nontraditional Dinner Dates

A dinner date usually means that two people get together between about 6 and 9 p.m. to share a meal. However, you may also spend that time together without eating a thing. If you decide that the meal part of the date is not that important, you open up a whole world of possible activities:

- Go for a run, stop at a nearby lake, and watch the sunset or the stars twinkle.
- Take a painting or language class together and stimulate your minds.
- Take advantage of stores that stay open late and do your Christmas shopping early; then you won't be so frazzled when the holidays roll in.

✔ Take in an early movie, when the lines aren't so long, and dine on buttered popcorn and Raisinets.

✔ Give each other massages; then meet some friends at a bar and empty the nut dishes over beers and good conversation.

✔ Take advantage of the last hours of daylight to work on your garden; then have a salad from the greens you picked in your back yard.

In other words, a nontraditional dinner date means that you set aside your dinner time to do something different together, rather than sit at home, eat leftovers, and watch TV.

Warm-Up Dates

One problem with traditional dates: Most of these dates include food and perhaps a drink or two. If you've worked a long day, you're already fatigued. Then you fill your stomach with rich foods and have a couple of Fuzzy Navels to wash them down. By the time you and your partner get home from your traditional date, you may be too pooped to do much more than strip off your clothes and fall asleep.

Every date doesn't have to lead to a sexual episode. But what if sex is on your mind? What if you want the evening's activities to be just a warm-up to the main event? If that's your aspiration, plan a date that charges up your batteries, not one that depletes your energy and short-circuits your libido.

To stay alert on this kind of date, eat very little and limit yourself to one glass of wine. If you are tired already, avoid alcohol altogether.

To get your blood circulating, include some exercise on your date. You don't want to tire yourself out, so a brisk walk should do it. However, a little sporting action may be just what you need to fire up your furnaces. You may play a game of tennis or racquetball, glide on some roller-skates, or even swim at the Y.

When you get home, head for the showers — a great place to have foreplay while getting squeaky clean. Then, you'll be primed for some terrific sex.

Pick-Up Dates

Say you've been together for a dozen years (or feel like you have). You know your partner's stories backwards and forwards and can predict what he or she is going to say before the words come out. If that's the case, even the most romantic setting may not create the special ambience you seek. How do you overcome the staleness that can stem from familiarity? For starters, each of you can pretend to be someone else.

Set a date to meet at a particular bar at a certain time. Start the date as if you were strangers. (You may have played this game before and have favorite characters that you like to play. Feel free to slip into those personalities.)

How far you go with the role-playing is up to you. Your creative juices may run out after half an hour; then you can each have a good laugh and go back to being yourselves. On the other hand, if you can carry your act off for the entire evening, you may even be able to add some variety to your bedroom activities. Use positions that are taboo in "real life" but not on these special nights.

To widen the separation between the real you and your character, try using a foreign accent or wearing special clothes that you save in the back of your closet only for these evenings. For example, you could pretend that you're living in some bygone era and dress appropriately. Clothing from the '50s or '60s would work well. However, be careful about going Greek and wearing togas; you may draw more attention than you bargain for.

The selection of the bar can play an important role in the proceedings — choose it carefully. You don't want one that is too crowded and noisy. (How will your partner hear your accent?) Conversely, you don't want an empty bar where you and your partner may be conspicuous. Dim lighting, soft music, and a quiet gathering should be your goal. Then, let the games begin.

Maybe play-acting seems too daring for you. Break the ice by trying this game at home the first time. See whether you can pull your act off for a while. If the rehearsal goes well, you can try your new personality out in public.

The Cocoon Date

What makes a date ultra-romantic? Being able to truly concentrate on each other. Ideally, the two of you could wrap yourselves in a cocoon, where nothing could distract your attentions. Although that's not possible, I strongly suggest that at least every few months, you make an effort to configure a cocoon-like state.

If you stay at home, those pesky household chores stare you in the face and make you feel guilty for devoting some time to romance. If you go to a restaurant, you're surrounded by people and other distractions. My suggestion:

Take a room in a hotel that has room service. Hotel rooms are free of distractions — other than the TV, which you have to promise each other not to turn on. After you examine the paltry artwork and check to make sure that the toilet works, you can gaze into each other's eyes to your heart's content.

Sexual interplay is completely permissible inside this cocoon, but the main purpose of such a getaway isn't to have orgasms. Use the time to reconnect, because running in the rat race can easily drive a wedge between you and your partner.

Mini Dates

I'm saddened to say that people are too busy these days to plan dates with their partners. Unless you are willing to wait weeks for a matching window of free time in each of your schedules, you may never connect. Waiting for an opportune time to meet isn't a viable way to maintain a relationship. You need to make finding time a priority to keep any rifts from developing. Don't limit your dates to large blocks of time; fit some mini dates in whenever you can.

What qualifies as a mini date? Any time that you spend together focusing on just the two of you. (Having dinner with your children is *not* a mini date.)

Here are a few examples of how to have a mini date:

- He works late; you go home and eat dinner. Later in the evening, you drive to his office and pick him up. You stop at a bar that serves food and he has dinner while you sip a beer.

- You ask the teenager next door to come over at 9 p.m. while the kids are sleeping and the two of you go out for an ice cream soda.

- The kids watch cartoons; you tell them that mom and dad are going to be in the garage and that they shouldn't disturb you unless it's an emergency. You pop a pleasant CD in the car stereo, share some fresh fruit, and have a private conversation.

Whatever form your mini dates take, the point is that they require time put aside for just the two of you. Even when you can find only half an hour, it's better than nothing. You may have kids; try to establish the notion that mom and dad have a mini date every night at about the same time. Teach your children to accept the fact that the two of you share a cup of tea at 9:30, and those 15 minutes are sacred.

Extended Dates

How great would it be if you could hop on a plane Friday afternoon and spend the weekend in Paris? Such glamorous voyages don't mix with most people's budgets. However, you can find less extravagant ways of spending an entire weekend together.

Many people take weekend trips that involve getting into the family vehicle, picking a place on the map a few hours away, and enjoying whatever that community has to offer.

You may also have a particular goal in mind for your trip. If you like to shop for antiques, you could head for areas that have lots of antique dealers. If you want to check out the fall foliage, a nearby state park would be another great weekend destination. If the two of you are skiers, it's the slopes for you.

Some trips, like a visit to an orchard to go apple picking, are perfect for sharing with your children. However, your kids should know that some weekend trips are only for mom and dad. Set this precedent early and they won't howl quite as loudly when you leave them with their grandparents.

Don't try to pack too much into these long weekends. For a trip to qualify as a date, you need some time to unwind and get close to one another. That closeness is difficult to achieve if you never remove your seat belts.

Chapter 24

Ten New Twists on Your Everyday Sex Life

In This Chapter

▶ Shaking up your sex routine

▶ Creating your own positions

▶ Daring to experiment

Sexually active people may have sex with the same partner 1,000 times, 5,000 times, or more, depending on the length of their relationships and how frequently they make love. These folks may be adventurous types who try every position imaginable. Or they may settle into a rut and not really enjoy much variety in their sex lives.

How important is variety to your romance? Suppose that whenever you are hungry you eat the same exact meal. You may select a menu that contains your absolute favorite foods, but after eating 1,000 identical meals, how much would you really look forward to the next one? You would almost certainly crave something new once in a while.

Perhaps your time is limited, your energy is low, and your desire to experiment is lacking. You may have a favorite way to enjoy sex that you choose most of the time. At least once in a while, you need to spice things up a little, especially if you're interested in rekindling your romance. So here are ten ideas for adding some slight twists to your everyday sex life.

Switching Who's on First (And When)

Sex is initiated one of two ways: Either he lights the fire, or she does. Only one of you may originate the sexual act — not a lot of variety — but if only one of you *always* takes the initiative, you may already find yourselves in a sexual rut.

Look at sex as a sequence of activities, just as if the act is a series of notes. Change one note, and you play a different song. Change one part of your routine, and you enjoy a different way of having sex. Your first step is to share in taking the initiative.

The person taking the initiative carries a bit of a burden, because he or she risks being rejected. A fear of rejection may be preventing one of you from ever taking that first step. But you should realize that placing the entire burden of initiation on the shoulders of one partner is unfair.

Another twist that you can integrate into the initiation process regards its timing. For many couples, the initiation process begins right before the sex begins. If these couples usually have sex at around bedtime, the initiation occurs as they prepare for bed.

To add variety, make that request earlier in the day. Say he's taking his morning shower. You join him as he's rinsing off; you give him a hug and say, "Want to continue this tonight?" If he says yes, the two of you have all day to think about the possibilities.

Playing Hide and Seek

Couples almost always have sex in a comfortable bed, but sometimes a couple may get too comfortable. Adding a little variety to where you have sex definitely doesn't hurt. I'm not suggesting you make love in Times Square (although lovemaking outside your home may be a nice idea). I am speaking of relocating inside your dwelling.

How do you decide where to have sex on those nights when the bed is going to be for sleeping only? How about a game of hide-and-seek? One partner hides — and in this case the hiding place is in plain sight — by lying on the dining room table. The other partner, after counting to ten and getting just that much more excited, seeks. Where he or she finds the person "hiding" is where they have sex. If you live in a small apartment and you want to extend the seeking part a little longer, blindfold the hunter (a dab of perfume or some kissy noises may help the seeker in his or her search).

Beating the Clock

Another way to add some variety is to change the time when you have sex — especially if you most often have sex at bedtime.

If you don't have children or if your children flew the coop and you're empty nesters, any time the two of you are together is a good time for sex. But if some little angels share your living quarters, their presence limits your opportunities. If you're exhausted by bedtime, don't force yourselves to stick to the eleven o'clock start time. You may set your alarm to allow for a two-hour nap or just wake up earlier in the morning.

Remember that a man's level of testosterone, the chief male sex hormone, is highest in the morning, so mornings may offer the best time for him to have sex. This timing is especially important for older couples, because the man may only have a strong enough erection to penetrate his partner during the early hours of the day.

Changing the Rules of Foreplay

I hear many women complain that their partners begin foreplay exactly the same way every time they make love. First he touches one breast; then he touches her other breast; and then he reaches down between her legs. After many years of this routine, not only can she predict exactly what he'll do, but she also begins to dread this foreplay.

To add some spice to your foreplay, don't always be so quick to reach for the so-called erogenous zones. Yes, a women likes her breasts touched and her clitoris stroked in order to help her reach orgasm. But don't rush. Why not start by massaging your partner's feet? Or maybe offer a hand massage. Or massage her back. Or her scalp. Lick the back of her knees. Run your fingers along her spine. Nibble on her earlobe.

And even when you arouse the traditional areas, don't always follow the same pattern. Use your penis to tantalize her nipples. Stroke her clitoris with your big toe. Blindfold her one time so that she has no idea what you are doing. Give her a hand mirror the next time so that she can watch the show.

Instead of seeing your partner as the person with whom you make love over and over, imagine that this experience marks your first encounter with your favorite actress as you impress her with your skills at lovemaking.

Inventing Your Own Venus Butterfly

A TV program mentioned a sexual position called the Venus Butterfly. Everyone asked me about this position, but I had no idea what it was. All I know is that there *is* a Dr. Ruth/Dr. Amos position that was created for the book I co-wrote called *Dr. Ruth's Pregnancy Guide for Couples*. Like the stars that are named after astronauts, a position was named after me — I love that fact.

Maybe you want to invent your own position. Don't worry whether your position is already on page 52 of the *Kama Sutra,* just enjoy putting your bodies together in different ways. You may wind up back in your favorite position, and that's okay. The point is that you don't become a stick in the mud.

If inventing your own position taxes your creativity, peruse a book like the *Kama Sutra* or *The Joy of Sex* and see if you can replicate the illustrations. Don't take this challenge too seriously, because whether or not you can isn't the issue. Your goal is to break out of the rut you are stuck in. If you share a good laugh trying and decide to give up, you're still ahead of the game.

Taking a Lick

Oral sex was once something very few couples engaged in, but oral sex has gained acceptance in the mainstream. A young person may be more willing to engage in oral sex these days in order to maintain his or her virginity.

One reason that young people are opting for oral sex is that it can't cause an unintended pregnancy, but even if that's not your concern, there are plenty of other reasons why you might enjoy oral sex. It certainly gives each partner a different set of sensations, as well as an up-close view of the other's genitals.

Just because oral sex is more common does not mean that you need to include it in your sexual repertoire. If one partner really can't stand the thought of performing oral sex, the other shouldn't try to pressure him or her into it. But perhaps the unwilling partner may consider at least making an effort, rather than refusing out of principle.

Because the genitals serve a dual purpose — sex and urination — the cleanliness issue may be a mental obstacle to oral sex. If cleanliness is a problem for you or your partner, take a shower together first. Doing so may help to overcome your hesitations.

Even if you can't perform oral sex on your partner, this fact shouldn't stop your partner from giving you oral sex. You should experience pleasure in both the giving and receiving. By negating all oral sex, you may only further diminish your partner's enjoyment as well as cut off an entire avenue of variation.

Some women avoid kissing or licking their partners' penises because they don't like the thought of their partners ejaculating in their mouths. They worry that if they offer any oral attention, their partners expect them to carry oral sex through to ejaculation. Don't deny your partner pleasure because of this fear. Given the choice of having some oral-genital contact versus none, I'm sure most men would choose door number one.

Talking the Talk

Some people make a lot of noise when they have sex, while others are quiet. If you already make a racket, good for you. However, you and your lover may be the strong silent types, and giving voice to your feelings could be fun.

I am fully aware that some people (especially women) must concentrate in order to have orgasms. Voicing their feelings is enough of a distraction to prevent them from coming to climaxes. While you retain the right to remain silent, perhaps you could speak up a little before your final act. Again, this vocalization doesn't need to occur every time, but an occasionally more verbose lovemaking session may add some spark to your relationship.

As far as using vulgarity, the same principle holds true. If the shock of hearing four-letter words is too distracting, don't do it. On the other hand, you never know how you'll react unless you give it a try at least one time.

Changing the Order of Orgasms

You may follow a routine in which the same partner reaches orgasm first. Maybe the man usually reaches orgasm first, because the woman needs more time to reach her orgasm. I suggest that the man wait until his partner successfully climaxes before heading for home himself. Or, if his orgasm comes very early in the game (and not a premature ejaculation, but a calculated eruption), perhaps he can get another erection while he helps his partner reach her destination.

The point here is to try different things. Even if you like the old way better — even if it's more practical — don't let that stop you from trying different ways of making love. You may always return to your usual style. Sex is not used up, like the fuel in your gas tank. At absolutely no cost to you, your reservoir fills up again on its own and you derive sex's enjoyment again and again. Be a little daring; if the new twist isn't to your liking, you don't really lose anything.

Heading Left of Center

Some sexual practices may be too far out in left field for you to even contemplate. Anal sex may be a position you just can't imagine ever enjoying. And you may be too afraid of pain to want to experiment with S&M. I'm certainly not going to encourage you to go beyond your limits. As I say all the time, I'm old-fashioned and a square; I believe you can hold those traits and still have terrific sex. Of course, if you decide to take a trip to the outer limits, be my guest. Just make sure that nobody gets hurt.

But while I'm not advocating anal sex or S&M, you may be able to incorporate some aspects of these activities into your own sexual behavior and add some variety without crossing any major boundaries. While the thought of anal penetration may give you the heebie jeebies, many people derive pleasure from having their anuses touched. If you assure each other that you won't do any probing, you may try touching each other's anuses at some point during foreplay to see if either of you find this act pleasurable.

You may not enjoy giving or receiving actual pain, but you may find light bondage exciting. Allow your partner to tie you up and do whatever he or she wants to you. If you try some light bondage and hate it, you never have to do it again. But perhaps you may derive some pleasure from this sort of thing and may include bondage in your lovemaking every once in a while — even if it's only once a year on Halloween.

Sharing Your Toys

The term *sex toys* is a broad one, and you needn't only order from a catalog or visit a sex shop in order to acquire some. You may already have some toys at your disposal. For example, you may stock your kitchen with whipped cream, honey, or chocolate sauce — any one of which makes sex with your partner just a little more tasty. Some feathers plucked from your feather duster provide a ticklish way of arousing your partner. If you want to try light bondage, bring some of his old ties out from the back of his closet. Deal from a worn deck of cards for a game of strip poker.

Of the store-bought variety of sex toys, the vibrator is probably the best known. Vibrators are actually important tools for women who experience difficulties achieving orgasms. Vibrators also provide invigorating sensations that you both may enjoy.

Oils make massages more pleasurable, and some oils create a warming effect. Wearing edible underwear, watching an erotic video, or reading passages to each other from an erotic novel may steam up your bedroom windows.

For more ideas, order a catalog from a company like Eve's Garden or Good Vibrations. Just thumbing through the pages may get your pulses beating faster. Maybe these catalogs could be considered sex toys in their own rights.

Chapter 25

Ten Romantic Web Sites

*T*he World Wide Web is an amazing place, though I'm still confused about exactly where it is. (I guess it's like Santa's North Pole, which explorers have never found but which can yield a mountain of toys if you just believe in it.) Pick a subject, and you can find lots of information about it. Some of that information can be valuable, some is amusing, and some isn't worth one plastic peanut from the mound your computer came packed in.

With time as precious as it is, I don't want you to spend hours searching through every romance site on the Web, especially when you could be spending that time rekindling your relationship. Romance is a topic that many people have chosen to make the focus of their Web pages, but one person's idea of romance may not be another's (or anybody's for that matter).

Whatever the faults of the mass of Web sites dealing with romance, some sites can actually offer you nice dry firewood for your rekindling program. This chapter describes ten sites that you may find worth taking a gander at.

The RoMANtic's Guide

www.theromantic.com

This site was created by Michael Webb, who has written books on romance and has a syndicated newspaper column. I particularly like one aspect of his philosophy about romance, which I found in his description of "What is romantic." In it he says, "What is most romantic comes from your heart, not inside your wallet." Now, I'm the first one to enjoy freebies, but I also recognize that the high cost of a gift doesn't necessarily make it more romantic. With gifts, it really should be the thought that counts, which is why the gifts that mean the most to me these days are the little drawings and art works I get from my grandchildren.

This site has a lot going for it. You can find classic poems as well as letters written from Napoleon to Josephine and from Zelda Fitzgerald to F. Scott, which can inspire your own romantic missives. You also can find all sorts of trivia, tips, jokes, suggestions for romantic getaways, and, as the site itself says, "1000s of creative ideas and expert advice on love, dating, and romance." You can even subscribe to get a free weekly e-zine.

Barely Nothing

www.barelynothing.com

I know I said it's the thought that counts, so that shopping for gifts doesn't have to be part of rekindling your romance. However, I believe the people who created this shopping site did a lot of thinking when they were putting it together, so it's definitely worth a look.

I like that on the home page is a picture of the owners with their cat and their dog. They look like a very nice, average couple. While they are purveyors of materials that may shock some people, they aren't afraid to show themselves. I get the sense that they don't look at their site simply as a way of making money but as a way to offer a service to other couples.

Barely Nothing offer lots of lingerie, including teddies, bustiers, and baby-dolls. What I like is that they carry them in all sizes, including large sizes, and they have large sized models in some of their pictures.

But the shopping selection is not limited to sexy fashions. This site carries a full line of adult toys, including vibrators and dildos, and some things I'd never heard of, like dingers and vibro dongers. (Check out the site to see what these are.) They even have fantasy bedding.

I definitely recommend visiting this site, either alone or with your mate. Even if you don't order anything, you can have a good time poking around.

Virtual Kiss

www.virtualkiss.com

An important part of romance is kissing, and here's a site devoted to nothing but kissing. When I first looked at it I thought to myself, "How much can they say about kissing?" But it turns out there was a lot more than I ever imagined.

I am always getting questions about kissing, because people worry that they're not doing it right. Well, if they can't find the answers to their questions here, they're hopeless. This site covers lips, eyes, head movement, mindset, feedback, breathing, saliva control, tempo, tongues, and more.

Then you have kissing stories. Reading about people's first kisses is fun, and this site has hundreds of stories that people have sent in. You can also read stories about people's best and worst kisses.

And then you have all the kissing games. Everybody knows Spin the Bottle and Post Office, but have you ever played Ice Kold Kisser or Lifesaver Kandy Kisser? If not and you want to find out how, this is the place to go. And if you sign up when you visit, they send you a daily e-mail with tips on how to be a better kisser. If the whole country signed up, we'd all be champion kissers!

Romance 101

www.rom101.com

If you're looking for information about romance, here is the mother lode. I guess that makes sense, because the site was developed by college students. It began in 1993 as a presentation of the Pacific Affiliate of College & University Residence Halls and has been growing by leaps and bounds ever since. It's designed to look like a spiral notebook, and if you want to cram for an exam on romance, then this is the site to go to.

While this site has many of the features you can find on other sites, such as Make Your Own Greeting Card, Romantic Gifts, and Love Certificates, it also has lots of other information you won't find anywhere else.

If you want to laugh, this site lists sex laws that are actually on the books. For example, a law from Hastings, Nebraska says that the owner of every hotel in town is required to provide each guest with a clean and pressed nightshirt. No couple, even if married, may sleep together in the nude. Nor may they have sex unless they are wearing one of these nightshirts.

And when it comes to describing kisses, you can find more varieties on this site than on Virtual Kiss.

Among the other areas the site covers are love spells, flowers, unromantic laws, love in many languages, a history of Valentine's Day, diamond trivia, wedding ring origin, wedding horror stories, international sex, quiz games, word search, forums, dream meanings, and on and on.

Because they change the site every month, assuming you could possibly cram it all in during one session, you may want to revisit Romance 101 regularly to see what other goodies have been added.

Keeping certain sites in perspective

Many of the Web sites that fall under the banner of *Romance* are about romance novels. These novels helped me to learn English when I first came to the States, so I have absolutely nothing against them. But you should know that there may be some danger lurking amid the torrid language that fills their pages.

If you start to compare your own life to what is going on in a romance novel, then your own relationship is sure to fall short. A novelist controls the situation, the dialogue, and the outcome.

You and your mate have no such control over your very real life. So if you're drawn to these novels and to their accompanying Web sites, make sure that when you shut down your computer or close that book, you take off the rose-colored glasses that were put over your eyes while in one of these artificial worlds. Life in a romance novel cannot be the standard by which you judge the state of your own romance. If it is, you may as well give up ever finding satisfaction for yourself.

Marriage Pages on About.com

www.about.com

If you click on the topic of *Marriage* in About.com, you can find a wealth of information. The information isn't particularly romantic, but you can find useful ideas that may help you to fix problems in your relationship.

Among the dozens of articles I looked at were ones on Marriage Spirituality, Infidelity, Domestic Discipline, Conflict and Anger, Disillusionment, Coping with Your Partner's Passion for TV, and Ho'oponopono, which is a traditional Hawaiian problem-solving process.

If you and your spouse have a particular problem, you may well find ways of dealing with it on this site. Of course, you have to take anything you read with a grain of salt, first analyzing it with your own common sense before trying it out. Some people who give advice are professionals with training, and the feedback they offer comes from having a private practice. Other advice givers may have some good ideas but may not fully understand the consequences of what they are suggesting.

Isn't It Romantic?

www.geocities.com/heartland/hills/2587/romance.html

Though I haven't made an exact count, there are hundreds, perhaps even thousands of sites about romance on the Web that were created by individuals. I have made a point of viewing some, and I really like this one created by The Scott Family. Because it is so sweet, I found it very romantic. I suggest that the two of you check this one out together.

First of all, this site has music. On the first page you hear a melody with bells. I know they're not real bells and that the effect was created with a synthesizer, but I still find it charming.

Like other sites about romance, this one has coupons, but there, too, they are especially sweet. For example, one says "Coffee, Tea or Me, served anywhere in your home." The whole tone shows that somebody put a lot of care into this site, and you can feel it when you visit. It puts you in a pleasant, mellow mood — just perfect for stoking up those romantic fires in your own home.

Gone With The Wind

`http://community-2.webtv.net/tara50/gwtw`

The advantage of writing a book is that you get to include your personal favorites, and my all-time favorite romantic movie is *Gone With The Wind*. The Web features many sites on this film classic, and I happen to like this one best of those I have seen. It has lots of pictures from the film, and I especially like one background that is a picture of these incredible silk sheets. It may take a while for this part of the image to load, but it's definitely worth taking a peek. You may feel inspired to get similar sheets for your bed.

Loving You

`www.lovingyou.com`

Like several of the other romance sites I've mentioned, Loving You has many of the essential ingredients such as advice on dating, entertaining, food and wine, and so on. It also has chats, forums, clip art, postcards, and daily tips.

What this site also has that I did not find anywhere else is some very good advice on how to write about romance. Because each relationship is so personal and is built on so many personal memories, many people would like to write their own cards or poems. But if they're not good writers, they shy away from doing so. This site has a Love Library where you can find articles on how to describe emotions, what it takes to develop your writing style, and ten ways to avoid writing a bad poem. And the site uses real poems to illustrate, which makes it very interesting and educational. So if you've hesitated putting down your emotions in your own words or have felt that any writing you did do wasn't exactly what you wanted to say, check out this site.

Ring of Romance

www.webring.com

Web rings offer an excellent way of searching for what you want on the Web. If you go to the site www.webring.com, you can type in a word like *romance,* and you are given a list of various "rings" that touch this subject. A ring is a series of sites that are all linked, so that you can go from one to the other to the other with a click of the mouse.

You can choose absolutely any topic to search, but if you type in *romance,* you are led to many of the sites I've listed as well as many, many others. One ring in particular, the Ring of Romance, links about 80 sites that have romance as a topic. Each ring carries a description, so if you're looking for sites about romance but not those that cater to fans of romance novels, for example, you can head off in the right direction.

Drruth.com

www.drruth.com; **AOL keyword: Dr. Ruth**

I would be remiss if I didn't include my own site in this list. Certainly my site isn't geared to romance, but because romance often leads to sex, and that's my main topic, it fits. You can find sex tips, answers to many questions, my unique advice, and lots of other interesting information. If you check out the boards, you can find discussions going about a vast array of different topics (some too racy for even my tastes). You can contribute to the discussions and perhaps get tips from other visitors on solutions for what's bothering you.

Index

• S •

tennis, 153
testicles, 184
testicular cancer, 292
testing devotion, 87
testosterone
  erectile problems, 159
  morning sex, 164
therapy
  affording, 280–281
  catastrophes, following, 247
  deciding to seek, 269–270
  deeper problems, 279
  depression, 228
  empty nest syndrome, 198–199
  finding a therapist, 273–275
  homework assignments, 277–278
  initial visit, 275
  misusing, 279
  pregnancy issues, 173
  resistance, overcoming, 270–273
  second opinions, 278
  without partner, 276
threats, avoiding, 213
time together, finding
  business trips as vacation, 110
  communication time, 20–22
  distractions, 253–267
  importance of, 1
  long-distance romance, 217–218
  lunch, 306, 307
  martyr, playing, 212–213
  mate, making priority, 89, 209–212
  mini dates, 311
  pick-up dates, 309–310
  prioritizing romance, 215
  romance, prioritizing, 208
  routine, benefits, 267
  sex, making time, 213–215
  stress, 46–47, 218
  telephone dates, 307
  telling partner of need for romance, 216
  time to think of partner, 143
  women's increased presence in workforce, 207
touch, need in older men, 159
toys, sex, 117, 127, 318–319
travel. *See* vacations
trimesters. *See* pregnancy
tropical vacations, 301
truth
  faking orgasm, 127
  importance, 76
  lying during therapy, 279
  unemployment, 231
  white lies, 203

• U •

underwear, 116, 143, 205
unemployment, 228–232
Uprima, 162
urinating
  during sex, 287
  obstacle to oral sex, 316

• V •

vacations
  active, 113, 115
  adventure, 301
  beach, 112–113
  business trips, 110
  camping, 111–112
  children, including, 104–105, 107
  cities, 298–299
  cruises, 97, 110, 302
  extended dates, 312
  Holy Land, 300
  home hideaways, 297–298
  honeymoon hotel, returning, 302–303
  importance, 101–102
  packing, 115–116
  Paris, 300
  planning, 102–103, 202
  postpartum, 187–190
  renewing vows, 99–100
  road trips, 302
  seniors, 163
  sexual experimenting, 116–117
  short, 107–109
  tropical, 301
  woods, 299
vaginismus, 286
Vail, Colorado, 114
vengeance, 36, 37
Venice Beach, 113
venting, 34–36, 78
Viagra, 161–162, 291
vibrator, 127, 319
Virtual Kiss Web site, 323
voice
  lowering during argument, 38
  screaming during sex, 130
  venting, 78
volunteer work, 263
vows, renewing
  meaningful, 98–99
  planning, 99–100
  reasons, 93–98

IDG BOOKS WORLDWIDE
BOOK REGISTRATION

Register
This Book
and Win!

We want to hear from you!

Visit **http://my2cents.dummies.com** to register this book and tell us how you liked it!

- ✔ Get entered in our monthly prize giveaway.

- ✔ Give us feedback about this book — tell us what you like best, what you like least, or maybe what you'd like to ask the author and us to change!

- ✔ Let us know any other *For Dummies*® topics that interest you.

Your feedback helps us determine what books to publish, tells us what coverage to add as we revise our books, and lets us know whether we're meeting your needs as a *For Dummies* reader. You're our most valuable resource, and what you have to say is important to us!

Not on the Web yet? It's easy to get started with *Dummies 101*®: *The Internet For Windows*® *98* or *The Internet For Dummies*® at local retailers everywhere.

Or let us know what you think by sending us a letter at the following address:

For Dummies Book Registration
Dummies Press
10475 Crosspoint Blvd.
Indianapolis, IN 46256

BESTSELLING
BOOK SERIES